NASCAR
WINSTON CUP
2003

2003 NASCAR WINSTON CUP SERIES
AWARDS CEREMONY

Waldorf=Astoria, New York, NY
December 5, 2003

ACKNOWLEDGEMENTS

NASCAR WINSTON CUP SERIES 2003

It is with great pride that UMI Publications, Inc., presents NASCAR Winston Cup 2003, the season record presented in text and photos of the world's premiere stock car racing series. And what a season it was. In all, 17 different drivers visited victory lane and 11 names crowded the list of Bud Pole winners over the 36-race schedule, underscoring the competitive nature of the series. The winners' list included seasoned veterans and past champions such as Bill Elliott, Jeff Gordon, Terry Labonte, Dale Jarrett, Bobby Labonte and Tony Stewart, as well as many of the recent newcomers like Jimmie Johnson, Kurt Busch, Kevin Harvick and Ryan Newman.

As has been the rule rather than the exception, however, championships come down to consistency demonstrated throughout the 10-month racing season, and in that category, no one came close to Matt Kenseth and his DeWalt Tools team led by crew chief Robbie Reiser and fielded by veteran team owner Jack Roush. An early-season win at Las Vegas followed a week later by a fourth-place finish at Atlanta placed the fourth-year driver atop the point standings for the first – and the last – time. A total 25 top-10 finishes, 11 of those in the top five, accumulated enough points each week to thwart any serious challenge for the title. At Rockingham, N.C., in the season's penultimate event, Kenseth hoisted the championship trophy and handed team owner Jack Roush his first title in his 16 years of series competition.

In producing NASCAR Winston Cup 2003, many in the sport provided the support and assistance that made it possible for us to bring this book to you. We would like to thank all of our friends and partners at NASCAR for their help and guidance. To Brian France, Mike Helton, George Pyne, Jim Hunter, Jennifer White, Paul Schaefer and Ashley Costello, we are grateful for your help and efforts throughout the year.

We would also like to express our deepest gratitude and appreciation to the fine folks at R.J. Reynolds Tobacco Company in this, the last year of a long and pleasurable relationship. To Ned Leary, Rich Habegger, Denny Darnell, Mitch Cox, Rob Goodman, Jule Banzet, Guy Morgan, Mark Rogers, Chad Willis and all the former members of the Sports Marketing Enterprises team at RJR, we thank you for your support in producing the NASCAR Winston Cup Yearbooks, as well as your 33 years of outstanding service to the sport.

This year the stories of the 2003 NASCAR Winston Cup Series season were a team effort by our editors here at UMI. In addition, our good friend and motorsports journalist Jeff Huneycutt contributed articles on the champions of the Winston era and our special tribute to R.J. Reynolds. We'd like to express our appreciation to Jeff for his great work and help in the production of this book.

Of course, the NASCAR Winston Cup Yearbook would not be what it is without the contributions of our dedicated photographers. Once again, Don Grassman, Ernie Masche, Gary Eller and Tom Copeland of CIA Stock Photography, along with veteran free-lancer David Chobat filled our pages with some of the best imagery in the business, and we thank them for their fine work and attention to capturing the stories and details of the sport for us to enjoy for years to come. Thanks also to Sherryl Creekmore of Signature Racing Photos for her contributions in our tribute to past champions section.

Thanks also to Melissa Jones, our Senior Customer Service Representative at Quebecor World Kingsport Book Services, for her professionalism, patience and care in the production of this book.

Most of all, we'd like to thank you, the fans. Your continued support for the sport of NASCAR Winston Cup Series racing is, and has been, nothing short of incredible. We hope you enjoy this book as much as we enjoyed bringing it to you.

President and Publisher: **Ivan Mothershead**; Vice President and Associate Publisher: **Charlie Keiger**; Associate Publisher: **Rick Peters**; Controller: **Lewis Patton**; COO & VP and National Advertising Manager: **Mark Cantey**; Advertising Executive: **Paul Kaperonis**; Managing Editor: **Ward Woodbury**; Associate Editor: **Gary McCredie**; Art Director: **Brett Shippy**; Senior Designer: **Paul Bond**; Designer: **Mike McBride**; Manager of Information Systems: **Chris Devera**; Administrative Staff: **Stephanie Cook, Mary Flowe, Renee Wedvick**

Preproduction work provided by ISCOA (International Scanning Corporation of America).

ISBN# 0-943860-32-6

FOREWORD

The 2003 NASCAR Winston Cup Series season has to be considered one of the greatest and most historic years in our sport's history, and it must be recognized as one of the most competitive on record.

During the 36-race season we saw 17 different drivers celebrate victory in winner's circles across the nation, the result of superb driving skill, excellent teamwork both on pit road and in the teams' shops and garages, and the application of brilliant race strategy.

We also witnessed 11 different drivers winning Bud Pole Awards from their efforts in qualifying, each gaining entry into the 2004 running of the Bud Shootout at Daytona International Speedway next February.

It was a year in which victories were spread amongst seasoned veterans and past champions such as Bill Elliott, Jeff Gordon, Terry Labonte, Dale Jarrett, Bobby Labonte and Tony Stewart, as well as many of the sport's up-and-coming stars like Jimmie Johnson, Kurt Busch, Kevin Harvick and Ryan Newman, who led the series with eight victories to go with an outstanding 11 Bud Pole Awards.

The season also featured a tight race for Raybestos Rookie of the Year honors that ultimately was settled between two outstanding drivers, Greg Biffle and Jamie McMurray. Biffle was able to break into the winners' column with a victory in the Pepsi 400 at Daytona International Speedway in July. And although McMurray did not pick up a win, he posted consistently strong performances and ultimately ended the season by being named Raybestos Rookie of the Year.

We all celebrated Matt Kenseth's championship-winning effort in the DeWalt Tools Ford fielded by Roush Racing. Kenseth and his team, led by crew chief Robbie Reiser, put on a stunning show of strength and consistency throughout the entire season, gaining the top position in championship points after the fourth race of the season at Atlanta, a lead they would never relinquish for the remainder of the year.

We at NASCAR congratulate Matt, Robbie, and team owners Jack Roush and Mark Martin, along with all of the members of the DeWalt Tools team in their commitment and resolve to field a top-notch effort week in and week out, a challenge they successfully conquered that resulted in the NASCAR Winston Cup Series championship. We're sure those efforts will carry over into the future and establish the team as title contenders for years to come.

It was also a year in which we had to say goodbye to two outstanding and loyal partners in our sport, the R.J. Reynolds Tobacco Company with their Winston brand and ConocoPhillips with their 76 brand of racing gasoline. Both companies served racing and its fans superbly over their long relationships with NASCAR, and we thank them and wish them well in the future.

What has not changed are the exceptional fans our sport continues to enjoy. You are by far the most loyal fans in all of sports and we are blessed to have you and are grateful for your continued support.

I hope you will enjoy reliving the 2003 NASCAR Winston Cup Series season through this book. All of us at NASCAR look forward to seeing you at the tracks on the tour during the 2004 season.

Sincerely,

Brian Z. France
Chairman

TABLE OF CONTENTS

NASCAR WINSTON CUP SERIES 2003

2003 NASCAR WINSTON CUP SERIES MARKS THE END OF THE
"WINSTON ERA"

NASCAR WINSTON CUP SERIES 1971-2003

The arrival of R.J. Reynolds Tobacco Company on the stock car racing circuit in 1971 changed the face of the sport and spurred its phenomenal growth into a major national pastime known as the NASCAR Winston Cup Series.

It all began simply enough: Junior Johnson, a race team owner, just wanted R.J. Reynolds to sponsor his car and kick in a few bucks to help fund his racing operation. Johnson was a legendary driver during the sport's early days and one of the most successful car owners in the business at the time, so R.J. Reynolds executives found the idea of getting into motor racing with Johnson interesting. But the more they studied their options, the more they realized they wanted to be involved in the sport in a bigger way. A much bigger way.

Johnson referred RJR to Bill France Sr., the founder and president of NASCAR. After a few discussions, a plan that formed from the seeds of sponsoring a single car blossomed into title sponsorship of NASCAR's greatest series. Beginning in 1971 NASCAR's top racing series, the NASCAR Grand National Series, would be called the NASCAR Winston Cup Series, and it was the beginning of a partnership that would forever change the face of stock car racing.

The sponsorship included $100,000 for a point fund to be paid out to the top drivers at the end of the season. The driver who accumulated the most points during the season would receive $40,000 and the title of NASCAR Winston Cup Series champion, presently the most prestigious honor in motorsports in the United States.

Beginning in 1972, the first full season of RJR sponsorship through its Winston brand, the NASCAR Winston Cup Series schedule was reduced from 48 races to 31, marking the beginning of the sport's "modern era."

Richard Petty circles Homestead-Miami Speedway in November 2003 before the last of 987 NASCAR Winston Cup Series races.

NASCAR **Winston Cup**

NASCAR Winston Cup Series ... NASCAR Winston Cup Serie ... Winston Cup Series ... NASCAR Winston

NASCAR Winston Cup Series

NASCAR Winston Cup CHAMPION 17 MATT KENSETH

NASCAR Winston Cup CHAMPION 17 MATT KENSETH

NASCAR Winston Cup Series

NASCAR Winston Cup Series

NASCAR Winston Cup CHAMPION 17 MATT KENSE

NASCAR Winston Cup CHAMPION MATT KENSETH

NASCAR Winston Cup Series

NASCAR Winston Cup CHAMPION 17 MATT

RJR also spurred the development of modern sports marketing, which was instrumental in making the NASCAR Winston Cup Series what it is today. Ralph Seagraves, a member of the RJR sales force, and his successor, T. Wayne Robertson, guided the company's sports marketing programs into positions of national prominence. Seagraves, in turn, credited Bill Smith, who was chairman and CEO of RJR in 1971, as well as his successors Bill Hobbs, Ed Horrigan, Jerry Long, Jim Johnston and Andy Schindler, for understanding the marketing impact of sports sponsorships.

What began as a program just to help tracks survive eventually evolved into one of the most progressive and groundbreaking marketing programs in the country.

When RJR came on the scene in 1971, five race tracks on the circuit were in bankruptcy. Track operators couldn't afford to do what was needed to fill the stands. For the first six years of RJR's involvement, the number one objective was to put people in the stands. To do that, RJR bought ads in newspapers and magazines and space on billboards to promote races. The development of big in-store promotions at the retail level created added excitement for the races. Hat and jacket promotions at races provided extra sizzle for the ticket-buying fans. "Before anybody really knew what was happening, the promoters were filling up the stands," Seagraves said.

RJR then began assisting the tracks to build new grandstands, concession stands, rest rooms, sponsor suites, press boxes, scoreboards, expanded garages, bridges, entrance signs and flagstands. The rough edges were essentially smoothed to make race tracks a place where the entire family could come and enjoy a day together. "We stepped in wherever we were needed whether there was any immediate payback or not," Seagraves remembered.

One of RJR's most famous initiates was the creation of The Winston, in 1985, stock car racing's first true "All-Star Race," which pitted the greatest winners in the NASCAR Winston Cup Series against one another in a no-holds-barred, big money event.

Ten drivers formed the field for the first running of The Winston, held at Lowe's Motor Speedway the day before the Coca-Cola 600 on Memorial Day weekend. Bill Elliott, who was dominating the superspeedways at the time, had to be considered the favorite to win the inaugural event. But at the finish it was Darrell Waltrip who collected the winner's check for $200,000.

(Below Left) Ralph Seagraves was put in charge of RJR's new special events division, Sports Marketing Enterprises, in 1969. When the company, through its Winston brand, joined forces with NASCAR in 1971, it was Seagraves who established the plans that began the phenomenal growth the sport enjoyed for more than three decades.

(Below Right) T. Wayne Robertson, who joined RJR as an administrative trainee and show car driver in 1971, took the reigns of SME upon Seagraves' retirement in 1985 and remained in control until January 1998, when he was tragically lost in a boating accident.

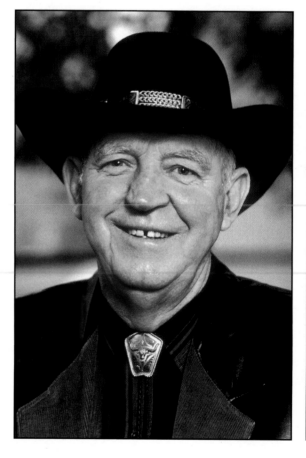

(Above) SME president T. Wayne Robertson presents 1991 NASCAR Winston Cup champion Dale Earnhardt with a check for $1 million as the champion's share of the point fund, which totaled $2.5 million at the time.

(Top Right) In 2002, Dale Earnhardt Jr. won the No Bull 5 at Talladega, Ala., the last time the special $1 million bonus was won. He was joined on the podium by Debra Polzun who, by virtue of being paired with Earnhardt Jr. through a special sweepstakes, happily collected a $1 million check of her own, courtesy of Winston.

(Right) Jimmie Johnson became the latest recipient of one of Winston's million dollar checks when he drove to victory in the 2003 running of The Winston at Lowe's Motor Speedway.

Over the years, The Winston gained a reputation as race filled with excitement and surprises, often with as much fireworks on the track as were provided following the event. In 1992 The Winston was run "under the lights" for the first time in front of a prime-time national television audience, which added even more to the color and mystique of the special non-points event.

And as if any driver needed more incentive to go all out to be named The Winston champion, RJR continually upped the purse, and this season Jimmie Johnson collected a winner's check for a cool $1 million.

Today, in a sports landscape where many sports organizations' all-star games are little more than an afterthought, The Winston has grown to become one of the most anticipated events on the NASCAR Winston Cup Series schedule by both the fans and the race teams.

RJR also announced in 1985 that it would sponsor the "Winston Million," an award to be paid to any driver who, during a single season, won three of four "crown jewel" events: the Daytona 500 at Daytona Beach, Fla., the Winston 500 at Talladega, Ala., the Coca-Cola 600 at Charlotte, N.C., and the Southern 500 at Darlington, S.C. Amazingly, Bill Elliott did the impossible when he won the award the very first year.

"When Bill Elliott won the Southern 500 in Darlington in 1985 to capture the Winston Million, he immediately became known as 'Million Dollar Bill,' and the sport reaped unprecedented publicity, reaching people throughout the country whether they were race fans or not," Robertson said.

The Winston Million went unclaimed for the next 12 years until Jeff Gordon became the only other driver to claim the lucrative prize by winning the Daytona 500, the Coca-Cola 600 and the Southern 500 during the 1997 season.

selected from the season schedule in which five different drivers would have a chance to collect a $1 million bonus if they could win the event. What made the Winston No Bull 5 so special was that fans were also selected and paired with each of the five participating drivers. If one of the participating drivers managed to win the event, the fan paired with him would win a million dollars as well. Between 1998 and 2002, RJR paid out a total of $26 million to drivers and fans as part of the Winston No Bull 5 program.

But the centerpiece of RJR's 33-year sponsorship of the series was the NASCAR Winston Cup Series point fund and the annual championship. Compared to the dollars thrown around today, the $100,000 that comprised the initial fund may seem meager, but in 1971 it was a princely sum. By 1985, it had reached $750,000. The next year, even though Winston had just paid Bill Elliott one million and paid out the first The Winston purse of another million, the point fund jumped to $2 million, with the champion being paid $400,000. In 1989 the point fund was increased again, this time to $2.5 million, and Rusty Wallace, the NASCAR Winston Cup Series champion, was paid $1 million at the end of the season.

The following year, RJR replaced the Winston Million with the "Winston No Bull 5" program, created as a tribute to NASCAR's 50th anniversary season. In this newest program, five races were

(Left) In addition to the annual point fund and special bonus programs, Winston also sponsored specific events, including regular-season races at Talladega Superspeedway and Winston Pole Day in Charlotte. Here, Jeff Gordon collects a trophy and check from Winston after winning the pole for the Mello Yello 500 in October 1993.

(Below) Special cars were prepared to honor all 15 drivers who became champions during Winston's 33 years as title sponsor. The cars and their drivers were featured at various tracks toward the end of the 2003 season as part of the NASCAR Winston Cup Series Victory Lap tribute.

YEAR	TOTAL $	CHAMPION'S SHARE $
1971	100,000	40,000
1972	100,000	39,000
1973	120,000	34,000
1974	140,000	46,000
1975	150,000	51,000
1976	150,000	44,000
1977	150,000	46,000
1978	175,000	49,000
1979	175,000	49,000
1980	210,000	49,500
1981	250,000	60,000
1982	300,000	75,000
1983	500,000	150,000
1984	500,000	150,000
1985	750,000	250,000
1986	2,000,000	400,000
1987	2,000,000	400,000
1988	2,000,000	400,000
1989	2,500,000	1,000,000
1990	2,500,000	1,000,000
1991	2,500,000	1,000,000
1992	2,500,000	1,000,000
1993	3,000,000	1,250,000
1994	3,000,000	1,250,000
1995	3,500,000	1,300,000
1996	4,000,000	1,500,000
1997	4,000,000	1,500,000
1998	5,000,000	2,000,000
1999	5,000,000	2,000,000
2000	10,000,000	3,000,000
2001	13,020,000	3,600,000
2002	14,000,000	3,750,000
2003	17,000,000	4,250,000
33 years	$101,290,000	$31,732,500

(Above) As part of the overall marketing plan instituted by RJR, signage such as this, at Pocono (Pa.) Raceway, appeared prominently at every track that hosted NASCAR Winston Cup Series events almost immediately after Winston began its sponsorship in 1971. The signs were updated and meticulously maintained throughout the 33-year period of RJR's involvement in the sport.

(Right) So long, Winston. And many thanks from all of us!

The NASCAR Winston Cup Series point fund continued to grow as RJR added to it on a regular basis. By 1995, the total point fund posted by RJR hit $4 million with the winner's share reaching $1.5 million. The sum increased to $5 million beginning in 1998, and in 2000 that figure was doubled to an unheard-of $10 million.

In 2003, the NASCAR Winston Cup Series point fund posted by RJR was an astounding $17 million, and thanks to RJR, the NASCAR Winston Cup Series champion, Matt Kenseth, became $4.25 million richer.

In June 2003, with the announcement that NASCAR had reached an agreement with communications giant Nextel to become the series' new title sponsor beginning in 2004, the "Winston era" began to draw to a close.

In an interview with Bill France Jr., the then NASCAR Chairman stated, "My dad (NASCAR founder Bill France Sr.) believed RJR's commitment to NASCAR would take us to new heights and make us a national sport. ... My father would definitely be proud."

In the 30-plus years NASCAR has had a relationship with the R.J. Reynolds Tobacco Company and its Winston brand, the sport has grown immeasurably. It is populated by the most loyal fans to be found in the American sporting landscape and is widely recognized as the most competitive form of motorsports to be found anywhere in the world. Much of that can be attributed to two companies, NASCAR and R.J. Reynolds, with a shared vision and a commitment to the sport that has been unmatched in American Motorsports history.

BOBBY ALLISON

NASCAR WINSTON CUP SERIES CHAMPION – 1983

Bobby Allison had been racing in the NASCAR Winston Cup Series for over 20 years before he finally won the championship. "Finally" is the correct term in Allison's case because seldom has an athlete with so much talent come up short so many times. In the 11 years between 1972 and 1982, Allison finished second in the point chase four times. The famed founder of the "Alabama Gang" wanted a championship so badly he could taste it, but somehow, something always happened to make him come up short.

Allison actually led the standings in both 1981 and 1982 only to have Darrell Waltrip make a late season run and steal the championship away. Plus, to add insult to injury, Waltrip did it driving Chevrolets for Junior Johnson, one of Allison's old teams!

In 1983 the situation appeared as if it were unfolding the same way all over again. Allison was entering his second year driving the No. 22 Chevrolet Monte Carlos for DiGard Racing (ironically, the team Waltrip left to join Johnson). During the off-season Allison had huddled with crew chief Gary Nelson and engine builder Robert Yates to determine how they could improve their finishes. The trio found it was on the short tracks where they were weakest and concentrated their efforts on fielding faster cars on the short courses.

The research paid off in spades for Allison. The DiGard team was already strong on the superspeedways, but in 1983 Allison and DiGard won twice on the shorter tracks, finished second four times, third three times and fourth once. The car was not out of the top four in any of the season's 10 short-track events, which resulted in Allison finding himself once again atop the point standings.

But given the circumstances of the past two seasons, Waltrip felt he had Allison and the DiGard team right where he wanted them. Waltrip began his usual push for the championship late in the season and actually began cutting into Allison's point lead. Waltrip and his crew were confident that Allison's effort would stumble as it had in past seasons, but they were wrong. Instead of tightening up and racing to protect the point lead, Allison and DiGard kept up their aggressiveness and instead raced for wins.

Down the stretch Allison put together a string of three straight wins, at Darlington, Richmond and Dover, that showed he had no intention of lying down and allowing another driver to steal his championship. Going into Darlington Waltrip had whittled Allison's point lead down to 41, but after that fantastic three-week stretch, Allison's lead had ballooned to 101 points.

Waltrip redoubled his efforts and began a new charge that eventually shaved Allison's lead down to 27 points with just two races remaining. But at Atlanta in the season's penultimate race Allison showed his mettle by going for broke and coming home third. That finish, combined with Waltrip's ninth, meant the chase was still too close to call and the champion would be determined in the season's final race at Riverside, Calif. Waltrip did his best at the California track and finished sixth, but Allison used a little good luck to make up a lost lap and battle to a ninth-place finish. It was enough to help Allison hold on to the lead over Waltrip by 47 points and give the fan favorite his first NASCAR Winston Cup Series championship.

Throughout his career, a lot of adjectives had been used to describe Allison's single-minded quest for the championship. Some called him hard-headed, others obstinate and stubborn. Those were some of the nicer phrases, especially during his heyday when his furious fender-bending battles with Richard Petty had brought him to prominence. Allison refused to be beaten either mentally or physically on the track.

Now, he finally had achieved his greatest goal. It had been a long quest – since the early days of racing in Florida before he moved to tiny Hueytown, Ala. – and it hadn't been easy by any means. But through it all Allison remained true to his belief that he could run with, and beat, the best stock car drivers in the world. The fans also appreciated Allison's drive and determination in finally achieving his longstanding quest to be the champion; for the fourth-straight year, and the sixth time in his career, the fans of NASCAR Winston Cup racing voted Allison the sport's Most Popular Driver.

DALE EARNHARDT

Few names in any sport are as widely associated with winning as Dale Earnhardt's. The son of Ralph Earnhardt, of one of the Southeast's greatest short track racers, Dale knew from an early age he wanted to be a race car driver like his daddy. But the younger Earnhardt's path to his goal wasn't an easy one. Ralph Earnhardt may have been a champion race driver, but that didn't give his son a free pass.

Dale Earnhardt slowly worked his way through racing's lower ranks. He often had to go into debt on Friday just to buy tires and fuel for his car, believing all along he could finish well enough over the weekend to pay off the debt on Monday.

Finally, Earnhardt received the break he needed when Californian Rod Osterlund, after a few tryout races in 1978, signed the driver to a full ride in his blue-and-yellow No. 2 Chevrolets. Earnhardt made the most of that opportunity, winning one time and finishing in the top five 11 times in 1979. The results were good enough to win Earnhardt Rookie of the Year honors and make his team believe their driver could do anything. Osterlund quickly signed the driver to his first long-term contract.

The next season was a surprise to everyone involved in the sport. With a sophomore driver and a rookie crew chief (20-year old Doug Richert) leading the way, Osterlund's team won five races while collecting 19 top-five finishes and 23 top 10s. All season long they held off determined charges by some of the sport's most respected teams and finished 19 points ahead of Cale Yarborough to win the championship. It was the first time in the history of NASCAR Winston Cup racing that a driver had won the Rookie of the Year crown one season and followed that up with the championship the next.

Earnhardt's next championship season didn't come until 1986, when he was driving for friend and car owner Richard Childress. After spending time driving Bud Moore's Fords and a few years with Childress helping build the team into a championship contender, Earnhardt knew that 1986 was his chance to return to the top. It was a season of great on-track battles as Earnhardt regularly fought with Darrell Waltrip and Tim Richmond for wins. Fans were rewarded with some of the greatest races ever to be seen on asphalt. At the end of the season Earnhardt won out over Waltrip on the strength of five wins and 16 top fives. Earnhardt brought home the first of six championships he would earn with Richard Childress and a whopping $1,783,880 in prize money.

A second-straight title followed in 1987 when the Kannapolis, N.C., native literally thumped the competition with 11 wins in just 29 races. His dominance was so complete that second-place finisher Bill Elliott trailed by 489 points in the championship standings - a mark that hasn't been bettered since.

Championship number four came with the turn of the decade. In 1990 Earnhardt and Childress needed a fantastic season, which included nine victories, to hold off a determined Mark Martin, who battled with Earnhardt for the championship into the closing laps in the final race of the season. Earnhardt returned in 1991 to finish off his second set of back-to-back championships. This time he bettered Ricky Rudd with four wins and a truckload of top finishes.

The next season, 1992, was a disappointment for Earnhardt, who managed only a single win. He and his crew returned to competition in 1993 with a vengeance, using "Black is Back" as their rallying cry. With six wins, Earnhardt maintained a comfortable lead throughout the season and coasted to his sixth title.

Earnhardt matched "King" Richard Petty's magical mark of seven NASCAR Winston Cup Series championships the next season. In 1994 Earnhardt strung together one top finish after another, gobbling up championship points by the handful. His consistency brought home four victories, 20 top-five finishes and 25 top 10s in 31 events. It was also the third time in five seasons he had exceeded the $3 million mark in winnings.

In the seasons after his final championship, Earnhardt struggled for a short period but seemed to have re-discovered his competitive edge late in his career. Before a tragic racing accident took his life early in 2001 the relentless competitor was back to his old form and publicly declaring himself in the hunt for a record-breaking eighth championship. Although he never got the opportunity to chase down that eighth title, the "Man in Black" will be forever remembered as one of NASCAR Winston Cup racing's greatest champions.

BILL ELLIOTT

NASCAR WINSTON CUP SERIES CHAMPION – 1988

Bill Elliott's life makes the perfect rags-to-riches story. Bill and his brothers, Ernie and Dan, seemingly came from nowhere when he made the field for his first NASCAR Winston Cup Series race at Rockingham, N.C., in 1976. The brothers raced a well-worn car on the meager budget that their father, George, could provide. Those early results were nothing to write home about - the team had trouble getting engines to last an entire race - but the Elliott brothers were learning what it took to be competitive at the NASCAR Winston Cup level.

After starting seven races in 1976, Elliott fared better the next season. He made the field for 10 starts with his family-owned team and even managed to post two top 10s. For the next few seasons Bill and his brothers had to pick their races carefully because the budget simply wasn't there to race the series full time.

Elliott's big break came in 1982, when Michigan industrialist Harry Melling purchased the team. George Elliott had taken it as far as he could, but there was so much promise left in Bill as a driver, Ernie as an engine builder and Dan as a specialist in gears and transmissions, that Melling was convinced that with more capital the team could become a contender.

Elliott raced well in 1982, finishing second three times and bringing home his best championship finish (25th) while still running a limited schedule. During the winter the Elliotts convinced their new team owner that if they were allowed to run the full schedule they could bring home a top-five finish in the end-of-season standings.

Melling went for the idea, and Bill and his team responded with a season that brought the team its first victory - at Riverside, Calif. - four second-place finishes, and 12 top fives. Best of all, the brothers made good on their promise, finishing third in the standings.

After the success of the 1983 season, the Melling Racing team went back to its shops hidden away in North Georgia and got right back to work. The brothers were convinced that their team needed only to find a little more speed in order to make the breakthrough to NASCAR Winston Cup champion.

The next season was another success. The team continued to improve, this time collecting three wins, but again finished third in the standings. Then came the season that put Melling Racing

on the map. Hidden out of sight in their shops in Georgia the Elliotts built a superspeedway program that was about to knock the rest of the NASCAR Winston Cup Series competition to its knees. Using a loophole in the NASCAR rulebook that stated no minimum tread width for the race cars, Elliott raced narrowed Thunderbirds that sliced through the air more easily than the rest of the field.

Elliott was so dominant on the big tracks in 1985 that he often had to hold back in order to keep from "stinkin' up the show." In all he won 11 times and collected the Winston Million, and along the way he picked up the nickname "Awesome Bill from Dawsonville." Unfortunately, Elliott and his team seemed to lose steam late in the season and allowed a 200-plus point lead over Darrell Waltrip to evaporate. The team eventually lost out to Waltrip for the championship, which was a bitter pill to swallow.

The hangover from that disappointment lasted into the 1986 season when Elliott could only manage ninth in the final standings. But in 1987 Melling Racing was back to its championship form with another second-place finish.

When the green flag dropped on the 1988 season Elliott and his team were no longer wide-eyed country boys. They were veterans in the NASCAR Winston Cup Series wars and now understood fully what it took to race for the championship. This time they were prepared for a year-long grind not just for victories, but also for consistent finishes at the top of the field.

Bill took the lead in the point standing for the first time after winning the spring race at Bristol, Tenn. He was chased by Darrell Waltrip, Rusty Wallace and Dale Earnhardt; three of the very best drivers ever to strap on a helmet. As the season drew to a close in the final race at Atlanta, Elliott was still nursing a small lead over Rusty Wallace, who had charged hard over the final third of the season to draw within striking distance. Elliott, however, knew exactly what he had to do. The Georgian drove a conservative race, protecting his car and eventually finishing 11th. Wallace did everything he could do by claiming the victory, but it was still not enough. The NASCAR Winston Cup Series championship was Elliott's by a mere 24 points. After more than a dozen years and countless late nights spent in the shop, this was more than a championship for Bill Elliott, it was the realization of a dream for the entire Elliott family.

JEFF GORDON

NASCAR WINSTON CUP SERIES CHAMPION – 1995, '97, '98, '01

When Jeff Gordon made the jump to the NASCAR Winston Cup Series for the final race of the 1992 season in Rick Hendrick's No. 24 Chevrolet, few marked the occasion as the beginning of a dynasty. Gordon started that race 21st and was credited with a 31st-place finish. Still, for a rookie just trying to get a feel for NASCAR Winston Cup power, it was good enough.

The 1993 season was Gordon's rookie tour. The California native didn't win, but he did capture the Raybestos Rookie of the Year title thanks to seven top five and 11 top-10 finishes. Gordon showed he had a natural talent for driving stock cars and was picking up the finer points of piloting a 3,400-pound car at its mechanical limits pretty quickly. The next season the driver found victory lane twice and posted his first top-10 finish (eighth) in the championship standings.

It was 1995, however, that was truly Gordon's breakout year. The driver and his standout crew chief, Ray Evernham, had developed a rapport that made the No. 24 Chevrolet a force on the circuit. Evernham had a knack for making adjustments to the car throughout the race that always made it among the fastest on the track in the final laps, and Gordon, well,

Gordon could just flat drive. After finding victory lane just twice in his first 62 starts, the driver won seven races on the 31-event schedule in 1995 - including three of the first six. Gordon gained the point lead after winning at New Hampshire in July and never gave it up again. At the end of the season he bested Dale Earnhardt, who was shooting for a record eighth NASCAR Winston Cup Series championship, by 34 points. And at just 24 years old, he became the second-youngest champion ever and the youngest in the sport's modern era. He also gave Hendrick Motorsports, which had been fielding cars since 1984, its first title. Already blessed with movie star looks and now with the title of "Champion," Jeff Gordon became NASCAR's marquee name.

Gordon won 10 times in 1996 but lost out on the title to Hendrick Motorsports teammate Terry Labonte by a mere 37 points. The championship wasn't decided until the final race of the season at Atlanta where mechanical troubles put Gordon two laps down and effectively handed the title to Labonte.

A third-straight nail biter for the championship unfolded in 1997. This time Gordon battled Dale Jarrett all the way to the

wire. Again, the Hendrick driver posted an impressive 10 victories along with 22 top fives and 23 top 10s, but Jarrett's stats were nearly as impressive. The Robert Yates Racing driver collected seven victories, 20 top five and 23 top 10s. In the end, however, Gordon squeaked out a 14-point victory over Jarrett for the champion's title.

The string of tight point battles came to an end in 1998 when Gordon drubbed the competition with 13 victories in 33 races. That mark tied Richard Petty's record for most wins in a single season in NASCAR's modern era and helped Gordon set two other records. One was most money won in a season. Incredibly, the driver nearly broke the $10 million mark when he won in excess of $9.3 million. He also became the youngest three-time champion at just 27. This time around there was no drama in the season's final race; Gordon already had the championship wrapped up and went on to win the final race at Atlanta and claim the title by 364 points over second-place finisher Mark Martin.

Despite all the personal accolades heaped on him, Gordon was adamant that the real honor for the championship should go to the Hendrick Motorsports organization, the only NASCAR Winston Cup team he had ever driven for. "The most important thing, and perhaps the most overlooked thing, was that Hendrick Motorsports became the first team to ever win four-straight championships," Gordon said. "It is a tribute to Rick Hendrick ... and to every member of the entire organization."

Three years later the former Sprint Car driver was at it again. For the sixth time in seven years he posted more wins than any other driver; the mark, however, wasn't a personal best as Gordon only visited victory lane six times. The wins were almost all big ones, including his third victory in the Brickyard 400 and his seventh career road-course win (another series record). Gordon supplemented his six wins with 18 top-five and 24 top-10 finishes, both series bests. As the top finishes piled up so did the money, over $10 million in fact, which broke his own previously held record for most money collected in a single season.

Gordon's fourth NASCAR Winston Cup Series championship placed him third on the ladder behind only Petty and Earnhardt, who hold seven apiece. It was also his first with crew chief Robbie Loomis.

DALE JARRETT

NASCAR WINSTON CUP SERIES CHAMPION – 1999

Despite being a second-generation driver and the son of a NASCAR Winston Cup Series champion (Ned Jarrett in 1961 and '65), Dale Jarrett didn't get too many breaks in his quest to become a champion himself. The Hickory, N.C., native began his racing career in a Late Model Sportsman car at Hickory Motor Speedway and found himself competing against carpenters, plumbers and anyone else who had the racing bug. But Jarrett found success as a hobby-level racer and eventually graduated to the NASCAR Busch Series in 1982.

Jarrett began his NASCAR Winston Cup Series racing career with his first full-time season in 1987 and piloted cars for a number of different owners before finally getting his first win in 1991 while driving for the Wood Brothers. He began winning regularly while driving for car owner Joe Gibbs from 1992 through 1994, but he didn't become a regular player in the yearly chase for NASCAR's Winston Cup Series championship until he moved to Robert Yates' powerhouse team in 1995.

From 1996 through 1998 Jarrett posted championship finishes of third, second and third, respectively. It was obvious the driver had the talent to win big but hadn't yet found a way to break through. That came in 1999 when he finished the marathon 34-race season while piling up a mountain of top finishes. Jarrett pointed to the team's phenomenal consistency as the key to the championship chase. "Our reliability was there," he said, "and the consistency that had eluded the team in the last three years was there as well."

Jarrett and his No. 88 Ford team started out the season quite unimpressively when it failed to finish the season-opening Daytona 500, but that turned out to be the only DNF the team would turn in all season long. When it was over Jarrett, who was just five days shy of his 43rd birthday, had compiled a record that included 29 top-10 finishes. Twenty-four of those 29 were valuable top-five finishes, and four were victories.

A small group of drivers, namely Jarrett, Jeff Gordon, Bobby Labonte, Mark Martin, Tony Stewart and Jeff Burton, dominated victory lane that season. All told, that group of six claimed 23 of the schedule's 34 races. But none posted the consistency that Jarrett did, and late in the season the only

battle turned out to be who would finish for second behind the driver of the "88."

Unfortunately, the season started off about as poorly as possible for Jarrett and his team when he failed to finish at Daytona and was credited with 37th. The next weekend Jarrett and his race team started slowly but surely digging themselves out of that hole.

Going into the Pontiac Excitement 400 at Richmond, Va., in May, Jarrett had improved his standing in the season-long rankings considerably; he trailed only point leader Burton (by 55). But Burton faltered and finished 37th at Richmond while Jarrett collected the checkers. After that event it was Jarrett who sat atop the point standings by 63 points over the Roush Racing driver.

Jarrett strengthened his cause in the coming weeks when he recorded 10 consecutive top-10 finishes, which included victories at Michigan, Daytona and Indianapolis. It was enough that when the inevitable "slump" came over a four week stretch (consecutive finishes of 38th, 16th, fourth and 18th) he was able to survive it unscathed and even emerge with a 254-point lead over Bobby Labonte, who had moved into second place.

Though he was never a factor to win the season's next-to-last race, NASCAR Winston Cup's inaugural event at Homestead-Miami Speedway, a fifth-place finish was more than enough for Jarrett to secure the championship. The final race at Atlanta was basically Jarrett's victory party while the rest of the contenders raced for second. He finished second to Labonte in the race and ended the season with a 201-point lead over his friendly rival.

The championship was a popular one among both fans and fellow racers. Jarrett is a gentleman both on and off the track and labored for years to finally earn the championship. The honor was also the first for popular team owner Robert Yates, who had raced for 11 years before winning his first title.

For his efforts, Jarrett collected $6,649,596 in winnings. As a second-generation champion, he and his father, Ned, became only the second father-son tandem to win the championship (Lee and Richard Petty are the other).

MATT KENSETH

NASCAR WINSTON CUP SERIES CHAMPION – 2003

In 2002 Matt Kenseth led the NASCAR Winston Cup Series in wins with five victories. He took the checkers at Michigan, Rockingham, Phoenix, Richmond and Texas. On top of that he finished in the top five 11 times and in the top 10 an additional eight times. Still, winning the most races in the series didn't win him the NASCAR Winston Cup Series title. In fact, it barely got him into the top 10 in points. Kenseth finished eighth, 368 points behind winner Tony Stewart.

So it was a little ironic when people complained that Kenseth was "stroking" in 2003 while he was dominating the standings. Some felt the driver made the season boring by outdistancing his opponents in the championship chase because he piled up top-10 finishes like so many shells on the beach. Those critics conveniently seemed to forget that Kenseth went the route of racing for every win the season before and couldn't even crack the top five in the point standings.

The winning strategy devised by Kenseth and crew chief Robbie Reiser didn't exclude winning races, it just put the priority on consistency. And the results actually mirrored those of several past champions including Tony Stewart in 2002 (three wins), Terry Labonte in 1996 (two wins) and Alan Kulwicki in 1992 (two wins). Of course, Kenseth's single win was the lowest total for a champion since Benny Parsons performed the same feat in 1973.

Despite his success, Kenseth's season didn't exactly get started with fireworks and confetti. In the season-opening Daytona 500 the best finish he could turn in was 20th. But Daytona is a fickle track, because of the aerodynamics involved in running 200 miles per hour drivers can easily be shuffled from first to 10th in half a lap. Just finishing the "500" is a goal for many of the drivers, who consider the real start of the season to be at North Carolina Speedway, the second race on the schedule. Kenseth picked up the pace the next week at "The Rock" for the Subway 400. There the Wisconsin native finished third and moved from 20th in the standings all the way to sixth. He won the next week in the UAW-Daimler Chrysler 400, and in addition to the $365,875 in prize money he took home, he vaulted up to the rarified air of second in the point standings.

A fourth-place finish in the next event, Atlanta's Bass Pro Shops MBNA 500, moved the driver into the coveted first position in the NASCAR Winston Cup Series point standings. From there out Kenseth never looked back. Over the next 10 races he had only one finish outside the top 10.

The only driver to mount a serious charge on Kenseth's position at the top of the point ladder was Dale Earnhardt Jr. Early in the season Earnhardt Jr. gained 100 points on Kenseth in the span of three races. As the teams lined up to start Lowe's Motor Speedway's Coca-Cola 600 the driver of DEI's red Chevrolet was just 20 points behind the leader and on a hot streak. But Kenseth responded to the challenge with a second-place finish. Earnhardt Jr., meanwhile, struggled with brake problems and could only manage 41st. The lead was again a nearly 100-point cushion, and it only continued to grow from there.

Kenseth continued his assault on the rest of the competition. He raced smart, refusing to wear out his car early and avoiding situations where he could potentially be swept up into a wreck not of his making. If he had a weakness it was the team's qualifying program. Kenseth's average starting position was 21.3, which was mediocre at best. Kenseth and Reiser successfully overcame the weakness by utilizing fantastic pit work and smart driving to quickly slice their way to the lead pack race after race.

After the first two-thirds of the season were complete Kenseth had built his lead to a nearly insurmountable 351 points. A two-race slump where the driver of the No. 17 Fords finished 33rd and 36th allowed Kevin Harvick to briefly carve a large chunk from the margin, but it was too little too late. Kenseth wrapped up the championship with a race to spare. He and his Roush Racing team showed up at Homestead-Miami Speedway for little more than the fun of it.

"I'm just so thankful to have this opportunity," Kenseth said of his race team and the chance to race for the championship in just his fourth full year as on the NASCAR Winston Cup Series. "When you think about it, only 43 of us get to do this every Sunday. There are so many great race drivers who never get the chance. I've been real lucky to be with a top-notch team, right from my rookie year."

22 • Matt Kenseth - 2003 NASCAR Winston Cup Champion   NASCAR Winston Cup Series Yearbook 2003

ALAN KULWICKI

NASCAR WINSTON CUP SERIES CHAMPION – 1992

Alan Kulwicki wasn't just aware of his long-shot status as a competitor in the NASCAR Winston Cup Series, he embraced it. A privateer who learned how to stretch a dollar like it was a rubber band just to be competitive, Kulwicki tagged himself Mighty Mouse like the cartoon character because he made a habit of exceeding everyone's expectations.

When the Wisconsin driver made his decision to leave the ASA wars and head south to try his hand in NASCAR Winston Cup competition, he did it with typical Kulwicki single-mindedness. He sold all his racing equipment, loaded up his few household possessions into the back of a pickup truck and trailer and set out for the South.

Kulwicki's first season, 1986, in NASCAR Winston Cup competition started out predictably rough. He had only one car, two leased motors and two crew members. But on the strength of a one-race sponsorship deal from Quincy's restaurants he loaded up what little racing equipment he had and headed to Daytona Beach, Fla., for the season opener. Kulwicki suffered his first setback almost immediately when he was involved in a practice session accident triggered by oil spilled from Bobby Hillin's blown engine. Kulwicki and his skeleton crew made repairs to the car, but

they failed to make the field for the 500 when the driver was passed by Lake Speed and Dick Trickle in the last corner on the last lap of his Gatorade 125 qualifying race.

Two weekends later Kulwicki finally made the field for his first NASCAR Winston Cup race. It was the 1986 spring event at Rockingham, N.C., and he finished 15th. By the end of the season he turned out to be the highest-finishing rookie in 18 of his 23 starts and had completed 94.7 percent of the possible laps in the events he ran. These performances helped the ultra-competitive driver beat out Michael Waltrip in a tight battle for Raybestos Rookie of the Year honors.

Kulwicki improved steadily over the years and appeared ready to have a breakthrough season in 1991 when he finally found stability with a sponsor: Hooters Restaurants. The restaurant chain had originally signed Kulwicki for a single-race sponsorship when their driver couldn't make the field at Atlanta, but after Kulwicki demonstrated to the company what he could do,

the decals never came off the No. 7 Fords. The driver who had turned down deals to drive for other owners for "more money than I ever could have imagined," because he wanted to run his own program, finally had all the necessary pieces in place.

The next season the man known as Mighty Mouse scored two wins and managed enough top finishes to stay near the top of the point standings through the early part of the season. But then he suffered a disastrous setback when he crashed three cars during one weekend at Dover and fell more than 200 points behind. After that setback he had declared himself out of the point battle. However, with some help from those in front of him on the point table, Kulwicki found himself back in contention when the teams arrived at Atlanta for the final race of the season. He was second, 30 points behind leader Davey Allison and 10 points ahead of third place Bill Elliott. Kulwicki still had a shot at the title, although highly unlikely.

But Allison's day ended early when he was collected in an accident with Ernie Irvan. The championship was now up for grabs between hometown favorite Elliott and the Atlanta-based Hooters-sponsored Ford driven by Kulwicki.

Kulwicki's crew knew exactly how many laps their driver needed to lead to grab the five-point bonus for most laps led during a race, and Kulwicki pushed the fuel-mileage envelope to get them. When he had led enough laps to grab the bonus, he made his fuel stop. Elliott won the race, but Kulwicki did what he had to do and finished second. Thanks to the lap-leader bonus, Kulwicki won the championship over Elliott by just 10 points - it was the tightest point battle in NASCAR Winston Cup Series history.

At the end of his cool-down lap, Kulwicki stopped his race car on the frontstretch, turned around and performed his signature "Polish Victory Lap." His triumph in the face of the most improbable odds was the stuff of which legends are made. Kulwicki's tunnel vision had proven once again that, given the right tools and an enormous amount of good old-fashioned sweat, great things do happen to the "little guys." What many thought to be an impossible goal had become a reality: Kulwicki was the first owner/driver to win the NASCAR Winston Cup Series championship since Richard Petty did it in 1979.

BOBBY LABONTE

NASCAR WINSTON CUP SERIES CHAMPION – 2000

It must run in the family. Bobby Labonte's older brother, Terry, was a NASCAR Winston Cup champion in 1984 and again in 1996, and by the time Bobby made the jump from Bill Davis racing to Joe Gibbs' team in 1995, he was regularly showing the potential to follow in his brother's footsteps. The younger Labonte was a NASCAR Busch Series champion in 1991 and many believed he could do it again at the NASCAR Winston Cup level given the right situation.

That situation proved to be in Gibbs' green-and-black Pontiacs sponsored by Interstate Batteries. After joining Joe Gibbs Racing, Labonte began climbing his way up the NASCAR Winston Cup ladder bit by bit every season. In 1996 he finished 11th in the standings. He improved from that mark to seventh the next season and finished sixth in 1998. In 1999 Labonte wound up one position away from his ultimate goal when he finished second to Dale Jarrett for the NASCAR Winston Cup championship. Instead of blaming the narrow miss on bad luck or fate, Labonte and his crew spent the off-season searching for ways to get better.

"When the 1999 season was over, (crew chief) Jimmy (Makar) and I sat down and went over the entire year, race by race, and tried to figure out exactly where we needed to improve to make an even stronger run for the title," Labonte explains. "We found some weak places in the program. That included the team in its preparation and work at the track as well as on pit road, and it also included the driver."

Whatever Labonte and Makar discovered, it paid off quickly, as Labonte finished sixth in the season opening Daytona 500. A week later he beat Dale Earnhardt by almost two seconds to win the Dura Lube 400 at North Carolina Speedway, which vaulted him to second on the point ladder, just five behind Jarrett. He finished in fifth place at Las Vegas in the next event, which was two spots better than Jarrett. The difference allowed Labonte to leapfrog the defending champion and take over the lead in the hunt for the championship by four points.

Jarrett won the pole for race number four, the Cracker Barrel 500 at Atlanta Motor Speedway, but he dropped out early with a blown engine and finished 36th. Labonte finished second, right on the rear bumper of race winner Earnhardt, and that put him 15 points in front of Mark Martin, who took advantage of Jarrett's poor luck to take over his spot in the standings.

Labonte lost the lead to Martin after a 21st-place finish in the Winston 500 at Talladega (the ninth race of the season), but he made up for it the next week at California Speedway by finishing second. After regaining the lead at Fontana, Calif., Labonte would not give it up again.

During the rest of the 34-race season Martin, Jarrett, Jeff Burton, Ward Burton and Earnhardt all took turns making runs at the leader, but none could ever sustain the push long enough to make the move from second to first in the standings. When the season came to an end, Labonte's cushion over Earnhardt was a comfortable 265 points.

Labonte earned the championship by virtue of four wins, 19 top fives and 24 top-10 finishes. Further, the driver of the No. 18 Pontiac was running at the finish of every race and had only two finishes outside the top 20. Of the 10,167 total laps run over the course of the season Labonte completed all but nine.

The season was amazing in terms of its consistency, which Labonte insisted was a tribute to the hard work of dozens of men who worked on his car every week. The championship was a first for both him and team owner Joe Gibbs, who had been fielding race cars since 1992.

When Bobby Labonte won his NASCAR Winston Cup Series championship, it made the Labonte brothers the first pair of siblings in all of professional stock car racing to be crowned champion in the same series. They both were honored in their home state of Texas in 2001 when they were inducted into the Texas Sports Hall of Fame. The Labontes' fellow inductees included Texas football greats Troy Aikman, Dick "Night Train" Lane, Bruce Matthews and Mike Munchak along with baseball player Norm Cash.

TERRY LABONTE

NASCAR WINSTON CUP SERIES CHAMPION – 1984,'96

Few drivers have made as big a splash in their first NASCAR Winston Cup Series race as Terry Labonte. Labonte, who earned his stripes on the short tracks of Texas, found a ride in Billy Hagan's Chevrolet at the tender age of 23. When he strapped in for his first event at Darlington Raceway, not only had the young man never seen the track before, it was his first time sitting in a NASCAR Winston Cup Series race car!

Labonte, however, acquitted himself well. He kept the car out of the wall in Darlington's tricky turns and came home fourth. Even Junior Johnson, who is a tough man to impress, remarked that Labonte would be a driver to watch: "That young boy from Texas," he said, "is going to be very, very good."

The next season, 1979, Hagan and Labonte teamed for the full racing schedule. Labonte planned to run for rookie honors, and soon found himself in a battle with what is considered to be the finest rookie class ever to enter the series in a single year. Along with Labonte, Dale Earnhardt, Harry Gant and Joe Millikan were all in the running for rookie honors. Labonte eventually lost out to Earnhardt for the rookie title, but there's hardly any shame in that.

Hagan's team was small and didn't have the funding the big guys had, but it did score a coup when Dale Inman joined the team as crew chief before the start of the 1980 season. From there out the team improved consistently. Labonte finished 10th in the championship point standings his rookie year in 1979, but in 1980 with Inman's help he improved to eighth. In 1981 the team made the move to fourth, and then improved another notch to third in 1982. Labonte suffered a broken leg in an accident in 1983 and the team stumbled to a fifth-place finish, but all the pieces fell into place for Labonte and Hagan's crew in what turned out to be a magical 1984 season.

That season turned out to be one of the great point battles of all time. The lead changed hands several times and no driver was ever able to pile up more than a 91-point lead. Although he was only able to bag two wins, steady and consistent finishes - including 17 top fives and 24 top 10s - kept Labonte in the title chase. After getting his second victory, at Bristol in August, Terry found himself atop the point standings.

Eventually, both Earnhardt and Darrell Waltrip, who led the standings earlier in the season, couldn't keep pace and fell by the wayside. Harry Gant remained as the only challenger capable of standing in against Labonte.

Going into the season's final race, the road course at Riverside, Calif., Labonte held the slimmest of leads over Gant, just 42 points. The advantage, however, had to be given to the Texan since he had already won there earlier in the year. Labonte put together a conservative run and went on to finish third. Gant could manage only an eighth-place finish. The driver who would become known as "The Iceman" won the championship by 65 points. At the time he was the third-youngest driver ever to win the title.

Twelve years later Labonte was back in the hunt again. In the intervening years Labonte's performance had dipped, and during the 12-year span he had finished 10th or worse five times. More skeptical fans and scribes had written him off as a middle-of-the-pack driver that was past his prime. But in 1996 Labonte, who was entering his third year racing for Hendrick Motorsports, unbottled some of the old magic for a second push for the title.

The 1996 season did, in fact, greatly resemble Labonte's previous championship run in 1984. Again, the driver managed to capture only two wins (North Wilkesboro, N.C., in April and Sears Point, Calif., in May) but more than made up for it with a career-high seven second-place finishes, 21 top fives and 24 top 10s. Labonte only failed to finish three races on his way to holding off Hendrick teammate Jeff Gordon by 37 points. The 12-year gap between championships is the greatest span in the History of NASCAR Winston Cup Series racing.

Given the years between Labonte's first two championships and the fact he says he's nowhere near retiring, the book is still open on this driver. Over a 25-year career Labonte has shown amazing resiliency in the course of nearly 800 starts. It just goes to show you can never count a champion out.

BENNY PARSONS

NASCAR WINSTON CUP SERIES CHAMPION – 1973

Benny Parsons became the unlikeliest NASCAR Winston Cup Series champion when he scraped together a miracle season to win the 1973 NASCAR Winston Cup title despite recording just a single victory. In a sense, it wasn't just the 1973 season, but Parsons' entire career that made winning a championship seem so unlikely.

Parsons spent a career as the classic underdog. He got his start in racing while working in his father's shop repairing taxi cabs. From Hobby Stocks, Parsons graduated step by gradual step until he was racing Fords in ARCA-sanctioned events. While at an ARCA race serving as a warm-up to the 1968 Daytona 500, Parsons first garnered attention in the NASCAR Winston Cup garage when he won the ARCA pole. By the time he won the 1968 ARCA championship and repeated the feat in 1969, he was getting regular mentions as a driver deserving of a NASCAR Winston Cup Series ride.

Parsons got his shot at when he signed on to drive for L.G. DeWitt's small team in 1970. Parsons won his first race for DeWitt in 1971 when he claimed the checkers in South Boston, Va.

After struggling in 1972, Parsons and DeWitt prepared for the 1973 season by throwing out all their over-used Ford equipment. DeWitt replaced the cars with new Chevrolets, and although the team was still under-funded compared to many of the teams they regularly raced against, Parsons found his second wind as a driver.

Although the wins were still somewhat rare, Parsons began racking up one top finish after another. The Parsonsville, N.C., native's strength was his consistency. Parsons drove smart, rarely damaged his car and almost always had his nose near the front at the finish. David Pearson may have captured most of the headlines with a series-leading 11 wins, but his partial schedule of just 18 races killed his chances in the points race. Cale Yarborough and Richard Petty split an additional nine victories, but it was Parsons' 15 top-five finishes that placed him in the top spot on the point ladder as the season wound down to the final race at North Carolina Speedway in Rockingham, N.C.

Entering the race, Parsons needed only to make laps to claim the title, but an accident early on appeared to make even that small feat impossible. A wreck in the early going severely dam-

aged the right side of Parson's Ford, and the driver figured his day was done as a tow truck hauled his battered car back to the garage area.

But after scrapping all season long, Parson's crew wasn't about to quit. Crew chief Travis Carter and his small team fell on the car in a feverish attempt to return it to the track. As they worked, members from other teams pitched in to help, bringing their tools and replacement parts with them. The biggest hurdle was the heavily damaged roll cage. NASCAR wouldn't allow the car back on the track with a damaged cage, and there appeared to be no way the crew could repair it in time. But then Ralph Moody, formerly of the famed race team Holman-Moody, came to the rescue. He fired up Bobby Mausgrover's Chevrolet, which hadn't made the race, and parked it beside Parson's damaged car. Using Mausgrover's Chevrolet as a donor car, the crewmen used cutting torches to cut sections of the roll cage out of the car and use it to rebuild Parson's cage. In a little over an hour, a small army of crewmen had fixed the right side of the roll cage and replaced the rear-end housing, the rear axle, the rear suspension, the sway bars, the entire brake system, the steering linkage and the wheel bearings. When Parsons returned to the track the car still lacked any sheet metal along the length of the right side, but it was drivable and deemed safe by NASCAR.

Even though he could do little more than limp around the race track, Parsons was able to make enough laps to gain the points he needed. At the end of the day, he beat out Cale Yarborough for the NASCAR Winston Cup Series championship by just 67.15 points. The small race team with no factory support had done the impossible, it had knocked off the giants of the racing world for the ultimate title. And Parsons – racing's version of the "average Joe" if there ever was one – was the embodiment of the team: single-minded, hard working, approachable and above all, crafty.

Parsons continued racing through 1988, winning 21 races and 20 poles along the way. In addition to winning a championship, he also made his mark on the stock car racing world when he became the first driver to qualify a stock car at more than 200 mph when he went 200.176 during qualifying for the 1982 Winston 500 at Talladega Superspeedway.

RICHARD PETTY

NASCAR WINSTON CUP SERIES CHAMPION – 1964,'67,'71,'72,'74,'75,'79

Records are made to be broken. In the years to come some driver may eventually break the mark of seven NASCAR Winston Cup Series championships (tied but not broken by Dale Earnhardt). Someone may break the modern era mark of 13 wins in a season (tied but not broken by Jeff Gordon). And although it is highly unlikely, someone may even break the astounding record of 200 wins in a career.

But no matter how many great drivers NASCAR Winston Cup racing will see in the future, there will never be another "King." Richard Petty was inarguably one of the greatest drivers ever to claim a checkered flag, but he earned his moniker as "The King" as much because of how he treated people as how he drove a race car.

Petty was born into a racing family, but as a youth it was by no means certain that he would follow in the family's line of work. When Petty first decided he wanted to drive a car, at age 18, his father, Lee, in fact rebuffed him. "Come back when you are 21," the elder Petty said. "You will be smarter then." Until then, he was expected to help work on and repair his father's cars.

When he turned 21 in 1958 Richard Petty did come back. Petty drove his first race in one of his father's castoff Oldsmobiles. The car was painted with the soon-to-be-famous number 43, chosen simply because it was the number next in line after his father's 42. The race was a 100-miler in Columbia, S.C., and Petty eventually finished sixth. The following year Petty thought he had bagged his first win when he took the checkers at Lakewood Speedway in Atlanta. But another driver protested while Petty sat in victory lane, and after a review in the scorer's stand the protest was upheld. The man awarded the victory? None other than Lee Petty. "When that boy wins one," Lee stated flatly, "I want him to win it right."

That win finally came at Charlotte in 1960. Petty won twice more that season to finish second behind Rex White in the point standings. The first of seven championships came in 1964 on the strength of nine wins. Petty repeated the championship in 1967.

In 1971 R.J. Reynolds stepped into the world of stock car racing in a big way when it became the title sponsor for NASCAR's Grand National Series. Beginning in 1971 it became known as the NASCAR Winston Cup Series.

An added bonus to R.J. Reynolds' Winston brand becoming a title sponsor was it pledged $100,000 to be split among the competitors at the end of the season - the champion's share alone was $40,000. Predictably, many drivers upped the competitive ante in an attempt to be the first to claim Winston's big prize. As a two-time champion, Petty was the default favorite, but a third championship was by no means a given.

The King, however, came out with guns a blazing. The Petty-blue No. 43 won at tracks across the country. In 46 events Petty won 21 times and collected 38 top-five finishes. The first NASCAR Winston Cup Series crown was his by a wide margin. The next season marked the first of NASCAR's modern era because the schedule was reduced to the now customary 30-something races. Despite the change in format, Petty proved his dominance in the series was no fluke by claiming eight more wins and his fourth championship.

Thirteen wins in 30 races helped Petty Enterprises reclaim its place at the front in 1974, and the team backed that up again in 1975 when The King claimed his sixth championship by a 722-point margin over second-place Dave Marcis. The sixth championship was a milestone because it was the first year of the redesigned point system that has remained in effect through the 2003 season.

Petty's seventh and last championship probably came the hardest. In 1979 Petty started the season off in a big way by winning the Daytona 500, but from there on out Darrell Waltrip looked like the driver to beat. Petty and his crew somehow managed to win five races and make a come-from-behind push in the late stages of the season to upset Waltrip for the championship by a meager 11 points.

When Petty retired at the end of the 1992 season he was the owner of seven NASCAR Winston Cup Series championships, 200 victories and more than $7.7 million in winnings. Just as important to Petty, however, was the legion of fans he had gained over the years. The King always said that the sport's foundation was its fans, not the drivers, and he proved he believed in what he said time and again when he stayed for hours after races and signed countless autographs.

TONY STEWART

NASCAR WINSTON CUP SERIES CHAMPION – 2002

It could hardly be considered fair when Joe Gibbs Racing announced in 1998 that its newest driver, Tony Stewart, would be competing for the NASCAR Winston Cup Raybestos Rookie of the Year title the next season. After all, even if he had never raced a NASCAR Winston Cup race car before, Stewart could hardly be considered a rookie. The young man already had more titles than many drivers had wins; they included championships in Karting, the Indy Racing League and USAC (three of 'em, all in different types of cars).

Expectations were understandably high for Stewart that first season, but no predictions even came close to what he actually accomplished. The man known as the "Rushville Rocket" won three races in his freshman season and finished the year an outstanding fourth in the standings. The driver of the No. 20 Home Depot Pontiac also collected 12 top-five finishes, 21 top 10s and dropped out early in only one race. As the first NASCAR Winston Cup rookie ever to win three races, Stewart quite literally stunk up the show when it came to the Raybestos Rookie of the Year competition. No other driver even came close.

Two seasons later Stewart came painfully close to his first NASCAR Winston Cup Series championship when he finished second to Jeff Gordon. Stewart had finished the season on a tear, but he had opened the season with several poor performances. Those poor finishes simply had created a point deficit that was too large to overcome.

The 2002 season started out much the same way. Just two laps into the first race of the season, the Daytona 500, Stewart's Pontiac left him stranded with a broken engine. He finished the race in last place.

The Home Depot team seemed to be on the rebound when Stewart finished a strong fourth the next week and followed that up with a fifth-place finish and then a victory at Atlanta Motor Speedway in the following two races. But then the driver was swept into a wreck not of his making at Darlington and finished 36th. That pattern continued over the first half of the season; Stewart would string together several top finishes only to be knocked right back down by a poor showing, often by events outside of his control. In 2002 the driver posted a career high six DNFs.

Finally, the top finishes began to outweigh the damage done

by the DNFs and he clawed his way to the top of the point ladder. Stewart found himself atop the point standings for the first time in the season after finishing second to Dale Earnhardt Jr. in the October 6 EA Sports 500 at Talladega Superspeedway.

Six races remained on the schedule after Talladega, and Stewart did what he had to through the stretch run to hang on to the lead. Although he was unable to post any wins during that span, he also didn't bomb in any of the races, either. Overall, the final six finishes were all between eighth and 18th. It wasn't pretty, but it was enough to hold off Mark Martin's charge and win the Indiana native his first NASCAR Winston Cup Series championship by 38 points.

Stewart's incredible competitive spirit had been his undoing in previous seasons when his mentality was to win or use up the car trying. This time around, though, that competitive spirit paid off when the driver simply wouldn't let up even when he found himself at the bottom of the championship totem pole after the debacle at Daytona. At the end of the season Stewart had collected $9,163,761 thanks in large part to his victories at Atlanta, Richmond and Watkins Glen. The total nearly doubled his previous best mark for winnings in a single season.

Because he was already a champion in other top racing divisions, the difficulty and honor of being crowned NASCAR Winston Cup Champion was not lost on the driver. "The sheer difficulty of winning the title is something you can't make people understand if they are not involved in this part of racing on a day-to-day basis," he said. "The caliber of the teams, the car owners, the crew chiefs and the drivers that make up NASCAR Winston Cup racing is so high that it truly makes you respect winning the championship.

"There is so much more work involved in NASCAR Winston Cup than there was with the others. To win this championship, to overcome the obstacles that are put in your place, to race on all the different types of tracks in a season that runs for 10 months and wears you out truly makes this championship a special one. I don't want to take away from any of the other things that I have won, but after going through the battle and winning the championship, you truly begin to appreciate just how difficult the task is."

Spoken like a true champion.

RUSTY WALLACE

NASCAR WINSTON CUP SERIES CHAMPION – 1989

In his first NASCAR Winston Cup Series race, in 1980, he finished second to Dale Earnhardt. He was an ASA champion in 1983. So when Rusty Wallace joined the NASCAR Winston Cup Series full time in 1984 driving for Cliff Stewart people took notice.

They took even greater notice when Wallace showed his willingness to bang fenders with the sport's established stars. Wallace was a natural as a stock car driver and relentlessly aggressive behind the wheel. But his willingness to mix it up on the track met with more than a few comments of disapproval from veteran drivers. Ironically, two of those were Darrell Waltrip and Dale Earnhardt, both of whom had been more than happy to bend some sheet metal when they came into the sport just a few years earlier.

"Some people sure have short memories, don't they?" was Wallace's only reply.

Wallace drove for Stewart for two seasons, and even won the Rookie of the Year title with the team in 1984. But he was still searching for his first victory in NASCAR Winston Cup action when he left after the 1985 season to join Raymond Beadle's Blue Max team.

It didn't take long to realize that Wallace's move was a good one. The driver who was once a terror on the Midwest's short tracks used his experience on the bullrings to claim his first career victory in April at Bristol. He followed that up with another win on another short track, this time at Martinsville.

As Wallace gained experience in the big leagues he learned to temper his aggressiveness a bit in order to claim the best finish possible when a victory just wasn't in the works. It was his improved consistency that made him Bill Elliott's biggest challenger for the 1988 championship. Despite winning six times and bringing home 19 top-five and 23 top-10 finishes, he still lost out to "Awesome Bill" by 24 points.

Wallace returned to the series with Blue Max in 1989 determined not to fall short again. Part of his strategy for the championship was to lead every lap possible. The driver who leads the most laps is awarded an additional five championship points after every race. That, combined with the five bonus points for leading just a single lap was, Wallace reasoned, an extra 300 points ripe for the taking, and if he had claimed the

bonus just five more times in 1988 it would have been enough to turn the tides in his lost battle with Elliott.

Wallace was a man on a mission in 1989, and he made good on his promise to himself and his team to collect as many lap-leader bonus points as possible. While keeping his eyes firmly on the big picture Wallace scored six wins and backed that up with 13 top fives, 20 top 10s and only four DNFs.

As the season wore down the only driver left in competition with Wallace was Dale Earnhardt. The battle seesawed back and forth between the two drivers as they traded top finishes and piled up championship points in the race to the finish. In the final event of the season at Atlanta, Wallace maintained a 79-point lead over Earnhardt and needed only to finish 18th or better to claim the championship.

But events transpired against Wallace at Atlanta and at first it looked as though the championship was slipping through his fingers faster than water through a sieve. He lost a lap pitting early under a green flag, and then lost another when he pitted again under green for a cut tire. Yet another stop to tighten loose left-rear lug nuts cost him a third lap.

Earnhardt, meanwhile, was dominating the race at the front of the pack and looked to be unstoppable. Wallace's only hope was to carve his way through the field high enough to hold on to his point lead.

Earnhardt led the most laps in the race and won the event, but Wallace's determined charge throughout the race resulted in a 15th-place finish, a fantastic result considering the circumstances. It was just enough to claim the championship. The final tally showed Wallace had bettered Earnhardt by just 12 points; it was the slimmest margin since Richard Petty bested Darrell Waltrip by 11 in 1979.

At the NASCAR Winston Cup Series Awards Banquet that winter in New York's Waldorf=Astoria Hotel, Wallace again made history when he became the first driver to be awarded a cool $1 million for the champion's share of the point fund. The bonus, coupled with his victory over Waltrip in The Winston at Lowe's Motor Speedway and his winnings throughout the year, put him over the $2.2 million mark for his championship season.

DARRELL WALTRIP

NASCAR WINSTON CUP SERIES CHAMPION – 1981,'82,'85

Make no mistake about it, stock car racing in the 1970s and '80s may have been a rough sport born from hillbilly moonshiners, but it was still steeped in the traditions of Southern chivalry. Things were done a certain way; A driver may come to blows with another over what he thought was a dirty move on the track. That was OK. But what a driver could never do was brag or "be uppity."

That all changed when a certain Kentuckian named Darrell Waltrip came on the scene. After several seasons racing with his own, homegrown team, Waltrip signed with DiGard Racing and soon began racking up wins consistently. It was obvious the young man came loaded with talent, and that threatened some of the more established drivers. Waltrip also caused friction because he was part of a new generation of drivers. Other than Richard Petty, most racers of the time were uncomfortable with any media attention. They considered themselves drivers - working class men - and not stars. But the landscape of the sport was changing with increasing television and other media exposure. The limelight was there for anyone willing to stand in its glare.

Waltrip was one of those people, and he was a good

fit. The driver had a quick wit and was willing to give honest, candid answers to the questions posed him. Plus, he was young and handsome with an attractive, well-spoken wife. It was no wonder the media loved him. The problem was when his words were transferred to print, the reader didn't have the advantage of hearing his tone, the quick wink or the body language that told him Waltrip was saying things all in fun. Many things Waltrip said in jest sounded just plain mean and sarcastic when read in the newspaper.

Because of that Waltrip was labeled with many names during the early days of his career, many of them not printable on these pages. But the best - and best known - was given to him by rival Cale Yarborough when the driver tagged him with the name "Jaws" because of his willingness to talk to anyone who would listen.

Waltrip's public perception, however, never bothered his ability to get results on the race track. Waltrip spent six years racing for DiGard. The relationship was successful on the track – Waltrip collected 26 wins during that span – but acrimonious off it. To get out of his long-term contract Waltrip was forced to

put up a significant amount of money to buy himself out, but once he did he never looked back.

In 1981 Waltrip signed on to drive for Junior Johnson's powerhouse team. Interestingly, he was filling the seat vacated by none other than Cale Yarborough. The two drivers may have had their differences, but their aggressive, take-no-prisoners style behind the wheel was nearly identical. Waltrip claimed his first NASCAR Winston Cup Series championship his first year with Johnson, winning 12 of 31 events. By winning, Waltrip became the first driver feted as champion in the "Big Apple." As part of its expansion into mainstream America, NASCAR moved the championship awards banquet to New York City that year, starting a tradition that has lasted ever since.

The next season Waltrip followed up that success by doing it all over again. The two seasons were nearly mirror images of each other. Both times Waltrip won 12 races, both times he had to make a come-from-behind push late in the season, and both times he beat out Bobby Allison (by less than 75 points). The pairing of Johnson and Waltrip was obviously a perfect match: In 163 starts with former team DiGard, Waltrip had won 26 races, but in just 61 events with his new team Waltrip had already won 24 times!

Bobby Allison beat out Waltrip for the championship in 1983, keeping him from becoming only the second driver ever to three-peat. But Waltrip wouldn't be down long. He came back in 1985 to win the title in what is probably the greatest comeback in motorsports history. 1985 started off as Bill Elliott's miracle year. He won the Winston Million the first time it was offered and was virtually unstoppable in his Thunderbird on the superspeedways. So commanding was Elliott's performance that he enjoyed a 206-point lead over Waltrip after his win in Darlington's Southern 500.

At the final race of the season, Waltrip actually held a slim, 20-point leader over Elliott. The buildup to a big showdown had been palpable, but a broken transmission took Elliott out of contention early and Waltrip went on to win his third championship by a comfortable margin. Besides winning the championship for the third time in five years, in 1985 Waltrip also became the first driver to collect over a million dollars in winnings in a single season.

CALE YARBOROUGH

NASCAR WINSTON CUP SERIES CHAMPION – 1976,'77,'78

The ranks of NASCAR Winston Cup Series drivers are filled with intense competitors. No surprise there, since race car drivers that lack a competitive fire soon fade into the gloom of failure. But Cale Yarborough - a fireplug of a man whose short stature belied his fearless personality - stands out even in that crowd as a man with a near ferocious appetite for winning.

Growing up near Darlington, S.C., Yarborough was bitten by the racing bug early. As a teenager in the mid-50s the young man somehow managed to talk several different NASCAR Winston Cup car owners into allowing him to drive their cars during practice sessions. John Bruner, NASCAR's chief steward, would stop practice to kick Yarborough off the track, only to find Yarborough back on the asphalt in a different car a short while later.

As soon as Yarborough turned 18, the minimum age at the time to drive in a NASCAR-sanctioned event, the South Carolinian began banging fenders wherever he could find a race. Yarborough proved fearless on the short tracks across the Southeast. Before long he was earning $200 to $300 for a night's worth of racing. Although he had other pursuits – he was South Carolina's Golden Gloves welterweight champ two times running and was

offered a scholarship to Clemson University to play football – Yarborough decided to cast his lot as a race car driver.

His first break at the NASCAR Winston Cup level came in 1966 when he was invited to drive one of the Wood Brothers' factory-supported Fords. Yarborough claimed his first NASCAR Winston Cup win in 1967 at Atlanta and raced for the Woods for three years. The pairing was a successful one, but when Ford pulled out of racing the Woods decided the best way to weather the financial drought was to run a partial schedule. Yarborough wanted to race at every opportunity and the parties agreed to go their separate ways.

For the 1973 season Yarborough landed a choice ride when Junior Johnson hired him to drive his Holly Farms Chevrolet. Yarborough and Johnson hit it off immediately, and the No. 11 Chevrolets soon became a tour-de-force.

Yarborough won his first NASCAR Winston Cup champi-

onship driving for Johnson in 1976. He rocketed to the point lead after the first 10 races and, with the help of nine wins and six second-place finishes, was never far from the top of the standings. By the final race of the season, at Ontario, Calif., Yarborough's lead was enough that he needed only to make the race and take the green flag to win the championship over second-place finisher Richard Petty.

Yarborough followed that up with nine more wins and six more seconds in 1977. Also, Yarborough again beat out none other than Richard Petty, but this time by a whopping 386 points. The driver was so dominant that this time around he was able to wrap up the championship with two races remaining on the schedule.

No driver in NASCAR Winston Cup Series history had been able to win three championships consecutively, so Yarborough, ever on the lookout for a new challenge, made that his goal for 1978. So determined was the driver to reach his new goal that he made the competition realize early on that they were essentially racing for second. This time around Yarborough upped the winning ante by claiming 10 victories, while also bringing home six second-place finishes. He also showed amazing consistency by finishing every single race, which was another first in NASCAR Winston Cup history. By the end of the season he had thoroughly pummeled the competition and held a 474-point lead over the next-best driver (this time Bobby Allison was the runner-up).

Yarborough continued racing and winning, and he likely had a few more championships in his future but instead decided to limit himself to a partial schedule beginning in 1981. At first it may seem out of character for the die-hard racer to limit his schedule, but the decision was entirely true to form for Yarborough. He decided that his family had sacrificed enough for his racing career and it was time to turn his attention to them. And with typical Yarborough gusto he pitched himself into his task wholeheartedly. Yarborough continued to race through 1988, winning 83 NASCAR Winston Cup Series races along the way. No driver has ever repeated his mark of three straight NASCAR Winston Cup championships.

PREFACE

NASCAR WINSTON CUP SERIES 2003

By the time the band had packed up and the lights were dimmed in the Waldorf=Astoria's Grand Ballroom following Tony Stewart's championship celebration in early December 2002, plans for the 2003 NASCAR Winston Cup Series season were nearly complete. Only a few remaining driver seats were yet to be claimed, and they were going fast.

Elliott Sadler prepares to start his fifth full season in the series after signing with Robert Yates Racing and M&M's to drive the No. 38 Ford.

It all started back in the summer of 2002, when, after great anticipation, Ricky Rudd announced he had reached a three-year agreement with Wood Brothers Racing and Motorcraft to drive the No. 21 Ford Tauruses formerly wheeled by Elliott Sadler. That one move triggered a "Silly Season" that would set the stage for the coming year.

Rudd's departure from Robert Yates Racing resulted in a vacancy that was quickly filled by Sadler, and M&M's jumped on board to sponsor the effort that would carry the number 38, replacing the "28" and Texaco's Havoline brand fielded by Yates since Davey Allison's rookie year in 1987.

Havoline had already agreed to cast its lot with Chip Ganassi and Felix Sabates, who had committed to provide a Dodge for 26-year-old Jamie McMurray in the fight for

2003 NASCAR Winston Cup Series Raybestos Rookie of the Year honors. McMurray, who was not scheduled to begin competition on NASCAR's top circuit until the start of the 2003 season, got an early initiation near the end of 2002 when Sterling Marlin was forced to sit out the rest of the year with a neck injury. McMurray, who worked his way through the ranks competing in NASCAR Touring, NASCAR Craftsman Truck Series and NASCAR Busch Series competition, responded to his sudden challenge by claiming a win at Lowe's Motor Speedway in only his second NASCAR Winston Cup Series start.

Joining McMurray at Chip Ganassi Racing with Felix Sabates – and in the battle for the 2003 rookie crown – would be Casey Mears, nephew of four-time Indy 500 winner Rick Mears. With a background in open-wheel competition and one full season in the NASCAR Busch Series, Casey, 24, prepared to climb behind the wheel of the No. 41 Target Dodge in place of the departed Jimmy Spencer, with crew chief Jimmy Elledge ready to call the shots on pit road.

Both McMurray and Mears would rely in part on veteran teammate Sterling Marlin's vast experience. Marlin, who led the points for most of the 2002 season, was more than ready to get back to the business of racing his Coors Light Dodge and, hopefully, pick up where he left off in 2002 as the series' most consistent performer.

After parting ways with Chip Ganassi, Spencer temporarily found himself without a ride until, just before New Years, he inked a deal to drive the No. 7 Sirius Satellite Dodge for team owner Jim Smith. Smith, after dissolving his relationship with Ray Evernham during the course of the 2002 season, hired crew chief Tommy Baldwin, who was available after leaving Ward Burton's Caterpillar team at Bill Davis Racing. Many speculated that the combination of Spencer and Baldwin – both men known for being "strong willed" – would be either a weekly contender for wins or quickly go down in flames.

Evernham would again head up the Dodge contingent with drivers Bill Elliott and Jeremy Mayfield. Elliott, with back-to-back wins at Pocono and Indianapolis in 2002, had proved he still kindled the internal fire to win on a weekly basis, while Mayfield was looking forward to bouncing back from a lackluster season that produced just two top-five and four top-10 finishes.

(Clockwise from top left) DeWalt driver Matt Kenseth was considered a preseason contender for the championship after leading the series in 2002 with five wins. Crew chiefs Philippe Lopez (left) and Frank Stoddard prepare to direct the Dodge teams fielded by Bill Davis Racing. 2002 runner-up Mark Martin heads up the powerful Roush organization with five teams capable of challenging in 2003. A smiling Ken Schrader arrives at Daytona ready for a fresh start at BAM Racing. Three new looks for 2003 include the "01" Pontiac with driver Jerry Nadeau, Schrader's No. 49 BAM Racing Dodge and Ricky Craven's Tide machine, this year wearing Pontiac sheet metal.

Kenny Wallace joined the Dodge ranks during the winter by joining Bill Davis Racing as teammate to 2002 Daytona 500 winner Ward Burton, bringing with him his Stacker 2 sponsorship from the NASCAR Busch Series. Burton, with wins in each of the last four seasons, looked forward to working the full schedule with crew chief Frank Stoddard, who joined the Caterpillar team midway through 2002.

Petty Enterprises cut their effort back to two Dodge teams during the off-season. John Andretti would continue to campaign the "43" Cheerios Dodge under the direction of crew chief Greg Putnam, while Kyle Petty shed the Sprint decals on his No. 45 Intrepid in favor of a red-white-and-blue paint scheme featuring Georgia-Pacific.

Ken Schrader, left without a ride and a sponsor at the end of the season, suddenly found himself with two options. He could sign on to drive for Andy Petree Racing, although Petree was without a sponsor and could not commit to a full schedule of events, or he could elect to join upstart BAM racing. Like Petree, team owner Elizabeth Morganthau had no primary sponsor for the coming season, but she was adamant that BAM Racing, after getting their feet wet with a partial schedule in 2002, was fully committed to running the complete schedule of events and would field a competitive effort. Schrader liked what he saw and signed on to drive the No. 49 BAM Racing Dodge.

The Dodge Boys also welcomed two new faces

after Rusty Wallace and 2002 Rookie of the Year Ryan Newman announced they would switch nameplates during the off-season, dropping from the Ford ranks to campaign Intrepids for team owner Roger Penske. Wallace hoped the potent Dodge engines would power him back into victory lane after going winless in 2002, the first time in the last 17 seasons Rusty had failed to win at least one event.

Newman, on the other hand, cast off any notions of a "sophomore jinx" and planned to make his own challenge for the championship and add that honor to his victory at New Hampshire, a win in The Winston, the annual Bud Pole Award, the Rookie of the Year crown and a sixth-place finish in the final points, all captured in 2002, his initial season on the tour.

Newman's strongest challenge for 2002 rookie honors had come from Jimmie Johnson, and over at Hendrick Motorsports, Johnson and crew chief Chad Knaus spent the off-season quietly going about the business of preparing the Lowe's Chevrolets for a championship run all their own. With three wins and a solid fifth-place finish in the final 2002 point standings, and with his team and sponsor still intact, Johnson had every reason to believe he could parlay a brilliant freshman run into a strong drive toward a title.

Johnson would, of course, have to get past his team's co-owner and Hendrick stalwart Jeff Gordon, who finished 2002 one spot ahead of his

New looks for 2003 include Rusty Wallace in a Miller Lite Dodge after driving Fords since 1994, Kenny Wallace in the No. 23 Stacker 2 Dodge from Bill Davis Racing and Mike Skinner, driving a Pontiac instead of the Kodak Chevrolets formerly fielded by Morgan-McClure Motorsports.

(Below) Richard Childress made the off-season switch to veteran crew chief Mike Beam on his No. 30 AOL Chevrolet, hoping the chemistry between Beam and driver Jeff Green would help the team realize its full potential.

(Bottom) Driver Dave Blaney (left) was paired with new crew chief Robert Barker, fresh off a third-place finish in the NASCAR Busch Series with driver Scott Wimmer in 2002. Many considered Barker, with a strong engineering background, one of the hottest prospects in the NASCAR Winston Cup Series.

rookie protégé in fourth. With three wins last season – matching his lowest tally since 1994 – Gordon was ready to put last year's distractions behind him and focus on grabbing his fifth NASCAR Winston Cup Series championship.

Joining Johnson, Gordon and Terry Labonte at Hendrick Motorsports was Joe Nemechek, who took the wheel of the No. 25 Monte Carlo in late May 2002. Joe and crew chief Peter Sospenzo used the summer months to gel and produced some solid finishes toward the end of the season. Unhappy with his team's performance on pit road, however, Sospenzo hired a new pit crew during the off-season, hoping to support Nemechek with more consistency on race days.

The rest of the Chevrolet forces would remain intact for the most part, with Richard Childress continuing to field Monte Carlos for Kevin Harvick,

Jeff Green and Robby Gordon. But with Green, Gordon and Harvick finishing 17th, 20th and 21st, respectively, in the final standings and with Harvick's win at Chicagoland the organization's only victory of the season, Childress fully expected bigger and better things from his drivers this year. The six-time championship team owner chose to keep the GM Goodwrench and Cingular teams intact for Harvick and Gordon, and he hired veteran crew chief Mike Beam to work with Green on the AOL Monte Carlo.

Like Richard Childress Racing, Dale Earnhardt, Inc., also kept their three teams largely intact, with Earnhardt Jr. and Michael Waltrip set to maintain their dominance at the restrictor-plate tracks while finding more consistency on the "intermediate" superspeedways. After missing the first four events of 2002, Steve Park was looking forward to beginning the season with a clean bill of health and regaining the competitive form he showed in early 2001.

The Bowtie Brigade also welcomed strong reinforcements in the form of 2000 NASCAR Winston Cup Series champion Bobby Labonte and reigning champion Tony Stewart, after Joe Gibbs made the decision to shed Pontiac sheet metal in favor of the reshaped Monte Carlo. Finishing his championship run with a flurry of top-five finishes, Stewart would have to be considered one of the favorites to grab a second straight title if the team could adapt quickly to the Chevrolet body. Longtime crew chief Jimmy Makar took on the role of team manager at Gibbs Racing, so Labonte prepared to work with Michael "Fatback" McSwain, who had moved to the team for the last few races of 2002 after leaving his post with Ricky Rudd at Robert Yates Racing.

With the departure of Stewart and Labonte, the Pontiac contingent prepared to field five full-time, single-car efforts led by Johnny Benson and crew chief James Ince at MBV Motorsports. After flashes of brilliance over several seasons, Benson finally broke into the win column at Rockingham in November as the 2002 season wound down. That, coupled with a second place at Martinsville two weeks prior, gave the team plenty of momentum to carry them through the winter.

The departures of sponsor M&M's and driver Ken Schrader set the stage for an entirely new look at MB2 Motorsports. On board for 2003 would be former Hendrick driver Jerry Nadeau, former Jasper crew chief Ryan Pemberton and new sponsorship from the U.S. Army.

Ricky Craven was set to join Benson and Nadeau in the Pontiac camp after team owner

(Far Left) After parting ways with Chip Ganassi at the end of the 2002 season, Jimmy Spencer was happy to join owner Jim Smith at Ultra Motorsports to campaign Dodge Intrepids with backing from Sirius Satellite Radio.

(Left) After getting his feet wet in six events last season, including a win at Lowe's Motor Speedway and a seventh at Atlanta, Jamie McMurray was clearly set to challenge for rookie honors driving the Havoline Dodge for Chip Ganassi and Felix Sabates.

(Below) The "49" BAM Racing Dodge welcomed new driver Ken Schrader and new sponsor 1-800-CALL ATT to begin the organization's second year of competition. Casey Mears grabbed the wheel of the No. 41 Target Dodge, ready to make his NASCAR Winston Cup Series debut in the 2003 Daytona 500. Bobby Labonte was hoping his new Interstate Chevrolet could bring a third championship in four years to Joe Gibbs Racing.

Cal Wells made the switch from Ford in hopes that factory support and a new in-house engine program will propel Craven upward after a career-best 15th-place finish in the final 2002 points.

Larry McClure also chose to go with Pontiac in place of the Chevrolets he had previously fielded for driver Mike Skinner. With a single top-10 finish in 2002, both McClure and Skinner prepared to

start the new season with every intention of returning to the more competitive form of years past.

Three-time NASCAR Craftsman Truck Series champion Jack Sprague threw his hat in the ring for rookie honors after spending 2002 in the NASCAR Busch Series, where he placed fifth in the final points. Sprague, with longtime crew chief Dennis Connor heading up the effort, prepared to

(Above) After an uncertain off-season, Andy Petree Racing arrived at Daytona with the No. 33 Chevrolet and backing from Monaco Coaches and driving prospect Christian Fittipaldi. Fittipaldi, nephew of CART and Formula 1 champion Emerson Fittipaldi, made his series debut late in 2002 at Phoenix.

(Right) Three-time NASCAR Craftsman Truck Series champion Jack Sprague prepares to challenge for 2003 rookie honors driving a Pontiac for Haas/CNC Racing. Sprague remained paired with long-time crew chief Dennis Connor, who also helped Sprague to a fifth-place finish in the 2002 NASCAR Busch Series final points.

pilot the NetZero Pontiac for new team owner Gene Haas and Haas CNC Motorsports.

Greg Biffle rounded out the freshman class, moving up to the NASCAR Winston Cup Series with powerhouse Roush Racing. Biffle's somewhat daunting resume showed three years in the NASCAR Craftsman Truck Series, where he was Rookie of the Year in 1998 and series champion in 2000. He then moved to the NASCAR Busch Series where he again took the rookie crown (in 2001) followed by the 2002 NBS championship.

The rest of the Roush organization remained largely intact during the off-season – and rightfully so. Mark Martin, 2002 runner-up to Stewart, prepared to start the season with crew chief Ben Leslie. Kurt Busch couldn't wait to get back in the saddle after ending 2002 on fire with three wins, a third and a sixth place in the last five events to finish one spot below Martin in third. After leading the series in 2002 with five wins, Matt Kenseth and crew chief Robbie Riser were making plans to challenge for the championship in 2003, their fourth full season together. And Jeff Burton, who went winless and finished out of the top 10 in points (12th) for the first time in six years, fully expected to return to contending form. Arguably the strongest team overall last year, no one in the NASCAR Winston Cup Series garage doubted that Roush Racing could end the season with the series' top rookie and the organization's first NASCAR Winston Cup Series championship.

With that, the short two months that separate Champion's Week in New York City and Speedweeks in Daytona Beach, Fla., vanished as competitors rolled into Daytona International Speedway for the start of the 2003 NASCAR Winston Cup Series season.

NASCAR WINSTON CUP SERIES CHAMPION 2003
MATT KENSETH

NASCAR WINSTON CUP SERIES 2003

First, winning the championship and being the last NASCAR Winston Cup champion is, to me, incredible. It's an awesome accomplishment, doing what the team did through a 38-race schedule and to be as consistent as they were in giving me such good cars. They didn't make any mistakes on pit road. So, it was a great year for me, all the guys at Roush Racing, my owners, Jack Roush and Mark Martin, Robbie Reiser, our crew chief, all our sponsors, and it is really neat to be the last NASCAR Winston Cup Series champion.

Winston has been a big part of this sport for the last 33 years, so to be the final champion is quite an honor.

Growing up in a small town like Cambridge, Wis., and especially in the Midwest, the NASCAR world seemed to be so far away. It was something I never thought I'd get to see in person when I was a little kid, much less be a part of it. So, it wasn't really something that crossed my mind. I had always dreamed of being a race car driver. It was something I thought was really cool, but it certainly never seemed like an attainable goal or what you'd call reality. NASCAR was just something you saw on television.

Robbie Reiser and Matt Kenseth display the symbol of a championship season!

I'd always wanted to be a race car driver and be in the racing business. I always liked the driving part and the competition side of it, so it was something I always strived to do. But I can't say I aimed to be a NASCAR Winston Cup driver. But as my career progressed it became a goal.

When I first started competing my main goal was to race full time and not have to work at some sort of non-racing job during the week. What I wanted to do was work on the race cars at night and race them on weekends. So, yes, I wanted to make that my job and earn a living at it. Once I got into racing and started doing better, that was my main goal. But I never dreamed we'd make it as far as we have and do the things we've accomplished.

I guess I got into racing because of the family. All my uncles on the Kenseth side raced at a little place in Wisconsin called Jefferson Speedway. My dad, Roy, did a little racing, too, and I really got into the sport with him. He and I started going to the races. He started driving and I began working on his cars when I was 13 years old (1985). It was a kind of father-son hobby. It was something for us to do to become closer and have a common interest.

We kind of had an informal agreement that he would buy a race car and drive it if I would keep it up. Then when I turned 16 I could be the driver. It was a lot of hard work, but it paid off because the experience taught me how to do more than just steer it. That's how it all started. One thing led to another. We started racing more and more, and I kept getting these different opportunities to drive other people's cars. One thing followed another, and we ended up as the NASCAR Winston Cup Series champion.

My mom, Nicki, was never that interested in auto racing. She started watching the races and has gotten into it because I'm part of it. She would go with us to lend her support and do all sorts of things for us. But she was never a huge fan. My dad, on the other hand, wanted to race, but the reason behind it was the father-son thing. He wanted to race, but with him being 45 years old and me being 13, obviously the goal was someday for him to go racing with me when I was driving.

It would be like switching roles. I think he started it so he could drive for a while and have me work on the cars and gain some knowledge and know what made them work.

I ran my first race at Columbus Speedway, in Wisconsin. It was probably May or June of 1988. It was a Late Model car for that track, but at most places it probably would have been called a Sportsman or Late Model Stock type of car. I raced on a lot of local tracks in Wisconsin and around the Midwest. I did some ASA (American Speed Association) races, some ARTGO (Late Model) stuff, some NASCAR All Pro events. I always ran what you'd call Late Model Stock Cars. Anywhere we could run our car where the rules were close enough is where we'd race. I won the third race I was ever in. I was 16 and a junior in high school.

We had a lot of good things happen this year, but one of the best places for us was Rockingham, N.C. It's a really great track to race on, a really fun place, and I'm kind of sad there will be only one race there next year. We've had a lot of good times there, and it's been good to me and my crew. They won the Union 76 Pit Crew Competition there two straight years (2002-01), and if we were to win the championship this year - which we ended up doing - I was hoping it would be at Rockingham. There have been a lot of special times there for me, and for Mark and Jack. They won their first NASCAR Winston Cup Series race there (1989), I won my first NASCAR Busch Series race there in 1998, and we had four top-10 finishes at Rockingham going into the race there in October.

It was also cool because Bill Elliott won it this year. It was where he ran his first race in 1976. Bill gave me my first NASCAR Winston Cup start at Dover, Del., in September 1998. He had to go to his father's funeral and we finished sixth in that race. Bill had already left the track when they

As a young man from Cambridge, Wis., a town of about a thousand people, Kenseth could not have imaged that one day he would drive some of the best equipment available and reach the pinnacle of the sport.

came and got me. I really don't know how that happened because I actually talked to Bill's crew chief, Mike Beam. He came down to the NASCAR Busch Series garage and asked me. I asked Mark and Jack if it would be OK, and they thought it would be a great idea.

As far as the entire season, we had a lot of great races and many opportunities to win. Maybe we didn't capitalize on things at the end of some races like I wish we could have, but basically we had good competitive car all year and the equipment was really reliable. The secret to being consistent is to be there at the end. It's having quality cars and the proper preparation at the shop to make sure everything is done right and is working properly. The first thing is to have quality equipment. The next is to have people who don't make mistakes and will give you reliable cars that will last 500 miles, or whatever, every Sunday.

One thing that got us the championship is that we've had basically the same guys on the team

for almost 4-1/2 years now. I think that's a big key. Whenever you can keep the same group of people together and keep them fired up and working as a team, that's a recipe for success. We've had a great team that have gotten along well, and we have all become buddies.

But anything can happen. Later in the year we broke an engine at Talladega (Ala.) and I crashed two cars at Kansas, and after those two weeks we lost a big pile of points. That was a little bit of cause for concern ... we hoped things wouldn't continue that way ... but other than that the year was pretty good. When you leave a track after running well, that makes you feel good and not too concerned about how things might develop.

But when you've had a week where you've lost some points and didn't run as well as you'd hoped you would, there is always a little cause for concern.

Thinking about that, I want to thank Tony Stewart for his advice. Tony knew we had two

"I had always dreamed of being a race car driver. ... I never dreamed we'd make it as far as we have and do the things we've accomplished."

bad weeks there and he called me. He went through the pressure last year when he was on his way to winning the championship. For him it came right down to the wire, and he had a lot of pressure on him those last couple of weeks. He told me what he went through and what he did to try and make it a little easier to deal with toward the end of the year.

Basically, Tony told me just to be myself and do the things I liked to do. Whatever you enjoy doing, just go do it. Don't sit around and think about the points 24 hours a day and seven days a week. All that does it get you all worked up. If you like going to the movies, do that or whatever it takes to keep your mind off it.

One thing about our team is that there are a lot of guys from the Midwest and Wisconsin ... guys that had helped Robbie and me with the Late Models. A lot of them have been with us a long time. Robbie and I have been together since 1997. We ran the NASCAR Busch Series together and we used to race against each other in Wisconsin. We work well together and he's a lot of the reason for our success. He came with me to Roush when we got the NASCAR Winston Cup Series. It was Mark Martin, though, who gave us this opportunity. Along with his and Jack's help, Robbie put the whole team together. He created the No. 17 team at Roush Racing and pretty much handpicked all the people.

Robbie used to race, too, and that helps a lot. I think because of that he could understand what I was going through on the track. He knew what to do and say when I was getting frustrated. He could see it because he drove and knows what it's like in certain situations.

Mark and I are alike in that we both raced a lot of the same kind of equipment before getting to the NASCAR Winston Cup level. Also, he ran in the ASA and a lot in the Midwest. So, in a way, we came from the same place and raced the same way. I think that's part of why Mark noticed me. I have a lot of respect for Mark and he's really helped me out a lot. Robbie picked me to drive his NASCAR Busch Series cars and Mark, I guess you

(Left) Kenseth started 18th in the Coca-Cola 600, in May, at Lowe's Motor Speedway, ran hard all day and finished second. It was one of 11 top-five finishes for the year.

(Below left) Crew chief Robbie Reiser was once a race driver himself. According to Kenseth, that was a plus that kept the No. 17 DeWalt Tools team on a successful path to the championship.

(Below) When Kenseth got into an accident late in the season at Kansas, his teammates didn't quit. They repaired his damaged Ford and got him back into race. He finished 36th and picked up valuable points.

could say, "discovered" me, took me under his wing and got me hooked up with Roush Racing. Through the years in the NASCAR Busch Series, Mark has taught me so much about both driving the cars and the business end that goes along with that. He's had so much experience, and I feel lucky that he was able to guide me. It would have been a lot more difficult without having someone like him there.

Winning the NASCAR Winston Cup Series Raybestos Rookie of the Year title in 2000 was helpful, too. It's neat that a company like Raybestos backs that program, and any time you race for a championship title or for points it's a learning experience. Everything in NASCAR racing is based on performance and consistency and keeping track of points for a whole year. So any time you go for a title like that it gives you knowledge and experience. So that was a big help getting me to where I am now.

Being the second NASCAR Winston Cup champion from Wisconsin is neat. I really never got to meet Alan Kulwicki. I saw him one time at Slinger (Wis.) Super Speedway. I was racing a Late Model there and he came back to run the Nationals (special event there). But it was unfortunate I never got the chance to talk to him. But whenever anybody from your home state can be a success in NASCAR ... especially the way he did it as an independent going up against the bigger teams ... that was always an inspiration.

This year, we definitely tried to be more consistent, and we certainly didn't want to win less races than we did in 2002. We still were trying just as hard to win races, but we were also trying to make our bad days not as bad. Last year we didn't do a very good job of managing that. We'd have a few good days and then a lot of terrible days. This year we tried to take those terrible days and turn them around. I think the team did a great job of that.

When it looked like we going to finish 25th, we'd get to work and pull a 10th-place finish out of it. When you do those things, that's what leads to a championship. When your bad days are 12th- and 14th-place finishes, that's what going to lead you to where you're supposed to be.

I don't think we could have had a much better year. We could have won more races - and we were in a position to do that - but you're just not going to win every race you think you should. A lot of times this year the fastest car didn't win the race, and that's been the case before. I've been the fastest car and not won. There are a lot of things that go into winning these races, and every-

thing's got to go perfectly. I certainly hope we can get into victory lane more often in 2004 than we did this year, but I also hope we can be consistent like we were this year.

So I really want to express my appreciation to everybody, especially Jack, Mark, Robbie, my family - and that includes my sister, Kelly - and all our sponsors. DeWalt Tools has been with us for years, and there's also the help we've received from Smirnoff Ice Triple Black; GE Lexan; Carhartt; American Woodworker; Kwickset; CITGO; Champion Spark Plugs; Comp Cams; Comcast; Sherwin-Williams; Mac Tools and Kraft. They have all helped make 2003 an unforgettable year.

I also want to thank all the fans of NASCAR Winston Cup Series racing. Whether or not you pull for me or someone else, your support and loyalty to the sport is what makes it work. And it's what makes it all worthwhile for those of us who compete week in and week out. I just want to express my appreciation for all the support you've given me over the years.

As for me, I'm just going to be myself and do the best job I can in representing my sport and NASCAR as its champion. Thanks to all.

Matt Kenseth
2003 NASCAR Winston Cup Series Champion

DAYTONA 500

February 16, 2003

The pages on the daily calendar had flipped over far too quickly for members of NASCAR Winston Cup Series teams during the winter months as they prepared for the coming season. For fans of stock car racing's premier division, however, February meant the anticipation would soon be over as the NASCAR Winston Cup Series rolled toward Florida for Speedweeks at Daytona and the opening of the 2003 campaign.

As further enticement to the start of the season, R.J. Reynolds had announced one week earlier that $3 million would be added to the point fund this season, bringing the championship fund to a whopping total of $17 million. The 2003 champion would receive at least $4.25 million, and the drivers finishing second, third and fourth would all be awarded more than $1 million each.

To kick off the 2003 edition of Speedweeks, this year's Budweiser Shootout at Daytona would be run under the lights for a prime-time television audience on Saturday night. Under a new format, the 70-lap sprint for a purse of nearly $1 million would be divided into two segments with a 10-minute break after the first 20 laps, during which teams would be allowed to change tires and make minor adjustments to the cars. With the smaller fuel cells mandated by NASCAR for the restrictor-place tracks, an additional pit stop would be required during the final 50-lap segment, and, although laps run under the yellow flag would be counted, a required "green-white-checkered" finish meant the race could not end under caution.

Tony Stewart was among the 19 drivers in this year's field for the Budweiser Shootout at Daytona, and the defending NASCAR Winston Cup Series champion was hoping to get his

> **"People ... just don't know what Daytona means ... unless you've lived your life pursuing dreams that come true here."**

Daytona 500 pole-winner Jeff Green drives his AOL Chevrolet up the middle behind Jerry Nadeau (01) with Mike Skinner (4) and rookie Jack Sprague (0) on his flanks as the 2003 NASCAR Winston Cup Series season gets underway at Daytona.

(Left and Above) Dale Earnhardt Jr. flashes under the flagstand in the second Gatorade Twin 125 to pick up the win and make his second trip to victory lane in less than a week. Earnhardt had already won the Budweiser Shootout at Daytona.

(Below Left) Daytona 500 winners Michael Waltrip (right) and Ward Burton discuss what it means to win the season's biggest race during an interview on national television. Waltrip, winner of the event in 2000, was followed in 2001 by Burton.

season started off right by taking a third consecutive win in the event. Other favorites included Jeff Gordon, picked just ahead of Stewart to capture his fifth championship in NASCAR's preseason poll, and of course, Dale Earnhardt Jr., who had dominated restrictor-plate racing over the past several seasons.

With a handful of laps remaining in the Shootout, Earnhardt picked up some drafting help from Ryan Newman and slipped past Gordon on the outside to take the lead. Try as he might, the DuPont Monte Carlo driver could not catch the swift Budweiser Chevrolet as Earnhardt powered to the win, beating Gordon by 0.180 second. Matt Kenseth took third in the furious pack that had the top 15 cars cross the finish line within one second of each other.

With the Budweiser Shootout in the books,

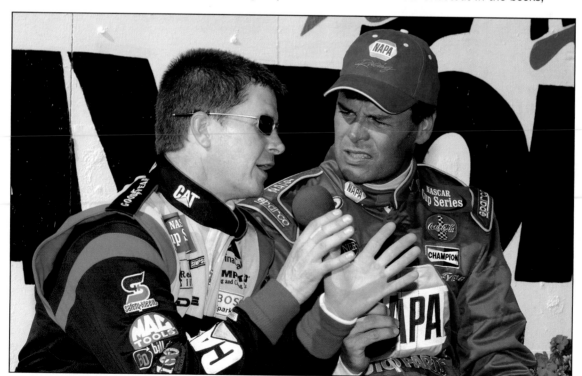

(Right) Robby Gordon claims victory after taking the win in the first Twin 125. He and teammate Jeff Green dominated the event and showed the competitiveness of their Richard Childress Racing Monte Carlos.

(Far Right) Dale Jarrett (88), Jeremy Mayfield (19) and Elliott Sadler (38) take the banks evenly spaced in three-wide formation trailed by Jeff Gordon (24), Matt Kenseth (17) and Mike Wallace (09). Wallace, driving a Dodge for owner Ray Evernham, took a top-10 finish in ninth place.

(Below) In the early laps, pole-winner Jeff Green (30) got shuffled back in the middle lane while Michael Waltrip (15), Todd Bodine (54), Ricky Rudd (21) and Sterling Marlin (40) hooked up on the bottom, with Robby Gordon (31), Earnhardt Jr. (8), Tony Stewart (20), Jimmie Johnson (48), John Andretti (43) and Bill Elliott (9) bunched up on the high side.

everyone's attention turned to Sunday's Bud Pole qualifying session that would determine the front row for the Daytona 500 and starting positions for the Gatorade Twin 125s. Most expected Dale Earnhardt Jr. to continue his heroics of the night before and capture the pole, but when time trials concluded, Jeff Green had posted at lap at 186.606 miles per hour, edging the Budweiser Chevrolet driver by just under six-hundredths of a second to gain his second career Bud Pole. It was the second straight Daytona pole for team owner Richard Childress after driver Kevin Harvick took the top starting spot for the 2002 Pepsi 400.

The rest of the Daytona 500 field through the 30th position would be determined by the results of the Gatorade Twin 125 qualifiers to be run on

Thursday. In the first Twin 125, Jeff Green and his Childress Racing teammate, Robby Gordon, worked together at the front of the pack, with Green leading the first 31 laps before pitting for fuel. With nearly half the field following the leader down pit road, Green overshot his pit stall a bit and was momentarily blocked by Jeff Burton. That slight delay was enough to turn the lead over to Robby Gordon, who led the final 17 laps on the

way to the win. Green recovered to finished second ahead of Ricky Rudd, Sterling Marlin and Jeff Burton.

Dale Earnhardt Jr. led the field under green in the second Twin 125 and, other than an early challenge from Kevin Harvick, dominated the event, further staking his claim as the odds-on favorite to win the Daytona 500. Earnhardt's DEI teammate, Michael Waltrip, followed Earnhardt

(Above) Veterans Rusty Wallace (2), driving a Dodge for the first time in his NASCAR Winston Cup career, and Mark Martin (6) cross the stripe side by side amidst the thunderous pack. Despite 87 wins between them, both drivers were looking for their first trip to a Daytona victory lane.

(Left) The field fans out in a relatively "comfortable" three-wide pack along the 18-degree banked tri-oval. Many drivers felt the new "common templates" that dictate aerodynamics made the cars feel more stable in the draft than in years past.

across the line in second, with Todd Bodine third, Rusty Wallace fourth and Tony Stewart in fifth.

In post-race inspection, Wallace's Dodge was found to have a carburetor that did not meet specifications for a restrictor-plate track, and his fourth-place finish was disqualified, dropping the Miller Lite Dodge to the 38th starting spot for Sunday's race.

Qualifying times for those who were unable to gain a top-15 finish in the Twins set positions 31-36. In addition to Wallace, provisionals went to Ryan Newman, Dave Blaney, Johnny Benson, Terry Labonte, Jerry Nadeau and Mike Skinner. A disappointed Brett Bodine was among the drivers who failed to make the event.

Dale Earnhardt Jr. was one of a handful of NASCAR Winston Cup Series drivers who chose to compete in Saturday's NASCAR Busch Series event, and Earnhardt added to the already popular notion that he would be the man to beat in the "500" by grabbing his second straight win the 300-mile event.

With cloudy skies and a dreary forecast on Sunday, the weather promised to become a factor as the field of 43 rumbled under the green flag to kick off the 2003 NASCAR Winston Cup Series season. Before the cars could even get up to full speed, Jeff Green, Michael Waltrip and Robby Gordon headed into the third turn in a three-wide

tussle, with Waltrip asserting himself to take the early lead. Michael and his NAPA Chevrolet held that spot for the first 34 laps before the first round of green-flag stops for fuel.

As the race settled in, Tony Stewart and Earnhardt Jr. swapped the point, showing they, too, had contending cars, while facing strong challenges from Harvick, Robby Gordon and Elliott Sadler's M&M's Ford.

The second caution flag flew on lap 58 after Ken Schrader's BAM Racing Dodge got tapped from behind, hit the wall and shot across the track in the path of Ryan Newman. The resulting crash turned Newman's ALLTEL Dodge into a pile of rubble on the frontstretch grass, and Bobby Labonte and Ward Burton suffered damage as well.

Back under green, the "DEI Duo" of Waltrip and Earnhardt Jr. continued to thrash the field, showing very much the same form that brought them victories in six of the last eight restrictor-plate races, including three of the last four at Daytona. But, just past the 70-lap mark, Earnhardt radioed to crew chief Tony Eury Sr. that the red No. 8 no longer registered any battery voltage, the result of a failed alternator. An unscheduled pit stop to change the battery ultimately cost him two laps — and seemingly any chance to win his first Daytona 500. But that's not to say he wouldn't be a factor in the race.

(Left) Michael Waltrip (15) takes the final yellow flag ahead of Kurt Busch (97) with Dale Earnhardt Jr., a lap down, on the outside. This caution, brought out on lap 106, sealed the final running order as rain showers set in moments later.

(Below) Michael Waltrip's NAPA crew changes right-side tires and adds fuel during a round of green-flag pit stops. Fine work in the pits helped keep Waltrip out front, where he led 68 of the 109 laps run in the event.

Waltrip continued his battle at the front until lap 95, when a cut tire sent pole-winner Jeff Green spinning into the wall, collecting Jimmy Spencer in the process. As the third caution flag of the race flew, crew chiefs turned an eye to the sky. Approaching storms would begin to dictate strategy.

When most of the leaders decided to pit for fresh tires and a load of fuel, Jimmie Johnson's Lowe's crew went to work. They performed their pit stop flawlessly, turning the second-year driver back to the track in the lead, followed by Waltrip, Stewart, Jeff Gordon and Robby Gordon.

Johnson was able to hold the point and, with storms approaching, appeared to be in position to win — until, in his rearview mirror, there appeared a sight that made him shudder. There was the big red Chevrolet with the word "Budweiser" strewn across the hood and driver Earnhardt aboard, determined to regain a lap. And on Dale's bumper sat the blue NAPA Chevrolet. Instantly, Johnson knew that without a drafting partner, he was in trouble.

Earnhardt dropped to the bottom and helped pull Waltrip into the lead, leaving Johnson help-less to defend the point. Moments later, Ward Burton lost control in the fourth turn and hit the wall. Waltrip headed toward the flagstand to take the yellow ahead of Kurt Busch, who also was

able to work past Johnson into second place.

While the field fell in line behind the pace car, raindrops again began to fall, bringing out the red flag on lap 109 and forcing Waltrip to sit patiently and wait. Track personnel tried desperately to dry the track, but a line of approaching showers forced NASCAR officials to call the race just before 5:30 p.m.

(Above) A very happy "Slugger" Labbe hoists his trophy as the winning crew chief of the Daytona 500. This was his second career win as a crew chief, the other coming here at Daytona in the 2001 Pepsi 400.

(Right) Family portrait. Michael Waltrip, with wife Buffy and daughters Caitlin and Margaret, are all smiles for photographers as they share the victory celebration at Daytona.

As the announcement was made, Michael sprang to his feet and charged in celebration onto the frontstretch grass. There would be no holding back in this victory celebration, which marked Waltrip's third career win, all coming at Daytona.

"People … just don't know what Daytona means," Waltrip said of winning at the storied superspeedway. "You can't know unless you've lived your life pursuing dreams that come true here."

Kurt Busch showed his continued prowess on the superspeedways of Daytona and Talladega where, with his second-place effort, he scored his fourth top-five finish in his last five restrictor-plate races. Jimmie Johnson held on to third place ahead of Kevin Harvick in fourth and Mark Martin in fifth. Robby Gordon, Stewart, Jeremy Mayfield, Mike Wallace and Dale Jarrett rounded out the top 10.

Daytona 500 *final race results*

Fin. Pos.	Start Pos.	Car No.	Driver	Team	Fin. Pos.	Start Pos.	Car No.	Driver	Team
1	4	15	Michael Waltrip	NAPA Chevrolet	23	16	38	Elliott Sadler	M&M's Ford
2	36	97	Kurt Busch	Rubbermaid Ford	24	39	77	Dave Blaney	Jasper Engines & Transmissions Ford
3	10	48	Jimmie Johnson	Lowe's Chevrolet	25	38	2	Rusty Wallace	Miller Lite Dodge
4	31	29	Kevin Harvick	GM Goodwrench Chevrolet	26	25	32	Ricky Craven	Tide Pontiac
5	26	6	Mark Martin	Pfizer/Viagra Ford	27	29	41	Casey Mears	Target Dodge
6	3	31	Robby Gordon	Cingular Wireless Chevrolet	28	42	01	Jerry Nadeau	U.S. Army Pontiac
7	8	20	Tony Stewart	Home Depot Chevrolet	29	32	1	Steve Park	Pennzoil Chevrolet
8	20	19	Jeremy Mayfield	Dodge Dealers Dodge	30	41	5	Terry Labonte	Kellogg's/got milk? Chevrolet
9	18	09	Mike Wallace	Miccosukee Resort Dodge	31	19	42	Jamie McMurray	Havoline Dodge
10	11	88	Dale Jarrett	UPS Ford	32	14	9	Bill Elliott	Dodge Dealers Dodge
11	9	99	Jeff Burton	CITGO Ford	33	33	74	Tony Raines	Staff America Chevrolet
12	13	24	Jeff Gordon	DuPont Chevrolet	34	12	43	John Andretti	Cheerios Dodge
13	30	45	Kyle Petty	Georgia Pacific Dodge	35	34	33	Christian Fittipaldi	Monaco Coaches Chevrolet
14	24	0	Jack Sprague	NetZero Pontiac	36	2	8	Dale Earnhardt Jr.	Budweiser Chevrolet
15	5	21	Ricky Rudd	Motorcraft Ford	37	43	4	Mike Skinner	Kodak Pontiac
16	21	23	Kenny Wallace	Stacker2 Dodge	38	17	22	Ward Burton	Caterpillar Dodge
17	7	40	Sterling Marlin	Coors Light Dodge	39	1	30	Jeff Green	America Online Chevrolet
18	6	54	Todd Bodine	National Guard Ford	40	23	7	Jimmy Spencer	Sirius Satellite Radio Dodge
19	40	10	Johnny Benson	Valvoline Pontiac	41	22	18	Bobby Labonte	Interstate Batteries Chevrolet
20	35	17	Matt Kenseth	DEWALT Power Tools Ford	42	28	49	Ken Schrader	1-800-CallATT Dodge
21	27	16	Greg Biffle	Grainger Ford	43	37	12	Ryan Newman	ALLTEL Dodge
22	15	25	Joe Nemechek	UAW-Delphi Chevrolet					

SUBWAY 400

February 23, 2003

Michael Waltrip barely had time to savor his emotional victory in the rain-shortened Daytona 500 before heading off to Rockingham, N.C., and North Carolina Speedway for the running of the Subway 400.

The super-sleek restrictor-plate cars were packed away in the team shops and now it was time to break out the "downforce" cars to tackle the high banks at the 1.017-mile track in North Carolina's Sandhills region. The track's gritty asphalt, characteristic of the area, would create challenges for drivers and crew chiefs completely different from those they had dealt with at Daytona. Chassis setups and tire management were foremost in their minds at the track where pit stops are predicated more on the need for fresh tires than for fuel.

"That's what makes this win (so) special ... to know that we really beat the hottest guy in NASCAR right now."

The Subway 400 would mark career milestones for two drivers: John Andretti would be making his 300th NASCAR Winston Cup Series start, while Rusty Wallace would roll of the line for the 600th time, making him 14th on the all-time list for NASCAR Winston Cup starts, just two behind 13th-place James Hylton. A far as Wallace was concerned, there was no better place to be than here at Rockingham, where he leads all active drivers with five career wins. After going winless for the first time in 17 seasons in 2001, Wallace was determined to put an end to his 63-race winless streak, the longest in his career.

Other drivers looking for success at "The Rock" included Ricky Craven, with three top-10 finishes in his last four starts at Rockingham and the Bud Pole winner in this event last season, and Dale Jarrett, who had found the formula for success at Rockingham while posting

Dale Jarrett exhibited patience and expertise gained from years of experience racing at Rockingham and, with well-cared-for tires on his UPS Taurus, held the advantage at the finish.

(Left) Dave Blaney (77) brings the starting field under green with Mark Martin (6) and Bill Elliott (9) behind him on the inside and Johnny Benson on his right. Blaney jumped to the early lead but quickly began battling a loose race car and finished a respectable 10th.

(Below) Steve Park (1) and John Andretti (43) run together along Rockingham's frontstretch. Park, the 2001 winner of this event, was not quite as quick this year and fell a lap off the pace, while Andretti suffered a broken radiator and finished 39th.

(Opposite) Rusty Wallace (2) leads the way for Larry Foyt (14) and Bill Elliott (9) in the event's early going. After weekend rains thoroughly cleaned the track, Wallace had his way while leading 182 of the first 219 laps, but when the groove came back, the Miller Lite Dodge became a handful and Wallace dropped to sixth at the finish.

12 straight top 10s, including one win, between 1996 and 2001. Jarrett, with a satisfactory 10th place at Daytona, was hoping for another strong finish to get his season started with the kind of consistency he enjoyed during his championship campaign in 1999.

To help counter the so-called "youth movement" of last year, Jarrett, perhaps the best natural athlete in the series, spent the off-season undergoing a vigorous fitness program and said he was in the best shape of his life when he began the season at Daytona. He knew that winning would require him to be razor sharp, both physically and mentally, if he were to mount a serious challenge against the bright new stars in the sport. Together with new crew chief Brad Parrott and a race team

that had undergone change over the winter, Jarrett was more than ready to get his team back on track toward a run at the title.

Perhaps the brightest of the new stars was 24-year-old Kurt Busch. With his second-place finish the previous week at Daytona, Busch extended a streak of six consecutive top-six finishes, including three victories, dating back to Martinsville last fall. Within that string was a third-place finish here at Rockingham in early November, and Busch was intent on adding yet another win to his remarkable hot streak.

Another driver looking forward to the Subway 400 was Johnny Benson, who scored his first career win in the series' last visit to Rockingham. In Bud Pole qualifying, Benson turned a fast lap at 154.553 mph, but that was only good enough for second on the starting grid. Dave Blaney sank his foot into the Jasper Engines Ford and clicked off a lap that was nearly a half-second faster than Benson's to grab his first career Bud Pole in his 113th NASCAR Winston Cup Series start.

The weather forecast called for rain throughout weekend, which curtailed practice sessions and left drivers and crew chiefs guessing on their setups for a "green" race track on Sunday. To aid all the teams, NASCAR announced it would throw a competition caution early in the event so crews could check tire wear and make necessary adjustments to the cars.

Blaney squirted away from Mark Martin as the green flag fell on a cold and blustery Sunday, and the Jasper Ford driver led the first eight laps before Mark Martin and Ricky Craven emerged stronger in the early going, swapping the lead between them over the first 25 circuits.

That's how long it took for Rusty Wallace to settle in with his Miller Lite Dodge. Working from his eighth-place starting position, Wallace powered to the point for the first time on lap 27 and began to motor away from the field. Wallace was clearly the fastest, leading four times over the next 182 laps and giving up the lead only briefly to Mark Martin during pit stops.

Meanwhile, Kurt Busch had been carefully slicing his way through the field from his 27th starting position. On the restart after the fifth caution of the race for a Dale Earnhardt Jr. spin, Busch lined up directly behind Wallace at the front of the field. For the next 15 laps, Busch dogged Wallace, making several challenges for the lead, but he was unable to overtake the 1989 champion. Finally, on lap 220, Busch closed up on the Miller Lite Dodge and dove to the inside in turn one to take the point. Over the next 25 laps,

Wallace made several runs at Busch but, with the racing groove now fully worn in, the setup on Rusty's Dodge caused him to begin slipping in the turns, allowing Busch to motor off and dominate the second half of the event.

Behind the hard charging Busch, Dale Jarrett was carefully picking his way through the field, gaining position by position while taking care of the tires on his UPS Ford. Six times between 1996 and 1999, Jarrett finished second at Rockingham, and, in two of those, he led the most laps but was passed near the finish with worn-out tires.

Not this time.

Relying on experience, Jarrett methodically closed on Busch, watching him, sizing him up. With 10 laps remaining in the race, Jarrett pulled alongside Busch in the first turn and dropped low to take the lead for the first time in the event.

Busch fought back, regaining the lead with less the five to go, but Jarrett noticed the Rubbermaid Ford was loose in turns three and four. On the next lap, Jarrett slid the nose of his Taurus right up to Busch's bumper – just enough to loosen it up and force him high and out of the groove. As Busch fought to keep his car off the wall, Jarrett

Kurt Busch congratulates Dale Jarrett during the victory lane celebration. Busch later said he was proud of the way the two had raced during their exciting duel over the final laps, while Jarrett expressed satisfaction in beating the series' hottest driver.

dropped to the inside and took the lead for the last time.

In victory lane, Jarrett celebrated his 31st career win, his second at North Carolina Speedway. "That's what makes this win (so) special," said Jarrett of his victory over Busch, "to know that we really beat the hottest guy in NASCAR right now."

Busch held on to second place and, combined with his runner-up finish at Daytona, took over the point lead for the first time in his young career. Last year's event winner, Matt Kenseth, took third place ahead of Ricky Carven and Jamie McMurray. Rusty Wallace faded to sixth place after leading the most laps in the event, while Mark Martin took seventh ahead of Jimmie Johnson and Elliott Sadler. Pole-winner Dave Blaney fought a loose race car nearly all day, but held on for 10th place at the finish.

Subway 400 *final race results*

Fin. Pos.	Start Pos.	Car No.	Driver	Team		Fin. Pos.	Start Pos.	Car No.	Driver	Team
1	9	88	Dale Jarrett	UPS Ford		23	14	25	Joe Nemechek	UAW-Delphi Chevrolet
2	27	97	Kurt Busch	Rubbermaid Ford		24	35	49	Ken Schrader	BAM Racing Dodge
3	18	17	Matt Kenseth	DEWALT Power Tools Ford		25	26	29	Kevin Harvick	GM Goodwrench Chevrolet
4	6	32	Ricky Craven	Tide Pontiac		26	24	01	Jerry Nadeau	U.S. Army Pontiac
5	7	42	Jamie McMurray	Havoline Dodge		27	31	5	Terry Labonte	Kellogg's/got milk? Chevrolet
6	8	2	Rusty Wallace	Miller Lite Dodge		28	36	7	Jimmy Spencer	Sirius Satellite Radio Dodge
7	3	6	Mark Martin	Pfizer Ford		29	19	31	Robby Gordon	Cingular Wireless Chevrolet
8	37	48	Jimmie Johnson	Lowe's Chevrolet		30	16	41	Casey Mears	Target Dodge
9	11	38	Elliott Sadler	M&M's Ford		31	39	30	Jeff Green	America Online Chevrolet
10	1	77	Dave Blaney	Jasper Engines & Transmissions Ford		32	5	9	Bill Elliott	Dodge Dealers/UAW Dodge
11	28	21	Ricky Rudd	Motorcraft Ford		33	12	8	Dale Earnhardt Jr.	Budweiser Chevrolet
12	38	99	Jeff Burton	CITGO Ford		34	34	0	Jack Sprague	NetZero Pontiac
13	2	10	Johnny Benson	Valvoline Pontiac		35	30	45	Kyle Petty	Georgia Pacific Dodge
14	21	12	Ryan Newman	ALLTEL Dodge		36	41	14	Larry Foyt	Harrah's Dodge
15	23	24	Jeff Gordon	DuPont Chevrolet		37	42	74	Tony Raines	BACE Motorsports Chevrolet
16	10	18	Bobby Labonte	Interstate Batteries Chevrolet		38	17	23	Kenny Wallace	Stacker2 Dodge
17	20	4	Mike Skinner	Kodak Pontiac		39	32	43	John Andretti	Cheerios Dodge
18	15	22	Ward Burton	Caterpillar Dodge		40	4	40	Sterling Marlin	Coors Light Dodge
19	22	15	Michael Waltrip	NAPA Chevrolet		41	29	19	Jeremy Mayfield	Dodge Dealers/UAW Dodge
20	33	20	Tony Stewart	The Home Depot Chevrolet		42	40	54	Todd Bodine	National Guard Ford
21	25	1	Steve Park	Pennzoil Chevrolet		43	43	37	Derrike Cope	Friendly's Ice Cream Chevrolet
22	13	16	Greg Biffle	Grainger Ford						

UAW-DAIMLER CHRYSLER 400

March 2, 2003

With two runner-up finishes in the first two races of the 2003 season, new point leader Kurt Busch had to be thinking, "There's no place like home."

The 24-year-old returned to his hometown of Las Vegas, Nevada, riding a hot streak of seven consecutive finishes of sixth or better, dating back to November 2002. He sat atop the points for the first time in his young career, and he was well aware that the powerful Roush Racing Fords had an unprecedented record of success at the desert speed palace known as Las Vegas Motor Speedway. Certainly, there was no better time or place than here and now to log his first win of the season and extend his lead in the standings.

But no win comes easily in NASCAR's top series, and Busch's toughest competition, he knew, would likely come from within his own organization. Mark Martin, winner of the inaugural event as Las Vegas in 1998 was riding his own streak of seven consecutive top 10s and was the only driver to have finished in the top 10 in all five of the events run at the 1.5-mile superspeedway.

Jeff Burton followed Martin's 1998 win with back-to-back victories in 1999 and 2000. In his five starts at the track, Burton boasted three top fives and a top 10 while leading a total of 204 laps, far more than any other driver in the series. With his 12th-place finish at Rockingham the previous week, Burton moved into the top 10 in points and arrived at Las Vegas hungry to notch his 18th career victory after going winless in 2002.

And then there was Matt Kenseth, last season's winningest driver and fresh off a third-place finish – behind Busch – in the Subway 400. Kenseth had

"Last week the crew was down on itself because we didn't have quite the pit stop we wished for at the end. ... This week they won the race for me."

Morning sun breaks the horizon over the Nevada desert as work is already underway on the Dodges of Rusty Wallace (2) and Ryan Newman in the garage at Las Vegas Motor Speedway. Newman fared the best of the Penske cars with at third-place effort in qualifying and a strong seventh-place finish, Newman's first top 10 of the season.

yet to score a top 10 at Las Vegas in three career starts, but he was determined to end that statistic by resuming his winning ways this weekend.

All four drivers were among the top seven in the early-season point standings, and everyone in the NASCAR Winston Cup Series garage considered the powerful Roush Fords the early favorites as the weekend's activities got underway.

With his win less than a week ago at Rockingham, Dale Jarrett moved into second in the points, and he, too, was looking forward to the UAW-Daimler Chrysler 400. Jarrett had proven to be fast at LVMS as the only driver to win two Bud Poles in the five events run to date and with finishes among the top 10 on three occasions. Counting the pole position won by Ricky Rudd in 2000, Robert Yates Racing Fords owned three poles in the five events run at Las Vegas.

When Bud Pole qualifying got underway, the best of the Yates and Roush Fords was Kurt Busch, who turned the fifth-fastest speed on his two-lap run. Fastest on the track was Bobby Labonte and his Interstate Batteries Chevrolet, breaking Todd Bodine's track record set last year with a lap at 173.016 miles per our. The Texan's 33rd career pole was his first since April 2001 at California, 65 races ago.

Labonte's speed just nipped the lap turned by Jeff Gordon, moving the 2001 winner of this event to the outside of the front row. Ryan Newman

(Left) Hideo Fukuyama happily fields questions during a press conference to announce support from Kikkoman Soy Sauce for a limited number of races in 2003 on the No. 66 Fords fielded by BelCar Racing. Fukuyama used a provisional to make the field and finished 33rd on race day.

(Below) Front-row starters Bobby Labonte (18) and Jeff Gordon (24) bring the starting field across the line to begin the NASCAR Winston Cup Series' sixth event at Las Vegas Motor Speedway. Labonte went on to score his first top five of the season in fourth. Gordon led the first 50 laps but was later caught up in a wreck and did not finish.

(Above) Dale Earnhardt Jr. (8) fends off a challenge from Kurt Busch (97) as the two duke it out on the Las Vegas straightaway. Earnhardt Jr. made it to the front and led the most laps before taking second at the finish, a result that vaulted him from 38th to 18th in the points. Busch stayed among the leaders until an accident handed him a DNF and dropped him from the point lead to sixth in the standings.

(Right) Michael Waltrip's NAPA Chevrolet was stout at Las Vegas and took him to a satisfying third-place finish that put him back atop the standings.

wheeled the fastest Dodge to third on the starting grid, just ahead of Dale Earnhardt Jr.'s Budweiser Chevrolet.

Among those using provisionals to make the field were Hideo Fukuyama, set to make his first start of the year, the third of his career, driving the No. 66 Ford for owners Travis Carter and Sam Belnavis, and Derrike Cope, also making his first start of the season. Rookie Greg Biffle failed to make the field in his No. 16 Roush Ford, along with newcomer Brandon Ash.

An estimated crowd of 140,000 packed the grandstands under clear and sunny skies for the sixth running of the UAW-Daimler Chrysler 400, and Jeff Gordon took control immediately after the drop of the green flag, passing Bobby Labonte on the outside in turns one and two with Kurt Busch in tow. Gordon remained at the point through the first round of green-flag pit stops until Dale Earnhardt Jr. tracked him down at took the lead on lap 51.

Another round of stops under green followed, with "Little E" able to retain the lead after everyone had pitted for fresh tires and fuel. But it wasn't long before Earnhardt's mirror began to fill with the blue-and-yellow colors of Michael Waltrip's NAPA Chevrolet. After working his way toward the front from his ninth-place starting spot, Waltrip began putting pressure on Earnhardt's Budweiser Monte Carlo. For three laps, Waltrip dueled with his DEI teammate until, on lap 91,

he was able to overtake Earnhardt in the first turn to become the event's third leader.

The race ran caution free for the first 100 laps until Ricky Craven and Larry Foyt got together off turn four, with Craven spinning through the grass along the frontstretch.

As so often happens, cautions breed more cautions. And that's how it went, with six yellow flags thrown for various incidents, slowing the field for 30 of the next 83 laps. Among the victims were Dale Jarrett, who hit the wall hard after contact with Steve Park, and Rusty Wallace, Jeff Gordon and Kurt Busch, all out of the event after a Wallace-Mike Skinner skirmish in the second turn that collected a total of seven cars.

By the first restart, which occurred at lap 107, Kenseth, who started 17th, had worked his way into the fifth position. He remained fifth after the second caution and moved into fourth place before the third yellow flag on lap 127. When Dale Jarrett spun a handful of laps later, the leaders chose to pit again, and the DeWalt crew

flag flew on lap 171, and it took Kenseth just a lap and a half to overtake Gordon and power to the front for the first time in the race.

Kenseth's car was dialed in, and the Wisconsin native, just a week away from his 31st birthday, drove the perfect line around the 1.5-mile super-speedway. With just under 100 laps remaining, Kenseth faced one more challenge: a final stop for tires and fuel.

Running hard under green, Matt peeled off the fourth turn and headed down pit road with 40 laps to go, giving up the lead to Jimmie Johnson. Waiting behind pit wall was the reigning two-time world champion pit crew, and, although the team had undergone several personnel changes over the winter, the Robbie Reiser-led gang reeled off a spectacular 13.2-second stop and sent their driver back into action.

When all the leaders had completed stops of their own, Kenseth held a commanding four-second lead – an advantage he was able to stretch to more than nine seconds before taking his first

(Left) Tony Stewart's Home Depot Chevrolet shows a fender patch resulting from a collision with Jeff Green on pit road. Stewart and his team recovered from the incident nicely and the defending series champ pulled off a strong fifth-place finish.

(Below) Matt Kenseth blasts off pit road after his championship pit crew reeled off a sparkling 13.2-second pit stop under green in the closing laps of the race. The four-tire stop gave Kenseth a cushion at the point that he stretched into a commanding lead.

turned Kenseth back onto the track in second place behind Earnhardt Jr., who held the point for the next 30 laps.

The race slowed again for a fourth-turn spin by Jamie McMurray, and Jeff Gordon's DuPont crew put the No. 24 Chevrolet out front for the restart, followed by Kenseth and Earnhardt Jr. The green

(Right) Matt Kenseth (17) leads the way in front of Dale Earnhardt Jr. (8), Jimmie Johnson (48), Sterling Marlin (40) and Bobby Labonte (18). Kenseth took the lead for the first time on lap 172 and was untouchable from there.

(Below Right) Matt Kenseth displays his trophy belt after pounding the competition in the Las Vegas ring. The win was his first of the year and the seventh of his career, coming in his 115th NASCAR Winston Cup Series start.

win of the season, the seventh of his NASCAR Winston Cup Series career.

"Last week the crew was down on itself because we didn't have quite the pit stop we wished for at the end. ... This week they won the race for me," Kenseth said of his team's late-race heroics.

DEI teammates Dale Earnhardt Jr. and Michael Waltrip swept second and third, respectively, squelching some who had been critical of the teams' performances on tracks other than those using restrictor plates, while the Joe Gibbs Racing Chevrolets of Bobby Labonte and Tony Stewart took fourth and fifth in the final running order.

UAW-Daimler Chrysler 400 *final race results*

Fin. Pos.	Start Pos.	Car No.	Driver	Team	Fin. Pos.	Start Pos.	Car No.	Driver	Team
1	17	17	Matt Kenseth	DEWALT Power Tools Ford	23	21	31	Robby Gordon	Cingular Wireless Chevrolet
2	4	8	Dale Earnhardt Jr.	Budweiser Chevrolet	24	32	74	Tony Raines	BACE Motorsports Chevrolet
3	9	15	Michael Waltrip	NAPA Chevrolet	25	20	22	Ward Burton	Caterpillar Dodge
4	1	18	Bobby Labonte	Interstate Batteries Chevrolet	26	42	0	Jack Sprague	NetZero Pontiac
5	8	20	Tony Stewart	Home Depot Chevrolet	27	14	30	Jeff Green	America Online Chevrolet
6	7	99	Jeff Burton	CITGO Ford	28	28	49	Ken Schrader	dakota imaging, inc. Dodge
7	3	12	Ryan Newman	ALLTEL Dodge	29	43	37	Derrike Cope	Friendly's Chevrolet
8	34	40	Sterling Marlin	Coors Light Dodge	30	33	23	Kenny Wallace	Stacker2 Dodge
9	26	25	Joe Nemechek	UAW-Delphi Chevrolet	31	19	45	Kyle Petty	Georgia Pacific Dodge
10	39	1	Steve Park	Pennzoil Chevrolet	32	12	42	Jamie McMurray	Havoline Dodge
11	10	48	Jimmie Johnson	Lowe's Chevrolet	33	41	66	Hideo Fukuyama	Kikkoman Ford
12	16	10	Johnny Benson	Valvoline Pontiac	34	35	77	Dave Blaney	Jasper Engines & Transmissions Ford
13	22	29	Kevin Harvick	GM Goodwrench Service Chevrolet	35	31	14	Larry Foyt	Harrah's Dodge
14	30	9	Bill Elliott	Dodge Dealers/UAW Dodge	36	37	32	Ricky Craven	Tide Pontiac
15	18	41	Casey Mears	Target Dodge	37	2	24	Jeff Gordon	DuPont Chevrolet
16	36	5	Terry Labonte	Kellogg's/got milk? Chevrolet	38	5	97	Kurt Busch	Rubbermaid Ford
17	15	7	Jimmy Spencer	Sirius Satellite Radio Dodge	39	40	4	Mike Skinner	Kodak Pontiac
18	6	43	John Andretti	Cheerios Dodge	40	25	2	Rusty Wallace	Miller Lite Dodge
19	38	21	Ricky Rudd	Motorcraft Ford	41	27	88	Dale Jarrett	UPS Ford
20	24	54	Todd Bodine	National Guard Ford	42	23	38	Elliott Sadler	M&M's Ford
21	13	19	Jeremy Mayfield	Dodge Dealers/UAW Dodge	43	29	6	Mark Martin	Pfizer/Viagra Ford
22	11	01	Jerry Nadeau	USG/Sheetrock Pontiac					

BASS PRO SHOPS
MBNA 500

March 9, 2003

The results from Las Vegas shuffled the early-season point standings considerably. Kurt Busch and Dale Jarrett, first and second in the points after Rockingham, both fell victim to accidents and dropped to sixth and 10th at the end of the UAW-Daimler Chrysler 400, ending Busch's hot streak of seven straight top-six finishes. Mark Martin's streak of seven top 10s also ended in a cloud of smoke when his engine let go before the halfway point, and Martin dropped out of the top 10 altogether.

Others moved the opposite direction in the standings. On the strength of Matt Kenseth's win at Las Vegas, the DeWalt driver jumped from sixth to second in the points, while Michael Waltrip used his third-place finish to retake the top spot in the standings. For Waltrip, this was the third time in his career he was listed on top, the first time not directly following the Daytona 500. Jimmie Johnson remained third after just missing the top 10 at Vegas, and Jeff Burton moved from seventh to fourth in the points with a solid sixth place in the Nevada desert.

"I didn't have a prepared plan. I just had to give it my best shot, because we'd led too many laps and had too fast a car to not try."

Two other beneficiaries of the Las Vegas results arrived at Atlanta Motor Speedway particularly optimistic about the weekend's events. Tony Stewart and Kevin Harvick had jumped from ninth and 10th in the points to fifth and seventh, respectively, and were looking forward to competing at Atlanta where both had enjoyed success in the past.

As the defending event champion, Stewart knew he had a chance to establish himself quickly as the man to beat in defense of his series title. He was just 52 points behind Kenseth and well ahead of where he was a year ago when he began his season-long charge at the title. Including his win a year ago, he was riding a string of three straight top 10s at AMS.

The Interstate Batteries team supported Bobby Labonte's strong efforts on the track with quick and efficient stops in the pits. That helped Labonte lead more than 50 percent of the laps in the race and pick up the early-season win.

(Left) Crew chief Raymond Fox III (left) and team manager Todd Parrott check the progress of their driver, Elliott Sadler. Sadler bounced back from a disappointing day at Las Vegas with the third-best run in qualifying and a sixth place in the final rundown from Atlanta.

(Below Left) Eddie O'Hare works on the rear hub assembly of Jeremy Mayfield's Dodge before Friday's qualifying round.

(Below Right) Ryan Newman (12) leads the starting field under the green flag to begin the the Bass Pro Shops MBNA 500 at Atlanta, with Georgia native Bill Elliott on his right.

For Harvick, Atlanta garnered fond memories as the track where, after taking the wheel of the GM Goodwrench Chevrolet following the death of Dale Earnhardt in 2001, he scored a stirring victory in just his third career NASCAR Winston Cup Series start. Further bolstering Harvick's mindset was the announcement on Saturday before the race that he, Goodwrench and Richard Childress had all signed contract extensions through the 2006 season, putting to rest the flurry of rumors that had surrounded the team regarding how long Harvick would be retained after a disappointing 2001 season that included a one-race suspension levied by NASCAR.

No one in the garage, however, was discounting the two names that topped the list of career wins among active drivers at Atlanta with five victories each. Bill Elliott and Bobby Labonte had enjoyed

their share of success at AMS as well. Labonte, in particular, was the current holder of the track race record, event race record and event qualifying record, set in 1997, '98 and '99, respectively. In his last 13 AMS starts, Labonte racked up 10 top fives, half of those victories. Including Stewart's win a year ago, Joe Gibbs racing accounted for six of the last 13 wins at Atlanta.

In addition to Elliott's five wins, the last of which finished off an Atlanta sweep in 1992, he also led all active drivers with five pole positions at his "home track," the most recent coming one year ago. And during this year's Bud Pole qualifying session, the driver from Dawsonville, Ga., spun off a lap at 191.232 mph – good enough for a front-row reservation, but just a tick of the clock slower than the lap posted by Ryan Newman.

Newman went out 15th in the session and

(Top Right) Bill Elliott (9) and Jimmy Spencer run together in early-race action. After starting second, Elliott suffered engine failure before the midpoint in the race, while Spencer, who started fifth, grabbed his first top 10 of the year in seventh.

(Bottom Right) Ryan Newman gets service on a car that was never quite fast enough to challenge the leaders during the race. In qualifying, however, Newman re-entered the annual Bud Pole Award competition with a lap in excess of 191 miles per hour.

(Below) Dave Blaney (77) inches ahead of Ricky Craven (32) in their race for position along the frontstretch. Blaney and his Jasper team had a strong showing and finished eighth at Atlanta.

lapped the 1.54-mile trioval at 191.471 mph to set an early pace no one was able to match. It was the first pole of the year for last season's annual Bud Pole Award winner and his fourth in the last nine races, looking back to the end of 2002 when he reeled off three straight.

Elliott Sadler captured the inside of the second row next to Bobby Labonte in fourth, and Jimmy Spencer tied his career best start at Atlanta by nailing down the fifth starting position. Dale Earnhardt Jr. was among those forced to use a provisional to make the starting field, along with Kyle Petty, Terry Labonte, Kenny Wallace, Larry Foyt, Ken Schrader and Jack Sprague.

Newman proved his qualifying lap was no fluke when he took the lead at the drop of the green flag on Sunday and held it for the first 20 laps before Atlanta master Bobby Labonte worked around the ALLTEL Dodge in the fourth turn. Also moving toward the front was Joe Nemechek who, 16 laps later, was able to successfully challenge Labonte for the lead.

Jeff Gordon took control after the first round of green-flag stops for fuel, but not for long. Bobby Labonte had his Interstate Chevrolet flying around the track and surged to the front where he was

able to open up a lead over Gordon of more than four seconds. He led handily for 113 of the next 117 laps, giving up the point only briefly during three short cautions and putting all but 11 of his competitors at least one lap down.

It became clear to drivers and crew chiefs that anyone who expected to win the event would first have to deal with Labonte. So, when the fourth yellow flag flew for Ken Schrader's blown engine on lap 186, decisions had to be made regarding track position. When the leaders began to pit, Earnhardt Jr. elected to remain on the track, while Newman and crew chief Matt Borland decided to take two tires instead of four.

Drivers say they like Atlanta Motor Speedway because they can run high or low on the track and race three wide through the turns, giving them the

ability to race and pass. Now, with the field shuffled and Labonte fourth on the restart, it was time to go racing.

Earnhardt Jr. led the field from the restart and he, Ryan Newman, Jeff Gordon, Tony Stewart and Jimmie Johnson each took turns trading the top spots among them as they jostled for position. In the middle of it all was Labonte, confident of his car's ability while sizing up his competition.

With 44 laps remaining, Labonte had seen enough. He tracked down then-leader Jeff Gordon and, with a move off turn four, retook control of the race. Within 15 laps, Bobby had opened up a gap of more than two seconds over Gordon and began to set his sites on the checkered flag.

Not so fast.

The mechanical stress imposed by the fastest non-restrictor-plate track on the circuit began to take its toll with less than 25 laps to go. First, Ricky Rudd's engine let go, then, those of Jimmie Johnson and Jeff Burton ignited simultaneously, bringing out the final two cautions of the day and, more importantly, eliminating any margin Labonte had been able to build. All the leaders took the opportunity to pit for four fresh tires and, as they lined up for the final sprint to the finish, Bobby Labonte held the point ahead of Gordon and Earnhardt.

Gordon wasted no time as the green flew once again, pulling alongside the Interstate Chevrolet in the first and second turns and powering to the

(Left) Defending event champion Tony Stewart grabbed his second straight fifth-place finish, his third top 10 in four starts this season, and jumped from fifth to second in the point standings.

(Below) Among those who attempted to challenge Labonte at Atlanta were Dale Earnhardt Jr. (8) and Matt Kenseth. Both drivers managed to hang around the leaders all day and eventually finish together, with Earnhardt in third and Kenseth fourth. That result put Kenseth atop the points and moved the Budweiser driver into the top 10 for the first time this season.

(Above) Bobby Labonte and Jeff Gordon battle for the point, with Michael Waltrip giving way on the inside. Gordon and his DuPont Chevrolet were on form at Atlanta and took the lead briefly after the final restart, but no one had the muscle – or the moves – to beat Bobby Labonte.

(Right) After taking the lead for the final time, Labonte begins stretching his advantage to what would become a 1.274-second margin of victory in his seventh career win at Atlanta. Gordon's runner-up finish was his first top 10 of the season and moved him from 20th to eighth in the standings.

front as they raced down the backstretch. The two former champions battled furiously around the track until, going into turn one, Labonte nudged the DuPont Monte Carlo, causing Gordon to lift to correct his wiggling race car. That was all Labonte needed as he dropped low and took over the lead once again. Try as he might, Gordon had nothing

for Labonte, and Bobby drove off to a 1.274-second margin of victory.

"I didn't know if it would work," Labonte explained to reporters about his move on Gordon. "I didn't have a prepared plan. I just had to give it my best shot, because we'd led too many laps and had too fast a car to not try."

The win marked Labonte's sixth at Atlanta and the seventh for Joe Gibbs over the last 14 events there. It was also the first for Labonte with new crew chief Michael "Fatback" McSwain since his move from Robert Yates Racing before the end of the 2002 season.

Gordon remained second to pick up his first top-10 finish of the season, while Earnhardt Jr. took third. Matt Kenseth and Tony Stewart finished fourth and fifth in the race and moved to the top two spots in the points, with Kenseth in first. Mark Martin, Bill Elliott and Kurt Busch had particularly costly days, all falling victim to engine failures.

Bass Pro Shops MBNA 500 *final race results*

Fin. Pos.	Start Pos.	Car No.	Driver	Team	Fin. Pos.	Start Pos.	Car No.	Driver	Team
1	4	18	Bobby Labonte	Interstate Batteries Chevrolet	23	33	41	Casey Mears	Target Dodge
2	30	24	Jeff Gordon	DuPont Chevrolet	24	36	74	Tony Raines	BACE Motorsports Chevrolet
3	37	8	Dale Earnhardt Jr.	Budweiser Chevrolet	25	28	30	Jeff Green	America Online Chevrolet
4	24	17	Matt Kenseth	DEWALT Power Tools Ford	26	40	23	Kenny Wallace	Stacker2 Dodge
5	8	20	Tony Stewart	Home Depot Chevrolet	27	6	15	Michael Waltrip	NAPA Chevrolet
6	3	38	Elliott Sadler	M&M's Ford	28	35	54	Todd Bodine	National Guard Ford
7	5	7	Jimmy Spencer	Sirius Satellite Radio Dodge	29	19	43	John Andretti	Cheerios Dodge
8	27	77	Dave Blaney	Jasper Engines & Transmissions Ford	30	32	4	Mike Skinner	Kodak Pontiac
9	13	25	Joe Nemechek	UAW-Delphi Chevrolet	31	14	01	Jerry Nadeau	U.S. Army Pontiac
10	1	12	Ryan Newman	ALLTEL Dodge	32	11	48	Jimmie Johnson	Lowe's Chevrolet
11	23	10	Johnny Benson	Valvoline Pontiac	33	26	99	Jeff Burton	CITGO Ford
12	22	32	Ricky Craven	Tide Pontiac	34	38	45	Kyle Petty	Brawny/Georgia Pacific Dodge
13	20	16	Greg Biffle	Grainger Ford	35	21	21	Ricky Rudd	Motorcraft Ford
14	34	40	Sterling Marlin	Coors Light Dodge	36	31	42	Jamie McMurray	Havoline Dodge
15	7	2	Rusty Wallace	Miller Lite Dodge	37	43	0	Jack Sprague	NetZero Pontiac
16	15	1	Steve Park	Pennzoil Chevrolet	38	42	49	Ken Schrader	BAM Racing Dodge
17	18	31	Robby Gordon	Cingular Wireless Chevrolet	39	2	9	Bill Elliott	Dodge Dealers/UAW Dodge
18	12	22	Ward Burton	Caterpillar Dodge	40	9	97	Kurt Busch	Rubbermaid Ford
19	17	29	Kevin Harvick	GM Goodwrench Service Chevrolet	41	25	11	Brett Bodine	Hooters Restaurants Ford
20	39	5	Terry Labonte	Kellogg's/got milk? Chevrolet	42	29	6	Mark Martin	Pfizer/Viagra Ford
21	16	88	Dale Jarrett	UPS Ford	43	41	14	Larry Foyt	Harrah's Dodge
22	10	19	Jeremy Mayfield	Dodge Dealers/UAW Dodge					

CAROLINA DODGE DEALERS 400

March 16, 2003

In every sport there are those special moments when, on a given day, competitors come together in the heat of battle, seemingly equal, neither willing to give. Inevitably, someone must win, the other will not. Fittingly, those special moments often occur at venues steeped in tradition, almost magical in resurrecting memories of great moments gone by. Yankee Stadium, Boston Garden, and Chicago's Soldier Field among them.

And then there is venerable old Darlington. How many times has NASCAR's original superspeedway hosted a battle royale that has found its place not only in the record book, but also in legend? Richard Petty, David Pearson, Ned Jarrett, Cale Yarborough, Dale Earnhardt and others who have shaped the sport's history have all contributed to the fabled history of the oddly shaped oval affectionately known as "The Lady in Black."

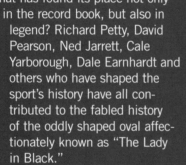

"It's the most fun I've ever had in my life. This is exactly what you dream about, the perfect way to win at the perfect track."

This year, in this race, another chapter was added to Darlington's rich history. The event had been called a "Milestone Weekend" as the Carolina Dodge Dealers 400 marked Darlington Raceway's 100th NASCAR Winston Cup Series event.

Other milestones would also be reached this weekend. It would be Terry Labonte's 750th career start, the 700th for Bill Elliott, number 650 for Kyle Petty, the 500th for Dale Jarrett and Jeff Burton's 300th start in the NASCAR Winston Cup Series.

Two of those drivers already had found success at the 1.366-mile egg-shaped track and were hoping to build on that success. Dale Jarrett's record included nine top-five finishes in his last 12 Darlington races, including three wins, all coming in the spring 400 miler. In that same stretch of 12 events, Jeff Burton posted 10 top 10s, eight of

Ricky Craven (32) and Kurt Busch take the checkered flag at Darlington, their cars virtually locked together after battling furiously over the final laps. The margin of victory was the smallest ever recorded in NASCAR Winston Cup Series competition.

(Above) Elliott Sadler displays his first career Bud Pole Award after besting the competition with a lap at more than 170 miles per hour.

(Left) Defending event champion Sterling Marlin (right) counsels rookie teammate Jamie McMurray on the finer points of getting around the track "too tough to tame."

(Below) Although Michael Waltrip did not lead a lap, he was able to bounce back from his 27th-place finish at Atlanta with a fifth place result at Darlington and maintain his third-place standing in the points.

those being top fives, including two wins – a season sweep in 1999.

Most in the garage at Darlington, however, were well aware that Jeff Gordon would likely be a threat to win. Gordon came to Darlington leading all active drivers in victories with six, third on the all-time list behind David Pearson with 10 and Dale Earnhardt with nine. In his last 15 starts, Gordon's record boasted 13 top-10 finishes, 11 of those in the top five. Five of his wins came in the Southern 500, including a four-year sweep of the Labor Day Classic from 1995-98. Gordon's runner-up finish at Atlanta just days ago was his first top 10 result of the season and vaulted him into the top 10 in points for the first time in 2003, from 20th position the week before to eighth as he prepared his assault on Darlington.

Bud Pole qualifying takes on added significance at the tricky South Carolina oval. In the 99 previous races run at Darlington, only 12 winners started outside the top 10. Further emphasizing the importance of qualifying well, 19 of the 99 previous winners started from the pole – more than any other position – while 35 came from the front row and exactly two-thirds from the top five starting slots.

With that in mind, all competitors had their game faces on for Bud Pole qualifying and, when the session was competed, Elliott Sadler and the M&M's team wore the biggest smiles. Sadler took

the track 16th of the 43 competitors, mashed the gas in his powerful Robert Yates Ford and held on tight as he lapped the track at 170.147 mph to earn his first career Bud Pole.

Sadler's closest challenge came from qualifying ace Ryan Newman, whose lap at just under 169.4 mph put him on the outside of the front row. Jerry Nadeau and Jimmy Spencer, building on his strong Atlanta weekend, locked up the second-row positions, while Jeff Gordon and Kurt Busch took the third row.

Two-time Darlington winner Ward Burton turned the seventh-fastest lap, while Sterling Marlin, defending winner of this event and intent on regaining the consistently-fast form he displayed a year ago, would start eighth.

Hopefuls Dale Jarrett and Jeff Burton had disappointing qualifying speeds, with Jarrett the final driver to gain entry in the race based on speed and Burton taking the first provisional to start 37th for the race. After blowing an engine in practice, Kurt Busch relinquished his sixth-place qualifying effort and was forced to line up in last place due to an engine change.

It didn't take long for the action to begin after the green flag dropped under an overcast sky on Sunday. The first caution flag flew on lap seven for a Jerry Nadeau spin in turn one that also triggered contact between Jamie McMurray and Matt Kenseth. Four more yellow flags appeared over the first 70 laps, causing changes among the frontrunners as the leaders pitted for tires and early-race chassis adjustments.

Taking advantage of the frequent cautions were Dale Earnhardt Jr. and Mark Martin, who both were able to gain track position in chunks from their mid-pack starting slots. On the fifth restart at lap 75, Earnhardt Jr. held the lead with Martin right behind in second.

The race ran under green for the next 115 laps, and Earnhardt Jr. took control, eventually leading 91 of the first 116 laps until Martin hit his stride and powered past the Budweiser Chevrolet on the inside. Once in front, the Viagra Ford looked like the car to beat as a long green-flag run played into Martin's hands and allowed him to lead until the sixth caution flew for John Andretti's spin just before the 200-lap mark.

Jeff Gordon and Elliott Sadler managed to beat Martin off pit road and, as the leaders lined up for the restart, Ricky Craven found himself in fourth ahead of Dave Blaney, Michael Waltrip, Tony Stewart and the hot-running Kurt Busch. Once in the lead and in clean air, Gordon stayed there for the next 78 laps, leaving many to feel that the DuPont driver would add victory number seven to his Darlington resume.

But the complexion of the race changed during the seventh and final caution. Mark Martin, who had been running a solid second to Gordon, left his pit missing a lug nut and was forced to return to pit road, which dropped him to 11th place – last on the lead lap – for the restart. Gordon's crew returned him to the front ahead of Sadler, Busch, Craven and Blaney.

The final restart occurred with 52 laps remaining, and Busch immediately put the challenge to Gordon, trying him on the inside along the backstretch on consecutive laps, but to no avail. Suddenly, Busch keyed his microphone and radioed to crew chief Jimmy Fennig that his power steering was gone. Forced to manhandle his Rubbermaid Ford, Busch acquiesced second place to Sadler, who set his sites on the DuPont Monte Carlo.

With the sun now shining, the track became slick, and The Lady in Black was about to have her say. Entering the first and second turns, Gordon slipped and brushed the wall, followed seconds later by Sadler. As the two leaders gathered their wits, Kurt Busch made a daring move for the lead

by going three wide inside Gordon and Sadler along the backstretch, bringing the fans instantly to their feet. Sadler moved around Gordon into second, followed by Craven and Blaney.

While Gordon and Sadler struggled with the slippery racing surface, Craven found the track conditions well suited to his Tide Pontiac and slowly began to close on Busch, still wrestling with the steering in his car. Lap by lap, little by little, Craven closed the gap on Busch and, with just three laps remaining, caught the rear bumper of

(Left) Mark Martin got his Roush team back on track with a strong fourth place at Darlington after dismal finishes of 43rd and 42nd at Las Vegas and Atlanta.

(Below) Ricky Craven (32) tries to advance against Elliott Sadler (38) with Dave Blaney creeping up from behind. Sadler's late-race challenge on Jeff Gordon for the win was thwarted when he – and Gordon – brushed the wall. Blaney had another strong run in the Jasper Engines Ford, racing to a career-best third-place finish, his third top 10 in the first five races of the season.

the Rubbermaid Ford. With three to go, Craven went low in turn four, almost pulling even with Busch but unable to complete the pass.

On the next lap, Craven made the same move in the fourth turn and the two drivers charged down the frontstretch side by side with Craven on the inside. As they entered the first turn, Ricky crowded Busch up toward the wall. They touched, and Craven edged into the lead. But the scrappy Busch gave the Tide Pontiac a tap in the right rear and then swept to the low side and took the lead once again as the two drivers headed for the white flag.

With the crowd screaming wildly, Craven prepared to make his final move. They charged down the backstretch for the last time and into turns three and four. Everything was on the line now with neither driver willing to give an inch. As they entered turn three, Busch got a touch loose, which gave Craven the opening he was looking for. Ricky instantly dove low under power, spinning his own tires in the process.

As they came off the fourth turn, Craven slammed into the side of Busch, momentarily yanking the wheel out of Kurt's hands and causing him to veer back into Craven's Pontiac. Into the final stretch to the checkers, the cars were virtually locked together, fenders scraping, sparks flying, tires smoking. Craven on the inside, Busch near the wall.

They crossed the line together, neither driver sure of the outcome as Craven's Pontiac began to turn toward the outside wall. Both drivers regained control in the first turn, and as Craven checked the

scoring tower, he saw his number 32 on top.

NASCAR's electronic scoring and timing system showed Craven with a miniscule .002-second margin of victory, the closest finish recorded since the system went into effect in 1993.

Elated yet exhausted, Craven explained of his second career series win: "It's the most fun I've ever had in my life. This is exactly what you dream about, the perfect way to win at the perfect track."

With pure adrenaline masking the aching in his arms, Busch could only say, "That was the coolest finish I've ever seen and I'm glad I got to be a part of it."

Busch wasn't the only one to feel that way, as fans stood in the stands for nearly 20 minutes, stunned by the fact they had just witnessed one of the sport's greatest moments, at one of it's most storied venues.

Carolina Dodge Dealers 400 *final race results*

Fin. Pos.	Start Pos.	Car No.	Driver	Team	Fin. Pos.	Start Pos.	Car No.	Driver	Team
1	31	32	Ricky Craven	Tide Pontiac	23	21	23	Kenny Wallace	Stacker2 Dodge
2	6	97	Kurt Busch	Rubbermaid Ford	24	29	5	Terry Labonte	Kellogg's/got milk? Chevrolet
3	18	77	Dave Blaney	Jasper Engines & Transmissions Ford	25	22	10	Johnny Benson	Valvoline Pontiac
4	27	6	Mark Martin	Viagra Ford	26	40	45	Kyle Petty	Georgia Pacific/Brawny Dodge
5	9	15	Michael Waltrip	NAPA Chevrolet	27	14	48	Jimmie Johnson	Lowe's Chevrolet
6	16	8	Dale Earnhardt Jr.	Budweiser Chevrolet	28	30	31	Robby Gordon	Cingular Wireless Chevrolet
7	1	38	Elliott Sadler	M&M's Ford	29	7	22	Ward Burton	Caterpillar Dodge
8	12	17	Matt Kenseth	DEWALT Power Tools Ford	30	11	19	Jeremy Mayfield	Dodge Dealers/UAW Dodge
9	25	9	Bill Elliott	Dodge Dealers/UAW Dodge	31	43	57	Brett Bodine	CLR Ford
10	28	20	Tony Stewart	The Home Depot Chevrolet	32	42	14	Larry Foyt	Harrah's Dodge
11	23	4	Mike Skinner	Kodak Pontiac	33	5	24	Jeff Gordon	DuPont Chevrolet
12	17	16	Greg Biffle	Grainger Ford	34	24	41	Casey Mears	Target Dodge
13	38	25	Joe Nemechek	UAW-Delphi Chevrolet	35	3	01	Jerry Nadeau	U.S. Army Pontiac
14	2	12	Ryan Newman	ALLTEL Dodge	36	33	29	Kevin Harvick	GM Goodwrench Chevrolet
15	39	21	Ricky Rudd	Motorcraft Ford	37	20	18	Bobby Labonte	Interstate Batteries Chevrolet
16	13	2	Rusty Wallace	Miller Lite Dodge	38	26	43	John Andretti	Cheerios Dodge
17	15	49	Ken Schrader	1-800 CallATT Dodge	39	8	40	Sterling Marlin	Coors Light Dodge
18	36	88	Dale Jarrett	UPS Ford	40	34	0	Jack Sprague	NetZero Pontiac
19	32	30	Jeff Green	America Online Chevrolet	41	41	74	Tony Raines	BACE Motorsports Chevrolet
20	35	1	Steve Park	Pennzoil Chevrolet	42	37	99	Jeff Burton	CITGO Ford
21	4	7	Jimmy Spencer	Sirius Satellite Radio Dodge	43	10	54	Todd Bodine	National Guard Ford
22	19	42	Jamie McMurray	Havoline Dodge					

FOOD CITY 500

March 23, 2003

The garage dwellers at Bristol Motor Speedway were still buzzing about the fabulous finish at Darlington a week earlier when Ricky Craven and Kurt Busch duked it out over the last couple of laps before Craven literally inched ahead at the line to become the fifth different winner in as many races so far this season. All agreed that the thrilling battle would go down as one of the greatest finishes in the history of the sport, if not the closest as well.

Perhaps lost in the moment was the fact that the point chase was beginning to take shape, settling in a bit after the first five events of the season. Consistency remained the key in rising to the top of the standings and, at this point, Matt Kenseth and Tony Stewart had proved to be best at bringing home consistent results. Both led all drivers with four top-10 efforts in their first five starts, with Kenseth's win at Las Vegas and three top fives versus Stewart's two accounting for the defending champ's 57-point deficit to the DeWalt Ford driver.

Michael Waltrip left Daytona with the point lead, fell to fifth after Rockingham, regained the lead on the strength of a third place at Las Vegas, and then dropped to third at Atlanta, where he remained after finishing fifth last week at Darlington. Waltrip, whose three top fives tied him with Kenseth and Kurt Busch in that category, sat a paltry five points behind Stewart, and Michael was pleased at having the best start to a season in his 17-year career.

Waltrip's teammate, Dale Earnhardt Jr., jumped to fourth in the standings after taking his third consecutive top-six finish and virtually wiping out his disastrous start to the season. A finish of 36th at Daytona followed by a 33rd place at Rockingham landed him 38th in the standings after two events.

> "... I knew eventually we'd be able to piece things together and make sure that our car was competitive at the end of a run ... "

Mark Martin takes a spin down the frontstretch after getting tagged from behind, while Robby Gordon slides past on the outside. The incident was just part of a frustrating day for Martin, who was listed 29th in the final rundown.

But Little E turned things around by finishing second at Las Vegas, third the following week at Atlanta and sixth last week at Darlington, jumping 34 positions in the process and smack dab into the early-season hunt for the championship, 126 points out of first.

Ironically, Darlington's featured combatants, Ricky Craven and Kurt Busch, arrived in Bristol deadlocked at fifth in the points, 143 back of Kenseth. The Darlington win elevated Craven 11 positions from 16th place the week before and, combined with his fourth-place performance at Rockingham, had Ricky off to the best season start in his career.

For Busch, the season so far had been a case of feast or famine. Runner-up finishes at Daytona and Rockingham put him atop the points, but a blown engine that ended his hot streak at Las Vegas followed by another DNF due to an accident at Atlanta dropped him out of the top 10 to 14th place. His third runner-up result at Darlington filled his plate once again, and now, all that was missing in Kurt's mind was the icing on the cake – a win. Busch came to the Tennessee mountains optimistic; this was the site of his initial NASCAR Winston Cup Series win one year ago, and with a bit of early season bad luck behind him, this, he thought, would be a great place to notch his first win of the year.

Dave Blaney's career-high third place at Darlington put him seventh in the standings and confirmed the newly found competitiveness of the

Tony Stewart (20) gets out of shape on the first-turn apron in front of Elliott Sadler's M&M's Ford. Stewart had an unusually tough day at Bristol, being involved in at least four mishaps, the last of which ended his day with just a hand-ful of laps left in the race.

Jasper Engines team. He and rookie crew chief Robert "Bootie" Barker were definitely clicking and, had it not been for a failed clutch and result-ing 34th-place finish at Las Vegas, Blaney could be challenging Earnhardt Jr. for fourth place, just 31 points away.

Jimmie Johnson and Joe Nemechek were tied for the eighth position in the standings, just two points behind Blaney, while Darlington pole-winner Elliott Sadler and Johnny Benson were deadlocked in the 10th position 185 points behind Kenseth.

Ryan Newman, Dale Jarrett and Bobby Labonte were all within 15 points of the top 10 and within 200 of the leader, while Jeff Gordon, Mark Martin, Ricky Rudd and Kevin Harvick were clustered within 13 points of each other in positions 15-18. Certainly, this week's competition in the first short-track event of the year on the rough and tumble high banks at Bristol would shake things up among the top 20 in the standings.

Harvick was one of those drivers hoping to make big gains at Bristol. Earlier in the week, team owner Richard Childress announced that Todd Berrier would take over the duties of crew chief on the GM Goodwrench team and former chief Gil Martin would move into the team man-ager role at RCR. Harvick welcomed the change, reminding everyone that he and Berrier had worked together in the NASCAR Busch Series, where they nailed down the Raybestos Rookie of the Year title in 2000 followed by the series championship in 2001.

One year ago, Jeff Gordon set Bristol's track qualifying record at better than 127.2 mph, and this year, Gordon took to the track early in the Bud Pole session and again blistered the track, adding another tenth to his former record speed. Driver after driver fell just short of Gordon's mark, until Ryan Newman wheeled his ALLTEL Dodge onto the track. Newman screamed around the .533-mile oval and shattered the old record by

a qualifying time a mere .539 second slower than Newman's.

Some 160,000 fans packed the grandstands surrounding Bristol's concrete half-mile oval on Sunday afternoon, and the race had barely gotten underway when the first caution flew on lap three, setting the tone for the early part of the race. The yellow flag flew four more times in the first 75 laps and appeared a total of 12 times before the halfway point in the race.

Jeff Gordon took control of the event in the early going and led 174 of the first 201 laps, relinquishing the lead briefly to Rusty Wallace and Jimmy Spencer. Harvick gained the point at lap 202 and led the next 15 circuits until Spencer dove under the GM Goodwrench Chevrolet coming off the second turn on lap 217 and went on to lead the next 117 circuits. Behind Spencer, Kenseth, Stewart, Bobby Labonte and Kurt Busch jostled for positions among the lead group.

A pivotal point in the race occurred on lap 226 when Bobby Labonte went spinning after contact with teammate Tony Stewart, bringing out the 14th caution of the day. Behind them, Busch slowed to avoid the incident but was tagged by Kenseth, and Busch, too, went spinning.

Busch reported to pit road to replace his flat-spotted tires and, since the spin had already dropped him to the end of the lead lap, his team spent extra time making chassis adjustments on the Rubbermaid Ford to make it more competitive on long runs. And long runs are what they got. The race ran under green for nearly 130 laps, during which time Busch, Labonte and Kenseth all began to pick their way through traffic and back toward the leaders.

(Above) Bobby Labonte (18) and Kurt Busch (97) perform a synchronized spin after contact with Tony Stewart (20) near the midpoint of the race. Both Labonte and Busch recovered and fought their way back to the front, where the two drivers staged the final battle for the win.

(Left) With 17 cautions in the event, Bristol Motor Speedway's pit road was a very busy place throughout the day.

more than 1.5 mph to become the first driver in the track's 41-year history to beat the 15-second mark in qualifying and become the first multiple Bud Pole winner of the season.

Gordon remained on the front row for the start of the race, followed by Ken Schrader in the BAM Racing Dodge and nine-time Bristol winner Rusty Wallace in row two. Defending event champion Kurt Busch lined up ninth for the start next to Tony Stewart, while point leader Matt Kenseth used a provisional to make the field after posting

With about 150 laps to go, Kenseth had worked all the way back into the lead followed by Busch, Spencer, Gordon, Bobby Labonte and Jimmie Johnson. Busch overtook Kenseth on lap 359 and held the point for 19 laps before having to yield the position to Bobby Labonte, who appeared to have the advantage in his Interstate Chevrolet.

It quickly became time for a round of green-flag pit stops, and the leaders began dropping onto pit road for a final set of tires and enough fuel to carry them to the finish. Jimmy Fennig called for Busch to pit, but the driver noticed debris on the track and decided to stay out, anticipating another caution. Labonte had yet to pit as well, and when the caution indeed fell, Jimmy Spencer, Jimmie Johnson, Jeff Gordon and Matt Kenseth, all of whom had pitted under green, suddenly found themselves one lap down.

Labonte led on the lap-403 restart, but Busch wasted no time in getting around the Interstate Chevrolet and set sail toward the finish. Busch led the remaining 97 laps to gain his first win of the season, the fifth of his young career.

In a brilliant effort to come from two laps down, Matt Kenseth gutted out a second-place finish after passing Bobby Labonte with just a handful of laps remaining.

"We've been so close so many times this year, it's been a little bittersweet," Busch told reporters after the race. "But I knew eventually we'd be able to piece things together and make sure that our car was competitive at the end of a run – that's how we got beat at Rockingham and Darlington."

With the laps winding down, Matt Kenseth (17) stalks race leader Kurt Busch (97), but to no avail. Busch went on to take his first win of the year and move into second in points behind Kenseth, who fought gallantly throughout the race, having to come from the back of the field on two separate occasions.

Food City 500 *final race results*

Fin. Pos.	Start Pos.	Car No.	Driver	Team	Fin. Pos.	Start Pos.	Car No.	Driver	Team
1	9	97	Kurt Busch	Sharpie/Rubbermaid Ford	23	18	19	Jeremy Mayfield	Dodge Dealers/UAW Dodge
2	37	17	Matt Kenseth	DEWALT Power Tools Ford	24	33	11	Brett Bodine	Hooters Ford
3	12	18	Bobby Labonte	Interstate Batteries Chevrolet	25	28	15	Michael Waltrip	NAPA Chevrolet
4	34	21	Ricky Rudd	Motorcraft Ford	26	10	20	Tony Stewart	Home Depot Chevrolet
5	15	16	Greg Biffle	Grainger Ford	27	25	25	Joe Nemechek	UAW-Delphi Chevrolet
6	16	40	Sterling Marlin	Coors Light Dodge	28	13	01	Jerry Nadeau	U.S. Army Pontiac
7	27	29	Kevin Harvick	GM Goodwrench Chevrolet	29	19	6	Mark Martin	Viagra Ford
8	23	48	Jimmie Johnson	Lowe's Chevrolet	30	35	1	Steve Park	Pennzoil Chevrolet
9	2	24	Jeff Gordon	DuPont Chevrolet	31	43	43	John Andretti	Cheerios Dodge
10	40	23	Kenny Wallace	Stacker2 Dodge	32	39	41	Casey Mears	Target Dodge
11	26	42	Jamie McMurray	Havoline Dodge	33	11	22	Ward Burton	Caterpillar Dodge
12	7	7	Jimmy Spencer	Sirius Satellite Radio Dodge	34	32	45	Kyle Petty	Georgia Pacific Dodge
13	29	99	Jeff Burton	CITGO Ford	35	42	0	Jack Sprague	NetZero Pontiac
14	4	2	Rusty Wallace	Miller Lite Dodge	36	38	88	Dale Jarrett	UPS Ford
15	14	32	Ricky Craven	Tide Pontiac	37	3	49	Ken Schrader	1-800-CallATT Dodge
16	8	8	Dale Earnhardt Jr.	Budweiser Chevrolet	38	31	77	Dave Blaney	Jasper Engines & Transmissions Ford
17	36	31	Robby Gordon	Cingular Wireless Chevrolet	39	17	5	Terry Labonte	Kellogg's/got milk? Chevrolet
18	5	9	Bill Elliott	Dodge Dealers/UAW Dodge	40	41	54	Todd Bodine	National Guard Ford
19	20	10	Johnny Benson	Valvoline Pontiac	41	6	4	Mike Skinner	Kodak Pontiac
20	21	30	Jeff Green	America Online Chevrolet	42	22	74	Tony Raines	BACE Motorsports Chevrolet
21	30	38	Elliott Sadler	M&M's Ford	43	24	37	Derrike Cope	Friendly's Chevrolet
22	1	12	Ryan Newman	ALLTEL Dodge					

RACE

SAMSUNG/ RADIOSHACK 500

March 30, 2003

One might say that at this early point in the season, Matt Kenseth was in the catbird's seat as the NASCAR Winston Cup Series rolled into Texas Motor Speedway for the seventh race of the 2003 season.

A week ago at Bristol, Kenseth fought adversity for most of the afternoon, battling back from being a lap down on two different occasions and still was able to finish in second place, less than a half-second behind winner Kurt Busch. That effort, combined with mid-pack finishes on the part of his closest challengers, padded his lead in the standings by another 81 points to a total of 138. Kenseth became the only driver to score five top-10 finishes in the first six events, four of those top fives – including his win at Las Vegas – and now, he arrived in Texas as the defending race champion. Certainly, Kenseth had to be considered a threat to win the Samsung/RadioShack 500 and further increase his advantage in the points.

Kurt Busch, by successfully defending his win in the Food City 500 at Bristol, jumped from sixth to second in the standings, which dropped Tony Stewart, Michael Waltrip and Dale Earnhardt Jr. each down one rung on the ladder from where they stood a week before.

Jimmie Johnson's eighth place at Bristol was good enough to move him up two notches, from eighth to sixth, while Ricky Craven's 15th place caused him to drop two spots, from fifth to seventh.

Bobby Labonte's strong performance at Bristol and resulting third place put his name on the top 10 list for the first time this season in eighth place, which illustrated further that he and crew chief Michael McSwain were beginning to click in terms of the team's on-track performances. The Atlanta

"If you had an ill-handling car in clean air, it was faster than some of the other guys that were handling well back in the pack. ... [This win] is going to be a big confidence builder for the whole team."

Ryan Newman attacks the Texas asphalt in his ALLTEL Dodge. In four consecutive starts of third or better, Newman's best finish had been a seventh place. At Texas, he and the ALLTEL team completed the weekend with their first win of the season.

(Far Left) Christian Fittipaldi (left) attends a briefing with Kyle Petty (right) and crew chief Steven Lane before making his third career NASCAR Winston Cup Series start. Petty chose to sit out the Texas event while recovering from injuries sustained at Bristol.

(Left) The Home Depot Chevrolet sits alongside the NASCAR trailer, impounded after failing inspection on Friday. Tony Stewart qualified his backup car, which suffered engine failure before completing the 500-mile race distance.

(Below) Bobby Labonte grabbed his second Bud Pole of the year in his Interstate Batteries Chevrolet, but never quite got the handle in the race. Labonte faded out of the top 10 and then slapped the backstretch wall, which ended his day early.

win, a fourth at Las Vegas along with the third place at Bristol totaled three top fives in the last four events, and Labonte was upbeat about not only his team's performance, but also that he was returning to his native state of Texas where he had run well in the past, notching three third-place finishes and four top 10s in his six starts at TMS.

Ricky Rudd and Jeff Gordon both returned to the top 10 in the standings, Rudd now in ninth and Gordon in 10th, after top 10s at Bristol for both drivers.

Teams unloaded their transporters on Friday morning and rolled their cars toward the inspection line prior to the first practice session of the weekend, and Tony Stewart's Home Depot Chevrolet brought the inspection process to a screeching halt. Measurements taken diagonally across the rear window did not meet specifications, and NASCAR impounded the car so it could be taken back to the NASCAR R&D center to be analyzed, forcing the team to pull out the backup car for the remainder of the weekend.

Team owner Joe Gibbs responded in a statement on Saturday in which he apologized for the incident and characterized it as a mistake in the construction of the car at the team's shop. Stewart was able to place the backup car solidly in the field during Bud Pole qualifying in the 22nd starting position.

Stewart's teammate, Bobby Labonte, made the most of his Texas "homecoming" during his timed run, tripping the clocks at 193.514 miles per hour to win his second Bud Pole of the season. Although just short of the track qualifying record

(Above) Tony Stewart (20) and Jimmy Spencer (7) charge off the fourth turn in a very close side-by-side duel for position. Ironically, they finished together as well – in the garage – with Spencer out due to accident damage and Stewart with an expired engine.

(Above Right) Dale Jarrett's UPS Ford, already battered from an earlier incident on pit road, burns fuel from the exhaust while spinning off the fourth turn following a tangle with Christian Fittipaldi. In spite of his troubles during the afternoon, Jarrett was able to finish on the lead lap, in 13th place, his best finish since winning at Rockingham five races ago.

(Right) Elliott Sadler's M&M's crew flies through an early-race stop under caution to keep their driver at the front of the field. After starting second, Sadler led 91 of the first 157 laps before losing control on the backstretch and hitting the inside wall, abruptly ending his day in 41st place.

set last year by Bill Elliott, Labonte's lap was the fastest turned so far this season.

Elliott Sadler made it a Chevrolet-Ford front row with the second-fastest qualifying attempt, and Ryan Newman placed his Dodge in the third starting position, extending his personal streak of starting third or better in five straight races.

Jimmie Johnson was fourth fastest in qualifying but dropped to the rear of the starting grid due to an engine change, as did Todd Bodine and Sterling Marlin. Christian Fittipaldi also joined those at the back after he took over the wheel of the Georgia-Pacific Dodge for Kyle Petty, still ailing with injured ribs suffered in an accident at

Bristol. It would mark Fittipaldi's second start of the season, the third of his NASCAR Winston Cup Series career.

Kerry Earnhardt and NASCAR Craftsman Truck Series regular David Starr, making his first attempt at a NASCAR Winston Cup start, both missed the field.

A huge crowd estimated at 215,000 watched as Bobby Labonte took the green flag to begin the seventh running of the Samsung/RadioShack 500. Almost immediately, Sadler drove past Labonte in turns one and two to take the early lead.

A handful of laps later, Bill Elliott worked to the point from his sixth-place starting spot and led the

way for the next 43 laps, until his day suddenly ended when the engine in his Dodge erupted in a puff of smoke, sending Elliott to the garage in 43rd place.

That put Sadler back in control and, other than short stints during rounds of pit stops and a brief challenge from Jeff Gordon, Sadler had his way until the midpoint of the race, when a cut tire sent him spinning into the backstretch retaining wall, ending his day in 41st place.

Matt Kenseth, Jeff Gordon, Ryan Newman and Dale Earnhardt Jr. emerged as the challengers for the win as the second half of the race unfolded. Kenseth led a chunk of 63 laps, and then Newman took over on lap 224 and stayed out front for the next 60 laps until the 10th caution of the day.

Realizing that track position was paramount with the aero package in place, Newman and crew chief Matt Borland decided to gamble on a two-tire stop. Earnhardt Jr. opted four tires and lined up second for the restart, and Little E immediately moved to the point at the drop of the green flag and took over with 46 laps left.

Newman, seemingly unflappable in his steady demeanor, went to work in pursuit of the Budweiser Chevrolet. Little by little, the ALLTEL Dodge settled in the grove and, despite fighting a bit of aero push, began to close the gap.

In front of him, Earnhardt Jr. was feeling his race car tighten up with each lap, and, despite fresher tires, he was forced to fight the ill-handing

Chevrolet while watching Newman close from behind. Earnhardt tried to match Newman's line around the 1.5-mile superspeedway, hoping to keep the air off the nose of the fleet-running Dodge. But as they entered the turns, Earnhardt

Jeff Gordon (24) and Dale Earnhardt Jr. battle side by side for second place as the Samsung/RadioShack 500 draws to a close, a duel that ended with Earnhardt Jr. just edging out the DuPont Chevrolet.

was forced to stress his right-front tire on the badly pushing Chevrolet until, finally, Newman was able to make his move in turns three and four.

Newman pulled even with Earnhardt as they crossed the stripe with just 11 laps remaining and seized the lead coming off turn two. Once in clean air, Newman sailed to the win with a 3.405-second margin of victory.

Jeff Gordon was able to catch Earnhardt as well, and the two battled to the line with Dale Jr. able to edge out Gordon for the runner-up position. Jerry Nadeau brought his U.S. Army Pontiac home fourth in a very strong run, his first finish better than 22nd this season, while Mark Martin took fifth ahead of point leader Matt Kenseth, who

scored his sixth top-10 finish of the year.

"Track position outweighed everything today," Newman explained after the race. "If you had an ill-handling car in clean air, it was faster than some of the other guys that were handling well back in the pack. ... [This win] is going to be a big confidence builder for the whole team."

At post race inspection, crew chief Matt Borland popped the hood on the ALLTEL Dodge and stared blankly at two hose clamps that had come loose near the end of the race. When asked, Borland speculated that, had the race been five laps longer, Newman would not have been around for the finish.

Sometimes it pays to be lucky AND good.

Samsung/RadioShack 500 *final race results*

Fin. Pos.	Start Pos.	Car No.	Driver	Team	Fin. Pos.	Start Pos.	Car No.	Driver	Team
1	3	12	Ryan Newman	ALLTEL Dodge	23	40	23	Kenny Wallace	Stacker2 Dodge
2	11	8	Dale Earnhardt Jr.	Budweiser Chevrolet	24	42	49	Ken Schrader	1-800-CallATT Dodge
3	7	24	Jeff Gordon	DuPont Chevrolet	25	27	19	Jeremy Mayfield	Dodge Dealers/UAW Dodge
4	5	01	Jerry Nadeau	U.S. Army Pontiac	26	16	21	Ricky Rudd	Motorcraft Ford
5	32	6	Mark Martin	Viagra Ford	27	26	41	Casey Mears	Target Dodge
6	17	17	Matt Kenseth	Smirnoff Ice/DEWALT Power Tools Ford	28	20	16	Greg Biffle	Grainger Ford
7	14	30	Jeff Green	America Online Chevrolet	29	36	40	Sterling Marlin	Coors Light Dodge
8	4	48	Jimmie Johnson	Lowe's Chevrolet	30	35	14	Larry Foyt	Harrah's Dodge
9	30	97	Kurt Busch	Rubbermaid Ford	31	25	11	Brett Bodine	Hooters Restaurants Ford
10	24	42	Jamie McMurray	Havoline Dodge	32	13	10	Johnny Benson	Valvoline Pontiac
11	19	54	Todd Bodine	National Guard Ford	33	18	7	Jimmy Spencer	Sirius Satellite Radio Dodge
12	33	22	Ward Burton	Caterpillar Dodge	34	22	20	Tony Stewart	Home Depot Chevrolet
13	23	88	Dale Jarrett	UPS Ford	35	9	25	Joe Nemechek	UAW-Delphi Chevrolet
14	10	2	Rusty Wallace	Miller Lite Dodge	36	39	77	Dave Blaney	Jasper Engines & Transmissions Ford
15	8	29	Kevin Harvick	GM Goodwrench Chevrolet	37	1	18	Bobby Labonte	Interstate Batteries Chevrolet
16	12	5	Terry Labonte	Kellogg's/got milk? Chevrolet	38	28	45	Christian Fittipaldi	Georgia Pacific Dodge
17	37	15	Michael Waltrip	NAPA Chevrolet	39	15	1	Steve Park	Pennzoil Chevrolet
18	21	31	Robby Gordon	Cingular Wireless Chevrolet	40	41	4	Mike Skinner	Kodak Pontiac
19	43	43	John Andretti	Cheerios Dodge	41	2	38	Elliott Sadler	M&M's Ford
20	29	99	Jeff Burton	CITGO Ford	42	34	74	Tony Raines	BACE Motorsports Chevrolet
21	38	32	Ricky Craven	Tide Pontiac	43	6	9	Bill Elliott	Dodge Dealers/UAW Dodge
22	31	0	Jack Sprague	NetZero Pontiac					

AARON'S 499

April 6, 2003

In the days following the race at Texas Motor Speedway, much was written in the press about the problems found with Tony Stewart's Home Depot Chevrolet that gave NASCAR cause to impound the car and return it to their R&D center near Charlotte, N.C., to study the body and better understand the irregularities that caused it to be so far out of spec.

Stewart's crew chief, Greg Zipadelli, was emphatic that his team had not tried to skirt the rules in an effort to gain an advantage. On the contrary, Zipadelli explained that the problem was the result of errors in fabricating the car in the shops at Joe Gibbs racing and that steps had already been put in place to ensure a similar situation would not reoccur.

The entire episode brought to light the subject of "aero matching" of all body types, put in place by NASCAR over the winter to create a more level playing field and, therefore, enhance competition. The good news that resulted was that, in fact, the concept seemed to be working quite well judging by the results so far this season.

> It still didn't look good up until there at the end of the race. ... You really had to be tough or get knocked the hell out of the way."

In the first seven races, there were seven different winners. Three of those drove Fords to victory lane and two drivers took Chevrolets to the winner's circle. Ricky Craven scored a win for Pontiac at Darlington, and last week at Texas, Ryan Newman chalked one up for the Dodge Boys. In terms of Bud Poles, Chevrolet led the way with three, while Ford and Dodge had collected two each. Only Pontiac had yet to turn the fastest lap in qualifying so far this year.

Perhaps more telling when it came to how effective the so-called "common templates" had been was the fact that, so far, there had been little to no squabbling in the garage area about

Talladega fans watch the field flash past at nearly 200 miles per hour. The estimated crowd of 190,000 didn't use their seats much during an exciting race that featured 43 lead changes among 16 different drivers.

another, and NASCAR had not found cause to make any rule changes since the season began during Speedweeks at Daytona two months ago.

With that said, this week was a slightly different story. This was Talladega, and it was very clear that, based on the results at the two restrictor-plate tracks over the past few seasons, there was no matching – aero or otherwise – the powerful Chevrolets of Michael Waltrip and Dale Earnhardt Jr. fielded by the DEI organization.

If Dale Earnhardt Sr. had been the Talladega master during his storied career, far out-distancing any other driver in history with 10 wins at the mammoth superspeedway, then Dale Jr. picked up right where his father left off by leading all active drivers with three Talladega wins in his brief career, those coming consecutively in the last three events run there.

Add the fact that, together with Waltrip, DEI cars had won five of the last six restrictor-plate races and seven of the last nine, including three 1-2 finishes with Waltrip and Earnhardt Jr. Little E had won four of the last eight events run at Daytona and Talladega and, worse yet for his competition, he was on a roll of late. The red Budweiser Chevrolet had finished in second place

twice, third once and sixth once, all in the last five races – a hot spell that rocketed Dale Jr. from 38th to third in the point standings, where he now trailed second-place Kurt Busch by a mere nine points and leader Matt Kenseth by 166. No one in the garage at Talladega had to think very long when polled on who would be the man to beat in the Aaron's 499 this weekend.

(Above) Dale Earnhardt Jr. (8) and DEI teammate Steve Park (1) claim the inside line next to Ward Burton (22), Jeff Gordon (24) and Greg Biffle (16), with Jimmie Johnson (48) trying to push ahead on the outside. All of these drivers except Biffle took a turn at the front of the field, with Johnson leading on 10 occasions for 65 laps, topping both categories for the day.

(Right) Earnhardt Jr.'s Budweiser mates had their work cut out for them after their Monte Carlo was damaged in the early-race melee. Perseverance paid big dividends, however, as their work kept Little E on the lead lap and, therefore, able to take the win.

That notion was verified in practice before qualifying as Little E led the way with a fast lap at better than 187 miles per hour. But, during the timed Bud Pole qualifying session, his Budweiser Chevrolet was only good enough to nail down the 13th starting slot. Kevin Harvick set the early pace in the session with a lap at 186.166 miles per hour, but he was displaced five cars later when Jeremy Mayfield circled the 2.66-mile superspeedway in 51.349 seconds – a time that stood for the rest of the session and brought the Dodge driver his first Bud Pole of the season, the seventh of his career. Harvick remained on the front row in his Chevrolet, and Elliott Sadler slotted

his Ford in third with Jeff Gordon on his right.

David Green turned some heads in qualifying when he posted the fifth-fastest lap of the session to qualify for his first NASCAR Winston Cup Series race in two and a half years. Green's time was later negated, however, when his car failed post-qualifying inspection, sending Green to the back of the field for the start of the race. A similar infraction was uncovered with Larry Foyt's car, and when the field was set following the assignment of provisionals, Foyt was left out in the cold, unable make the field.

Earnhardt Jr. decided to run the NASCAR Busch Series race held on Saturday and furthered his Talladega dominance when he took the lead for the first time on lap 58 and led the remaining 60 circuits on the way to his second win of the year in that series, the first coming in the season opener at Daytona. A ray of hope glimmered for his NASCAR Winston Cup Series competitors, however, when his DEI crew found water mixed with the oil in the Budweiser Chevrolet and was forced to change engines before Sunday's race, relegating Dale Jr. to the 43rd starting position, one from which no one had ever won in Talladega's long history.

No matter.

The engines had barely come up to full song in the Aaron's 499 when Ryan Newman's ALLTEL Dodge cut a left-rear tire on lap four and triggered a 27-car accident, the biggest in Talladega history. Mired in the back of the pack, Earnhardt was unable to avoid the melee and clipped the nose of his Monte Carlo. Crew chief Tony Eury Sr. and his Budweiser crew immediately fell to work, using successive pit stops under the yellow to patch the nose of the car without allowing Little E to go a lap down.

Back under the green, Mayfield, Harvick, Jimmie Johnson and Michael Waltrip battled within the lead pack while Earnhardt went to work, dicing through the field, using bump drafts, daring passes and any advantage he could find to weave through traffic toward the leaders. And any doubts about his desire – or ability, considering the damaged Monte Carlo – to win the event were put to rest just past the halfway point in race.

Ironically, it was teammate Michael Waltrip who provided substantial aid to Earnhardt when he spun and hit the wall, bringing out the fourth caution of the day on lap 84. Until then, Earnhardt Jr. had been playing catch-up, sometimes as much as a quarter of a lap behind the leaders.

Aided by a total of five cautions over the first 100 laps, Earnhardt emerged at the front for the first time on lap 107. Five laps later, Jeff Gordon worked past Earnhardt's Chevrolet in the tri-oval, and from there, the battle was on. First Gordon, and then his Hendrick Motorsports teammate, Jimmie Johnson, took turns dicing with the determined Earnhardt, swapping leads back and forth in an event that featured 43 lead changes among 16 different drivers. Over the final 82 laps alone, there were 22 lead changes, with Earnhardt leading on nine different occasions for a total of 34 laps.

With less than five laps to go, Earnhardt found himself running third behind leader Matt Kenseth and Jimmie Johnson. Behind Earnhardt, Elliott Sadler chose his dancing partner and drafted up to Earnhardt's bumper, giving him the boost he needed. Earnhardt dove to the bottom of the track at the entrance to turn three and dispatched both Johnson and Kenseth, emerging off the fourth turn with the lead.

Kenseth pulled back alongside, and the Ford and Chevrolet battled all the way around the track, with Kenseth able to eek ahead at the line to lead lap 186, but not able to shut the door on Earnhardt. Little E charged back, staying low on the inside. The two drivers again blasted into the third turn with Earnhardt skirting the apron at the entrance to the turn, riding the yellow line at the bottom of the track as he cleared the yellow-and-

Dale Earnhardt Jr. charges into the lead ahead of Matt Kenseth (17) with Kevin Harvick challenging on the inside. Eventually, Harvick settled in behind the Budweiser Chevrolet and rode it's draft to a season-high, second-place finish.

Crew chief Tony Eury Sr. and driver Dale Earnhardt Jr. remind onlookers that their Talladega streak had reached four straight ... and counting. That they had done it from the back of the field and in a damaged race car made the accomplishment extraordinary.

black Ford for the final time and headed toward the white and checkered flags.

Behind him, Kevin Harvick slipped past Sadler and settled in on Earnhardt's bumper to seal second place for the GM Goodwrench Chevrolet, while Sadler fell in line to finish third.

Jimmie Johnson made contact with Kenny Wallace before taking the white flag and went spinning in the fourth turn. Although no caution was called, the incident affected the final running order, bringing Ricky Craven to fourth and Terry Labonte to fifth, his first top-10 finish of the year.

Kenseth was shuffled back to the ninth position at the finish, one spot behind Jeff Gordon in eighth.

With the win, Earnhardt Jr. became the first driver in Talladega history to sweep four consecutive races. To do it after starting last and with a damaged race car surprised even Dale, who said in post-race interviews, "The odds were against us to come in here and do it four times in a row. It still didn't look good up until there at the end of the race. ... You really had to be tough or get knocked the hell out of the way."

Tough indeed.

Aaron's 499 *final race results*

Fin. Pos.	Start Pos.	Car No.	Driver	Team	Fin. Pos.	Start Pos.	Car No.	Driver	Team
1	13	8	Dale Earnhardt Jr.	Budweiser Chevrolet	23	39	77	Dave Blaney	Jasper Engines & Transmissions Ford
2	2	29	Kevin Harvick	GM Goodwrench Chevrolet	24	16	15	Michael Waltrip	NAPA Chevrolet
3	3	38	Elliott Sadler	M&M's Ford	25	19	20	Tony Stewart	Home Depot Chevrolet
4	15	32	Ricky Craven	Tide Pontiac	26	9	6	Mark Martin	Viagra Ford
5	28	5	Terry Labonte	Kellogg's/got milk? Chevrolet	27	14	42	Jamie McMurray	Havoline Dodge
6	11	40	Sterling Marlin	Coors Light Dodge	28	35	54	Todd Bodine	National Guard Ford
7	24	22	Ward Burton	Caterpillar Dodge	29	30	30	Jeff Green	America Online Chevrolet
8	4	24	Jeff Gordon	DuPont/Pepsi Chevrolet	30	36	09	Mike Wallace	Miccosukee Resort Dodge
9	27	17	Matt Kenseth	DEWALT Power Tools Ford	31	42	4	Mike Skinner	Kodak Pontiac
10	6	31	Robby Gordon	Cingular Wireless Chevrolet	32	22	18	Bobby Labonte	Interstate Batteries Chevrolet
11	21	45	Kyle Petty	Georgia Pacific Dodge	33	41	49	Ken Schrader	1-800 CallATT Dodge
12	18	88	Dale Jarrett	UPS Ford	34	20	0	Jack Sprague	NetZero Pontiac
13	5	9	Bill Elliott	Dodge Dealers/UAW Dodge	35	38	99	Jeff Burton	CITGO Ford
14	40	43	John Andretti	Cheerios Dodge	36	23	01	Jerry Nadeau	U.S. Army Pontiac
15	7	48	Jimmie Johnson	Lowe's Chevrolet	37	31	2	Rusty Wallace	Miller Lite Dodge
16	43	74	Tony Raines	BACE Motorsports Chevrolet	38	34	7	Jimmy Spencer	Sirius Satellite Radio Dodge
17	25	23	Kenny Wallace	Stacker2 Dodge	39	8	12	Ryan Newman	ALLTEL Dodge
18	1	19	Jeremy Mayfield	Dodge Dealers/UAW Dodge	40	10	41	Casey Mears	Target Dodge
19	26	97	Kurt Busch	Rubbermaid Ford	41	17	10	Johnny Benson	Valvoline Pontiac
20	12	1	Steve Park	Pennzoil Chevrolet	42	37	21	Ricky Rudd	Motorcraft Ford
21	29	25	Joe Nemechek	UAW-Delphi Chevrolet	43	32	02	Hermie Sadler	Aaron's Dream Machine Chevrolet
22	33	16	Greg Biffle	Grainger Ford					

VIRGINIA 500

April 13, 2003

The results of the Aaron's 499 at Talladega left Matt Kenseth at the top of the point standings, but for the first time since Atlanta when he took over the lead, his margin over second place had actually shrunk. Each week, through his consistent top-10 performances, Kenseth had been able to pad his lead to where, going into Talladega, he possessed a bulge of 155 points over second-place Kurt Busch.

That trend ended abruptly when Dale Earnhardt Jr. passed Kenseth with two laps remaining at Talladega and drove to the win, moving into second place in the points and reducing the gap held by Kenseth from 155 to 129 markers.

Although few were surprised to find Earnhardt in Talladega's victory lane, the win was not without controversy. Some felt that when Dale Jr. dropped below the yellow line – considered out of bounds according to NASCAR rules – he was in violation and should have been penalized accordingly.

NASCAR determined at the time, that the move was not a violation and, after reviewing that decision following the race, explained that Earnhardt had not driven below the line to improve position, but rather, had already completed his pass on Kenseth and Jimmie Johnson in the third and fourth turns, and was merely avoiding a possible collision with the DeWalt Ford, which had begun dropping down from a slightly higher line.

The final results stood, and Earnhardt's jump into second place in the standings dropped Kurt Busch to the No. 3 position, 187 points behind Kenseth. Jimmie Johnson and Jeff Gordon both moved up one position and now stood fourth and fifth, respectively. For Gordon, the move completed a leap from 15th place to fifth over the last three events, and with three career wins at Martinsville,

"I was pretty determined to win this race. ... It was just hard to pass out there. I would have expected the same thing from anybody else."

In the tight confines of Martinsville's half mile, Jeff Gordon (24) finds himself in the thick of things between Matt Kenseth (17) and Dale Earnhardt Jr. (8), with Dave Blaney (77), Bill Elliott (9) and Steve Park (1) holding the outside line through the 12-degree-banked corners.

(Left) In Martinsville tradition, the field of cars awaits action on Sunday morning, lined up neatly on display in front of the frontstretch grandstand know as the Blue Ridge Tower.

(Below) Dale Jarrett looked at Martinsville as an opportunity to right the UPS ship that had gone awry not just on the track, but within the crew as well.

Gordon and crew chief Robby Loomis felt they had a great chance to continue their climb in the points with a strong finish this weekend in the Virginia 500.

Talk of the Earnhardt controversy quickly abated when Dale Jarrett and Doug Yates called a press conference at the track on Friday to explain that crew chief Brad Parrott had been released from his duties with the UPS Ford team. Additionally, it was announced that RYR competition director Todd Parrott had taken an indefinite leave of absence from the team while he and Yates evaluated the future direction of the organization.

Since beginning the season with a 10th place at Daytona followed by a win at Rockingham, Jarrett had not posted another top-10 finish and had fallen from second to 12th in the points. It was time to get that trend turned around, Jarrett felt, and with a current string of eight straight top-10 finishes at Martinsville, including a win in this event two years ago, this would be a good place to get started. While Brad Parrott immediately moved into a car chief role at Roush Racing to work with crew chief Paul Andrews and driver Jeff Burton, whom Parrott helped to five NASCAR Busch Series wins last season, Garth Finley and Richard Buck were slated to provide temporary leadership this weekend for Jarrett while the team considered its options for a permanent replacement.

Farther down the line in the Martinsville garage, Tony Furr was directing preparation of the NetZero Pontiac for driver Jack Sprague. Furr, who had already been with the team as shop foreman at

Haas/CNC racing, took over crew chief responsibilities from Dennis Connor, who had been with Sprague since 1995. Together, Connor and Sprague had three NASCAR Craftsman Truck Series championships and a full season in the NASCAR Busch Series where they finished fifth in the 2002 points with one victory. But Sprague's run for Raybestos Rookie of the Year in the NASCAR Winston Cup Series had so far yielded just one top-20 finish and a 38th place in the early-season point standings, and car owner Gene Haas felt it was time to shake things up a bit in an effort to get Sprague back in the hunt for rookie honors.

(Right) Robby Gordon charges off the fourth turn while Jack Sprague loops his NetZero Pontiac in front of Steve Park, Michael Waltrip and Bill Elliott. Sprague was driving for the first time under the direction of Tony Furr after Dennis Conner was released from his role as crew chief.

(Below) A sellout crowd of 86,000 takes in the action on a beautiful spring Sunday at Martinsville. The Virginia 500 marked the 95th NASCAR Winston Cup Series race at the pristine short track in southern Virginia.

The change seemed to produce immediate benefits: Sprague went out in the first practice session and was sixth fastest as he prepared for Bud Pole qualifying. To no one's surprise, Jeff Gordon led the way in practice followed by Tony Stewart, holder of the track qualifying record, Dale Earnhardt Jr., Jimmie Johnson and Mike Skinner in the Kodak Pontiac.

Gordon backed up his fast practice speed in qualifying by circling the 0.526-mile Martinsville oval at 94.307 miles per hour to claim his first Bud Pole of the year. Gordon's speed was one-tenth of a second faster than that posted by Dale Earnhardt Jr., who made it an all-Chevrolet front row ahead of Ryan Newman's Dodge in third. Ken Schrader became the surprise of the session by turning the fourth-fastest lap in his BAM Racing Dodge ahead of Rusty Wallace, wins leader among active drivers at Martinsville with six.

The UPS team appeared unsettled with the recent changes in personnel

when Dale Jarrett failed to make the field on his speed and had to take a provisional start. He was joined by Robby Gordon, Bobby Labonte, John Andretti, Todd Bodine, Derrike Cope and Hermie Sadler.

A sellout crowd packed the grandstands at beautiful Martinsville Speedway for the second

short-track event of the season, and Jeff Gordon took immediate control. With long green-flag runs interrupted by just one early caution (lap 80), Gordon led the first 120 laps without challenge. The DuPont Monte Carlo was so strong, Gordon began lapping cars on just the 28th circuit and took just 61 laps to drop point-leader Matt Kenseth a lap down.

The second caution of the day gave others a chance to adjust their cars, and Tony Stewart got off pit road first followed by Rusty Wallace, Gordon and Earnhardt Jr. It took just a handful of laps for Wallace to take the lead away from the Home Depot Pontiac and for Earnhardt Jr. to move into second place behind the Miller Lite Dodge. Earnhardt sized up Wallace for several laps, and then made his move at the entrance to turn three and took the lead for the first time in the race. Once out front, Little E led almost handily, fronting the field in large chunks of 95, 30

and 70 laps, and looking very much like the man to beat as the race entered its final stages.

But with just 65 laps remaining, the eighth caution flag of the day flew for a Ryan Newman spin, setting into motion a series of events that would change the complexion of the race. The leaders pitted, and Bobby Labonte decided to gamble for track position by taking just two tires. With the rest of the leaders all taking four, Labonte lined up first for the restart with Earnhardt Jr. and Jeff Gordon right behind.

As the green flag dropped on the restart, Labonte squirted away with Earnhardt in pursuit, but Ricky Craven, first of the lap-down cars starting on the inside, suddenly felt a wiggle in his Tide Pontiac. A cut tire sent Craven into Earnhardt, who could not avoid contact, and the two slid up the race track as the rest of the leaders scooted by on the inside. The Budweiser Chevrolet was not severely damaged but was shuffled back to fifth place with just 56 laps to go.

That left Jeff Gordon – with four fresh tires – in second place and in pursuit of Labonte. There was no doubt the DuPont Chevrolet was fast, having already led 176 laps during the day, and Gordon, Loomis and the entire team were anxious for their first win of the season, hoping to avoid a situation like last year's

(Upper Right) Bobby Labonte holds the point ahead of Jeff Gordon with the laps winding down. Labonte took control during the eighth caution of the day by taking two tires on the Interstate Chevrolet and exiting pit road first.

(Lower Right) Jeff Gordon takes the checkered flag under caution with Labonte riding his bumper in second. After tracking down Labonte, Gordon made a bump-and-run move to take the lead and held on for the win.

when they did not reach victory lane until late August at Bristol, the 24th race of the year.

Gordon stalked Labonte until, with 30 circuits left, he caught the rear bumper of the Interstate Chevrolet. For several laps, the two former champions ran together, with Labonte able to fend off Gordon's challenge. Gordon settled in behind Labonte to let his tires cool, and then began his charge again.

As they entered the turns, Gordon looked for room on the inside, but each time, Labonte would cut the turn short to protect his position and close the door on Gordon's bid. Finally, with 13 to go, Gordon pushed the nose of his Monte Carlo inside of Labonte's left-rear fender and, as the two entered the first turn, nudged the green-and-black Chevrolet and darted to the inside. As they came off the second turn, Gordon surged ahead and regained the lead he would keep over the final laps.

With no chance of catching the DuPont Monte Carlo, Labonte held on to the runner-up spot, while Earnhardt Jr. was able to fight back to third place before the checkered flag fell. Jeff Burton grabbed his first fop five of the year in fourth place ahead of Elliott Sadler, who scored his second straight top-five result.

When asked of his late-race "bump-and-run" on Labonte, Gordon responded: "I was pretty determined to win this race. ... I don't think anybody would have done any different. It was just hard to pass out there. I would have expected the same thing from anybody else."

After starting fourth, Ken Schrader finished a very satisfying 10th for BAM Racing, the best result to date for the second-year team. At the other end of the spectrum, Dale Jarrett's frustrations continued when loose lug nuts on a pit stop under caution forced him to return to the pits. That, followed immediately by a black flag for speeding on pit road, dropped the UPS Ford one lap down where he finished in 20th place.

Virginia 500 *final race results*

Fin. Pos.	Start Pos.	Car No.	Driver	Team	Fin. Pos.	Start Pos.	Car No.	Driver	Team
1	1	24	Jeff Gordon	DuPont Chevrolet	23	30	15	Michael Waltrip	NAPA Chevrolet
2	39	18	Bobby Labonte	Interstate Batteries Chevrolet	24	32	1	Steve Park	Pennzoil Chevrolet
3	2	8	Dale Earnhardt Jr.	Budweiser Chevrolet	25	12	22	Ward Burton	Caterpillar Dodge
4	10	99	Jeff Burton	CITGO Ford	26	35	30	Jeff Green	America Online Chevrolet
5	18	38	Elliott Sadler	M&M's Ford	27	17	32	Ricky Craven	Tide Pontiac
6	8	20	Tony Stewart	The Home Depot Chevrolet	28	36	97	Kurt Busch	Rubbermaid Ford
7	25	40	Sterling Marlin	Coors Light Dodge	29	14	0	Jack Sprague	NetZero Pontiac
8	5	2	Rusty Wallace	Miller Lite Dodge	30	40	43	John Andretti	Cheerios Dodge
9	7	48	Jimmie Johnson	Lowe's Chevrolet	31	15	77	Dave Blaney	Jasper Engines & Transmissions Ford
10	4	49	Ken Schrader	1-800 CallATT Dodge	32	28	10	Johnny Benson	Valvoline Pontiac
11	19	21	Ricky Rudd	Motorcraft Ford	33	27	74	Tony Raines	BACE Motorsports Chevrolet
12	9	23	Kenny Wallace	Stacker2 Dodge	34	33	45	Kyle Petty	Georgia Pacific Dodge
13	31	9	Bill Elliott	Dodge Dealers/UAW Dodge	35	21	4	Mike Skinner	Kodak Pontiac
14	16	5	Terry Labonte	Kellogg's/got milk? Chevrolet	36	22	41	Casey Mears	Target Dodge
15	6	25	Joe Nemechek	UAW-Delphi Chevrolet	37	41	54	Todd Bodine	National Guard Ford
16	29	29	Kevin Harvick	GM Goodwrench Chevrolet	38	3	12	Ryan Newman	ALLTEL Dodge
17	24	6	Mark Martin	Viagra Ford	39	11	42	Jamie McMurray	Havoline Dodge
18	20	16	Greg Biffle	Grainger Ford	40	23	19	Jeremy Mayfield	Dodge Dealers/UAW Dodge
19	13	7	Jimmy Spencer	Sirius Satellite Radio Dodge	41	26	01	Jerry Nadeau	U.S. Army Pontiac
20	37	88	Dale Jarrett	UPS Ford	42	42	37	Derrike Cope	Friendly's Chevrolet
21	38	31	Robby Gordon	Cingular Wireless Chevrolet	43	43	02	Hermie Sadler	GoTeamVA.com Chevrolet
22	34	17	Matt Kenseth	DEWALT Power Tools Ford					

AUTO CLUB 500

April 27, 2003

An off-week for Easter, the first of three open weekends in the long NASCAR Winston Cup Series season, gave competitors a chance to step back and take a breath. And those who studied the point standings could see that change was in the air.

Dale Earnhardt Jr. and Jeff Gordon, winners of the past two events, had slashed considerably into Matt Kenseth's lead in the point standings. A healthy margin of 155 points just two races ago had suddenly shrunk to a mere 51 over Dale Jr., who had put together an outstanding string of six top-six finishes in the last seven events, including a win, two seconds and two third-place results. More satisfying to Earnhardt was that fact that he had shown his prowess in not just the restrictor-plate race at Talladega, but also on the superspeedways at Las Vegas, Atlanta, Darlington and Texas, as well a his strong run on the half-mile at Martinsville, where he led the most laps and was a very real threat to win.

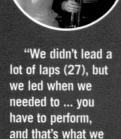

"We didn't lead a lot of laps (27), but we led when we needed to ... you have to perform, and that's what we did today."

For Gordon's part, a streak of five top 10s in the last six races, topped off with his first win of the year at Martinsville, vaulted him into third place in the standings, where he now trailed Kenseth by 139. Like Earnhardt Jr., Gordon was on a roll, and although it was still early in the season, he and crew chief Robbie Loomis felt the whole team coming together, building momentum for a run at a fifth NASCAR Winston Cup Series championship.

Jimmie Johnson remained in fourth place in the standings, 179 behind Kenseth, after three top 10s in the last four events, and he, too, was looking to pick things up like Gordon and Earnhardt had, by returning to his native California and the site of his initial NASCAR Winston Cup Series victory one year ago.

Bill Elliott charges through the California banking while hunting down the race leaders. Elliott jumped immediately to the point from his front-row starting spot, but a problem pit stop later in the race caused him to fight back to a fourth-place finish.

NASCAR. *Winston Cup Series*

Kurt Busch, Kevin Harvick, Tony Stewart, Michael Waltrip, Ricky Craven and Elliott Sadler all remained among the top 10 in the point standings, although all but Sadler, in 10th, had shuffled their positions either up or down based on the final Martinsville results.

In any event, the competitors of the NASCAR Winston Cup Series circuit were ready for a change of pace. They got just that by going from the confines of the series' smallest speedway in southern Virginia to one of its largest on the opposite side of the country – the two-mile California Speedway. Located in the Greater Los Angeles area, the Fontana track also draws its share of

show business literati and other denizens of "Tinsletown." Among the celebrities at the track was actor-strongman and aspiring politician Arnold Schwarzenneger, who was the event's official flagman.

Qualifying for the Auto Club 500 turned out to be something of a temporary reprieve for Steve Park, who placed the No. 1 DEI/Pennzoil Chevrolet on the pole with a speed of 186.838 mph. Park was elated with the accomplishment. Persistent rumors that his job might be in jeopardy had left him feeling he was being excoriated by the media, and he was a bit self-defensive after receiving his first Bud Pole award of the year.

Tony Stewart's Home Depot Chevrolet gets fresh rubber and fuel before returning to competition. Stewart appeared well in control of the race, leading 100 of the first 116 laps, but a blown engine put him in the garage early with a 41st-place finish.

(Above) The estimated crowd in excess of 120,000 settles in near the race's halfway point at the picturesque speedway in Fontana, Calif.

(Below) John Andretti (43) leads Dave Blaney (77) and Jeremy Mayfield (19) through California's fourth turn. Andretti picked up a solid eighth-place finish, his best of the season so far.

"My future with DEI is one that is strong right now," Park said. "We're not going to stop this year until we win."

Lining up beside Park was Bill Elliott, in the No. 9 UAW Dodge, while Tony Stewart, in the Home Depot Chevrolet, and Ryan Newman, in the ALLTEL Dodge, were third and fourth on the starting grid. Elliott Sadler was fifth quickest, in the No. 38 Pedigree Ford, while Jerry Nadeau was just a bit slower in the No. 01 U.S. Army Pontiac. Completing the first 10 starters were: Rusty Wallace, in the Miller Lite Dodge; Dale Earnhardt Jr., in the Budweiser Chevrolet; the UAW-Delphi Chevrolet of Joe Nemechek and Jeff Burton, in the CITGO Ford.

Soon after the drop of the green flag for the 500-mile event, Park's good fortunes came to a grinding halt, and he and Newman collided on the backstretch and brought out the first of eight yellow flags on just the second lap. That effectively ended the day for both drivers, who dropped out before the end of the race.

For about half the race, the star of the show was defending NASCAR Winston Cup Series champion Stewart, who was gunning for his first victory of the season. The Joe Gibbs Racing driver took the lead on lap 13 following the end of the second caution-flag period and held onto it until rookie candidate Jamie McMurray caught up and passed him on the 115th lap. Stewart got the lead back a lap later, but McMurray prevailed again on lap No. 117. Stewart then began to slow and a telltale plume of smoke sent him to the pits and finally to the garage on the 129th lap.

From there – and because of yellow-flag interruptions that broke the event into segments of

(Far Left) Matt Kenseth brings his DeWalt Ford through the turns ahead of Ricky Rudd's Motorcraft Ford and Ricky Craven's Tide Pontiac. Point leader Kenseth worked hard from his 23rd-place starting position to gain yet another top-10 finish, his eighth in the season's first 10 events.

(Left) Jimmie Johnson had been able to stay among the top 10 for most of the day, but a tangle with Mark Martin on the final lap ended his hopes of becoming a repeat winner in his native state. Johnson was able to get his car turned around and complete the race as the last car on the lead lap in 16th place.

(Below) Bobby Labonte (18) brings the field around for a restart with 28 laps remaining, followed by Jamie McMurray (42), Rusty Wallace (2) and Kurt Busch (97). Labonte lost his lead after a handful of laps under green, but was able to hold on and gain his second consecutive runner-up finish.

sorts – it was hard to pick an eventual winner. Kurt Busch put the Roush Racing/Rubbermaid Ford into the front spot on lap 131 (during the caution caused by Stewart's blown engine) and led through lap 145 before ceding the front spot to McMurray. Another yellow saw Wallace move into the lead and then hold off a strong challenge from Bobby Labonte.

Wallace held sway through the 215th lap. However, after he was passed by the lapped car of Dale Earnhardt Jr., he couldn't fend off a fast approaching Bobby Labonte, who took the lead but had to fight off McMurray. The rookie driver led one more lap (217), but Labonte was having none of that. He moved back by his rival as they headed into the first turn and led through the 227th circuit. Not to be denied, McMurray stole the lead from Labonte on lap 228 while Busch lurked in third place.

Caution No. 8 emerged with just 20 laps left

Kurt Busch (97) uses the outside to overtake Rusty Wallace (2) on his charge to the front. Busch grabbed his last lead with 12 laps to go and took the hard-fought victory to become the first repeat winner of the season.

and was caused by a seven-car crash involving Dale Jarrett, Jeremy Mayfield, Larry Foyt, Robby Gordon, Joe Nemechek and Casey Mears. While McMurray was still the leader when the event went green on the 238th lap, the stage was set for a four-way dogfight amongst McMurray, Labonte, Wallace and Busch.

Wallace – winless since this race two years ago – went to the front on the 248th circuit, but before the lap was complete, Busch and then Labonte overtook him, leaving Wallace to settle for third. Elliott and McMurray completed the top five, and Earnhardt Jr., Michael Waltrip, John Andretti, Matt Kenseth and Sterling Marlin completed the top 10.

"I really thought we had a great shot to win," said a disappointed Wallace, who led twice for 54 laps. "With two laps to go, I took the lead going down into (turn) three. But I slid up the track because I could not hold the bottom line, and Kurt got underneath me. Even when I slid up, I didn't know Kurt was there. When I came off four, it was like, 'Where did he come from?'"

"We put it to the mat and left them. I mean that car felt perfect at the end of the race," Busch, in becoming the year's first two-time winner, noted. "We didn't lead a lot of laps (27), but we led when we needed to ... you have to perform, and that's what we did today."

Auto Club 500 *final race results*

Fin. Pos.	Start Pos.	Car No.	Driver	Team
1	16	97	Kurt Busch	Rubbermaid Ford
2	19	18	Bobby Labonte	Interstate Batteries Chevrolet
3	7	2	Rusty Wallace	Miller Lite Dodge
4	2	9	Bill Elliott	Dodge Dealers/UAW Dodge
5	25	42	Jamie McMurray	Havoline Dodge
6	8	8	Dale Earnhardt Jr.	Budweiser Chevrolet
7	27	15	Michael Waltrip	NAPA Chevrolet
8	13	43	John Andretti	Cheerios Dodge
9	23	17	Matt Kenseth	DEWALT Power Tools Ford
10	30	40	Sterling Marlin	Coors Light Dodge
11	14	24	Jeff Gordon	DuPont Chevrolet
12	21	5	Terry Labonte	Kellogg's/got milk? Chevrolet
13	18	77	Dave Blaney	Jasper Engines & Transmissions Ford
14	6	01	Jerry Nadeau	U.S. Army Pontiac
15	15	32	Ricky Craven	Tide Pontiac
16	20	48	Jimmie Johnson	Lowe's Chevrolet
17	22	6	Mark Martin	Viagra Ford
18	29	16	Greg Biffle	Grainger Ford
19	10	99	Jeff Burton	CITGO Ford
20	28	4	Mike Skinner	Kodak Pontiac
21	39	22	Ward Burton	Caterpillar Dodge
22	31	23	Kenny Wallace	Stacker2 Dodge
23	5	38	Elliott Sadler	Pedigree Ford
24	35	21	Ricky Rudd	Motorcraft Ford
25	34	54	Todd Bodine	National Guard Ford
26	40	30	Jeff Green	America Online Chevrolet
27	26	31	Robby Gordon	Cingular Wireless Chevrolet
28	36	45	Kyle Petty	Georgia Pacific Dodge
29	37	29	Kevin Harvick	GM Goodwrench Chevrolet
30	41	49	Ken Schrader	1-800 CallATT Dodge
31	33	74	Tony Raines	BACE Motorsports Chevrolet
32	9	25	Joe Nemechek	UAW-Delphi Chevrolet
33	24	7	Jimmy Spencer	Sirius Satellite Radio Dodge
34	17	41	Casey Mears	Target Dodge
35	11	19	Jeremy Mayfield	Dodge Dealers/UAW Dodge
36	32	10	Johnny Benson	Valvoline Pontiac
37	38	88	Dale Jarrett	UPS Ford
38	42	14	Larry Foyt	Harrah's Dodge
39	12	0	Jack Sprague	NetZero Pontiac
40	1	1	Steve Park	Pennzoil Chevrolet
41	3	20	Tony Stewart	The Home Depot Chevrolet
42	4	12	Ryan Newman	ALLTEL Dodge
43	43	37	Derrike Cope	GBROnline.com Chevrolet

Joe Nemechek (25) gets a run on Dale Jarrett along Richmond International Raceway's frontstretch. Nemechek, who started on the outside of the front row, was able to lead the race in chunks throughout the night on the way to his third career win.

PONTIAC EXCITEMENT 400

May 3, 2003

With 10 of 36 scheduled points-paying races complete in the schedule comprising the 2003 NASCAR Winston Cup Series, two scenarios were playing out that few people would dared have predicted prior to the first event at Daytona Beach, Fla., in February. One was the tenacious hold that Matt Kenseth had on the lead in points. The other was the "decline and fall" of defending series champion Tony "The Tiger" Stewart.

Kenseth, in the No. 17 DeWalt Ford, was clearly the Roush Racing stable's most successful driver of the season. The Wisconsin native won the year's third race – the 400-miler at Las Vegas – and after finishing fourth in the following event at Atlanta Motor Speedway went into the lead in points and just wouldn't allow anyone to take it away.

Following a ninth-place showing in the Auto Club 500 at California Speedway, Kenseth had collected 1,473 points, 44 more than DEI/Budweiser Chevrolet pilot Dale Earnhardt Jr. Four-time NASCAR Winston Cup Series champion Jeff Gordon left California third in the standings with 1,321 points, with Kurt Busch, the California victor, uncomfortably close behind the DuPont Chevrolet driver with 1,305. Just 22 points separated fifth place Jimmie Johnson and sixth place Michael Waltrip, while Ricky Craven was 268 points behind Kenseth, in seventh place. Bobby Labonte was 28 points in front of ninth place Kevin Harvick, while residing 10th in the standings was Elliott Sadler with 1,149 points.

By virtue of his runner-up finish in California, Labonte cracked the top 10 in points, but he displaced Stewart, his Joe Gibbs Racing teammate, to get into the elite group. Stewart's bum luck continued at California with another DNF. It marked

> "We've got all the pieces to the puzzle right now ... I had a blast out there. When you get cars that good, you've got to take advantage of them."

the fourth time in the last six races he had failed to finish, and he dropped to 17th in points.

But with more than two-thirds of the races yet to be run, it was still anyone's horse race. So, the teams, at least for a week, stowed away their superspeedway equipment, bid the West Coast adieu and headed back East – specifically to the 0.75-mile Richmond International Raceway – for competition "under the lights."

It would be a long, somewhat wet weekend for the competitors that began on a low note when Jerry Nadeau was hospitalized because of an accident and ended on a high with a 10th different winner – Joe Nemechek – in 11 events.

For reasons not fully clear, Nadeau lost control of his MB2/U.S. Army Pontiac during a practice session the day before the race and ran, driver's-side first, into the second-turn wall. The likeable

(Left) Members of Matt Kenseth's DeWalt crew record tires temperatures after a pit stop. In a rough night on the track, Kenseth and crew had to fight back after suffering damage on the Roush Ford and succeeded in landing yet another top-10 finish, in seventh.

(Below) A crowd of more than 100,000 packed the Richmond grandstands to witness the excitement of NASCAR Winston Cup Series racing under the lights.

(Above) The glowing brake rotors on the cars of Elliott Sadler (38) and Todd Bodine (54) illustrate the importance of stopping power on the super-fast short track at Richmond.

(Right) Kenny Wallace's Stacker 2 Dodge was just one of many battered race cars on a night that saw the yellow flag wave on 15 occasions, a Richmond record.

Connecticut native was cut from his car and air-lifted to a nearby hospital with serious head and rib injuries. He was facing a long recovery period but would recover and likely race again. His replacement was NASCAR Busch Series stalwart Jason Keller, who qualified a backup car 12th quickest, but, according to the rules, would have to start at the rear of the field.

Bud Pole qualifying saw the pole go to Terry Labonte, driver of Rick Hendricks' No. 5 Kellogg's Chevrolet. In becoming the ninth different pole winner of the year, Labonte toured the Capital City track in 21.342 seconds at a speed of 126.511 mph. He was a tad faster than his teammate, Nemechek, while Dale Earnhardt Jr., Bobby Labonte, Ryan Newman and Jeff Gordon completed the first three rows on the starting grid. Kurt

Busch was seventh quickest, Kyle Petty eighth, Tony Stewart ninth and Jimmie Johnson 10th.

There was also the seemingly continuing Steve Park "story." Ill fortune continued to nip at the second-generation race driver's heels like an ill-tempered canine harrying a hapless urban mail

carrier. Park, however, kept insisting his place on the team was secure, and DEI officials said much the same thing.

Park, however, did – in a way – do as much as Nemechek to set the tone for the Pontiac Excitement 400 when the scheduled 300-mile chase got the green flag under threatening skies. Nemechek edged by Labonte's No. 5 "cereal" Chevrolet to lead the first lap, Labonte did the same to Nemechek's "union" machine to pace the third and then Nemechek shot around Labonte and took over and led through lap 45.

The tone for a long night – a track record 15 caution-flag periods for 91 laps – was set on the 44th circuit when Park hit the second-turn wall with the canary yellow Pennzoil machine. The incident also involved rookie contender Jamie McMurray, who continued to finish 22nd, while Park was done for the night.

Three more yellow flags between laps 64-211 didn't appear to deter Nemechek from going after the win, and he led on three occasions, laps 99-120, 128-129 and 205-228. It was the race's fifth interruption on lap 224, though (and one that eliminated Stewart for the night) that threw a scare into the eventual winner. Instead of immediately pitting for service, Nemechek, who was chatting on the radio with crew chief Peter Sospenzo, stayed on the track. By the time he realized his mistake and pitted on the 229th circuit, the damage had been done. The race went green on lap 231, and Nemechek found himself mired in the 25th position.

"In the heat of battle, I wanted to choke Peter," the driver later admitted. "We're leading and talking about pitting, then all of a sudden I'm past the

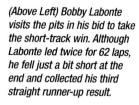

(Above Left) Bobby Labonte visits the pits in his bid to take the short-track win. Although Labonte led twice for 62 laps, he fell just a bit short at the end and collected his third straight runner-up result.

(Lower Left) Robby Gordon's Cingular crew outfits their Chevrolet with fresh rubber for their run at the victory. Gordon was able to maintain the lead for 29 laps during the final quarter of the race, but could not hold off Nemechek and eventually took fourth place.

(Bottom) Nemechek (25) puts a lap on Brett Bodine, running for the first time since the Texas event, four races ago.

pit entrance and couldn't turn in. That was very disappointing."

Nemechek, however, curbed his frustration and got back to work. A two-car incident slowed the race for a seventh time on lap 250, and Nemechek ducked into his pit for service. Thirty laps later, he was running 14th and 100 laps from the end there was some light at the end of the

tunnel. He stopped again for two tires under yellow on lap 301, and on the restart following the 11th caution (laps 318-321) was running third behind leader Robby Gordon and second-place Jamie McMurray.

Nemechek was basically home free and on his way to his third career win. He passed Robby Gordon for the lead on the 331st time around the oval and nothing – including four more caution-flag periods – would stand in his way. The last one came out on lap 391, and three circuits later the event came to a slightly abbreviated red-flag con-

clusion because of rain.

Bobby Labonte finished second, albeit he was several car lengths behind the race winner. Dale Earnhardt Jr.'s efforts paid off with a third-place showing, and R. Gordon and Mark Martin completed the top five. The race took 3 hours, 23 minutes and 47 seconds to complete, and Nemechek averaged 86.783 mph and won $159,375.

"We've got all the pieces to the puzzle right now," Nemechek said. "I had a blast out there. When you get cars that good, you've got to take advantage of them."

Pontiac Excitement 400 *final race results*

Fin. Pos.	Start Pos.	Car No.	Driver	Team		Fin. Pos.	Start Pos.	Car No.	Driver	Team
1	2	25	Joe Nemechek	UAW-Delphi Chevrolet		23	34	54	Todd Bodine	National Guard Ford
2	4	18	Bobby Labonte	Interstate Batteries Chevrolet		24	33	49	Ken Schrader	BAM Racing Dodge
3	3	8	Dale Earnhardt Jr.	Budweiser Chevrolet		25	19	19	Jeremy Mayfield	Dodge Dealers/UAW Dodge
4	32	31	Robby Gordon	Cingular Wireless Chevrolet		26	29	0	Jack Sprague	NetZero Pontiac
5	30	6	Mark Martin	Viagra Ford		27	8	45	Kyle Petty	Georgia Pacific Dodge
6	36	29	Kevin Harvick	GM Goodwrench Chevrolet		28	11	41	Casey Mears	Target Dodge
7	18	17	Matt Kenseth	DEWALT Power Tools Ford		29	14	23	Kenny Wallace	Stacker2 Dodge
8	7	97	Kurt Busch	Rubbermaid Ford		30	24	43	John Andretti	Cheerios Dodge
9	16	99	Jeff Burton	CITGO Ford		31	43	11	Brett Bodine	Hooters Restaurants Ford
10	17	2	Rusty Wallace	Miller Lite Dodge		32	12	01	Jason Keller	U.S. Army Pontiac
11	20	22	Ward Burton	Caterpillar Dodge		33	42	14	Larry Foyt	Harrah's Dodge
12	37	15	Michael Waltrip	NAPA Chevrolet		34	27	21	Ricky Rudd	Motorcraft Ford
13	21	40	Sterling Marlin	Coors Light Dodge		35	26	4	Mike Skinner	Kodak Pontiac
14	35	74	Tony Raines	BACE Motorsports Chevrolet		36	40	88	Dale Jarrett	UPS Ford
15	13	10	Johnny Benson	Eagle One/Valvoline Pontiac		37	39	38	Elliott Sadler	M&M's Ford
16	6	24	Jeff Gordon	DuPont Chevrolet		38	38	32	Ricky Craven	Tide Pontiac
17	15	16	Greg Biffle	Grainger Ford		39	5	12	Ryan Newman	ALLTEL Dodge
18	31	77	Dave Blaney	Jasper Engines & Transmissions Ford		40	41	30	Jeff Green	America Online Chevrolet
19	10	48	Jimmie Johnson	Lowe's Chevrolet		41	9	20	Tony Stewart	Home Depot Chevrolet
20	28	9	Bill Elliott	Dodge Dealers/UAW Dodge		42	25	7	Jimmy Spencer	Sirius Satellite Radio Dodge
21	1	5	Terry Labonte	Kellogg's/got milk? Chevrolet		43	23	1	Steve Park	Pennzoil Chevrolet
22	22	42	Jamie McMurray	Havoline Dodge						

THE WINSTON

May 17, 2003

Is it mostly "Survival of the Fastest?" Or "Luck of Inversion?" Take your pick. But late Saturday night Jimmie Johnson left Lowe's Motor Speedway with a smile as wide as a Pacific sunrise in his home state of California and a million greenbacks in his wallet.

The driver of the No. 48 Lowe's Home Improvement Warehouses Chevrolet (that's right, the track is named after the same company that sponsors Johnson) co-owned by Rick Hendrick and star driver Jeff Gordon had just won the 19th annual version of The Winston – NASCAR Winston Cup Series racing's high-profile all-star race for drivers who had won points races the year before and into the 2003 season. For the second straight year, the event carried the "Survival" moniker, and as it did in 2002, the 90-lap event played to an exciting conclusion in front of a packed house at the Concord, N.C., super-speedway.

"When those guys were caught up in the wreck, we figured we were the best car from then on ... There's nothing like winning at home."

As it was the year before, the special event consisted of three segments of 40, 30 and 20 laps, with the "winners" of the first two receiving a guaranteed payday of $50,000. This year's event consisted of 24 drivers - 23 winners - and Jeff Burton, who won the companion 30-lap Winston Open. The high-speed version of musical chairs, saw the final four finishers at the end of segment one eliminated from the race, while the top 14 finishers in the second were supposed to run the final 20 laps. As it turned out, segment three was a 12-car race because Tony Stewart (who finished first in the initial segment) and Terry Labonte (The Winston winner in 1988) were eliminated in a lap-69 crash.

Qualifying for the starting lineup occurred the night before the race. Each driver had to run three laps around the 1.5-mile track and make a mandatory four-tire pit stop, with the pole winner being the driver with the fastest overall speed and time.

Jeff Burton (99) surges ahead on the outside while Mike Skinner (4) and Jimmy Spencer (7) swap yellow and blue paint in a battle at the front during the Winston Open. Burton ultimately stayed clear of the scuffle and drove to the win, taking the final spot in the evening's main event, The Winston.

That honor went to Bill Elliott, driver of Evernham Motorsports' No. 9 Dodge. Elliott's total elapsed time was 1 minute and 3.192 seconds for an average speed of 131.502 mph, including a lightning quick 12.93-second pit stop. That was a tad quicker than Tony Stewart's one minute and 3.764-second effort in the Home Depot Chevrolet, while Kevin Harvick, Dale Earnhardt Jr. and Sterling Marlin were third through fifth quickest.

"As much as I don't agree with the format, it seems to sometime play into my hands," noted Elliott (who won the race in 1986) of his fifth The Winston pole.

Though it went off free of yellow flags, the 40-lap segment paved the way for drama yet to come. Kevin Harvick, in the No. 29 RCR Chevrolet, grabbed the lead on the first lap but relinquished it to Stewart on lap 13, who, in turn, passed it to Dale Earnhardt Jr. four circuits later when he made his mandatory pit stop. Subsequent pit stops put Stewart back out front and he drove to the "win." Johnson, Harvick, Elliott and Earnhardt Jr. completed the top five.

The intent of the format became clear on the 40th lap when Ricky Rudd snookered Rusty Wallace – the 1989 The Winston winner – and moved into the final transfer slot for segment No. 2. Joining Wallace in the locker room were Johnny Benson, Elliott Sadler and Jamie McMurray.

When the green flag dropped for the start of the 30-lap leg, Stewart shot out of the gate and led through the 56th lap overall until ceding the front

spot to Harvick, who paced the next eight laps. Six laps into the second run, Sterling Marlin and Jeff Gordon bumped and spun, and on the 65th circuit, Ryan Newman, Mark Martin and Ricky Craven triggered a wreck that red-flagged the event so the track could be cleared and cleaned.

(Right) 1998 The Winston winner Mark Martin started the evening 14th and pretty much stayed there. He was 14th at the end of the first leg and 15th in the second after tussling with Ryan Newman and Ricky Craven. Only Craven transferred to the final segment, where he finished 10th.

(Below Right) The Winston is, more than anything, the fans' race, and the pre-race ceremony is a production in and of itself. Here (from top) Ricky Rudd, Ryan Newman and Dale Earnhardt Jr. walk the gauntlet of high-fives followed by their crewmates.

When the race went back to green on the 69th lap – one lap from the end of segment two – Stewart got bogged down in traffic and was caught up in a six-car crash. That ended his night, as it did for Terry Labonte, Earnhardt Jr., Dale Jarrett, Martin and Elliott, who sustained a broken left foot, while Kurt Busch took the checkered flag first.

"I think I'm going to take the weekend off, and somebody else can drive this (car) for this race," said an upset Stewart. "I'll take the night off. It's starting to become not worth it."

Once again, the field for the final segment was inverted in an order determined by a vote of the spectators. The wily Johnson, who made his mandatory pit stop under yellow, appeared to gamble that the fans would opt for the optimum inversion – 10 cars. He finished seventh in the second segment and started fourth in the third, while Busch started 10th.

Gordon started on the "pole" (lap 71) in the final segment but lost his bid for a fourth triumph in the all-star event when his protégé passed him on the 75th lap and went on to win. Busch made a valiant effort but was 0.888-second – 300 feet – behind the winner in second place. Bobby Labonte, Joe Nemechek, and Michael Waltrip completed the top five, while Gordon faded to eighth at the finish.

"When those guys were caught up in the wreck, we figured we were the best car from then on," Johnson said. "Track position was everything. This is incredible. There's nothing like winning at home."

Johnson drove to a payday of $1,017,604

(vs. a "paltry" $265,104 for Busch) in 1 hour, 6 minutes and 46 seconds at an average speed of 133.297 mph. There were seven lead changes among five drivers and three yellow flags for 11 laps.

A second winner of sorts was LMS President H.A. "Humpy" Wheeler, who correctly predicted Johnson would win the race. It was the ninth time in 15 tries that Wheeler's crystal ball was crystal clear!

(Above) Jeff Burton (99) and Joe Nemechek (25) go at it side by side during the event's final 20-lap dash. Nemechek surged ahead to a fourth-place finish worth more than $85,000, while Winston Open winner Burton wound up ninth but with a payday in excess of $123,000 for the night.

(Left) Jimmie Johnson (48) runs alongside teammate/car owner Jeff Gordon (24) in the early stages of the all-star event. In the waning laps, the two would find each other again as Johnson overtook the DuPont Chevrolet with 15 laps remaining and went on to win it all.

Jimmie Johnson points out his status on the night during a celebratory victory lap. For his troubles, Johnson collected a check worth $1,017,604. That's $11,306 per lap!

The Winston *final race results*

segment 1 (40 laps)

Fin. Pos.	Start Pos.	Car No.	Driver	Team
1	2	20	Tony Stewart	Home Depot Chevrolet
2	16	48	Jimmie Johnson	Lowe's Chevrolet
3	3	29	Kevin Harvick	GM Goodwrench Chevrolet
4	1	9	Bill Elliott	Dodge Dealers/UAW Dodge
5	4	8	Dale Earnhardt Jr.	Budweiser Chevrolet
6	8	5	Terry Labonte	Kellogg's/got milk? Chevrolet
7	5	40	Sterling Marlin	Coors Light Dodge
8	10	24	Jeff Gordon	DuPont Chevrolet
9	11	97	Kurt Busch	Rubbermaid Ford
10	9	15	Michael Waltrip	NAPA Chevrolet
11	17	17	Matt Kenseth	DEWALT Power Tools Ford
12	6	25	Joe Nemechek	UAW-Delphi Chevrolet
13	7	32	Ricky Craven	Tide Pontiac
14	14	6	Mark Martin	Viagra Ford
15	22	88	Dale Jarrett	UPS Ford
16	12	12	Ryan Newman	ALLTEL Dodge
17	21	18	Bobby Labonte	Interstate Batteries Chevrolet
18	24	99	Jeff Burton	CITGO Ford
19	13	22	Ward Burton	Caterpillar Dodge
20	20	21	Ricky Rudd	Motorcraft Ford
21	18	2	Rusty Wallace	Miller Lite Dodge
22	23	42	Jamie McMurray	Havoline Dodge
23	19	38	Elliott Sadler	Pedigree Ford
24	15	10	Johnny Benson	Valvoline Pontiac

segment 2 (30 laps)

Fin. Pos.	Start Pos.	Driver	Fin. Pos.	Start Pos.	Driver
1	9	Kurt Busch	11	18	Jeff Burton
2	17	Bobby Labonte	12	20	Ricky Rudd
3	3	Kevin Harvick	13	6	Terry Labonte
4	11	Matt Kenseth	14	1	Tony Stewart
5	10	Michael Waltrip	15	14	Mark Martin
6	12	Joe Nemechek	16	4	Bill Elliott
7	2	Jimmie Johnson	17	5	Dale Earnhardt Jr.
8	13	Ricky Craven	18	15	Dale Jarrett
9	8	Jeff Gordon	19	16	Ryan Newman
10	7	Sterling Marlin	20	19	Ward Burton

segment 3 (20 laps)

Fin. Pos.	Start Pos.	Driver	Fin. Pos.	Start Pos.	Driver
1	4	Jimmie Johnson	7	8	Kevin Harvick
2	10	Kurt Busch	8	10	Jeff Gordon
3	9	Bobby Labonte	9	11	Jeff Burton
4	5	Joe Nemechek	10	3	Ricky Craven
5	6	Michael Waltrip	11	12	Ricky Rudd
6	7	Matt Kenseth	12	1	Sterling Marlin

COCA-COLA 600

May 25, 2003

While the ultimate outcome of the 44th annual Coca-Cola 600 at the venerable 1.5-mile track, "born" in 1960 as Charlotte Motor Speedway, could have been more favorable for Roush Racing driver Kurt Busch and Evernham Motorsports' Bill Elliott, at least they each had something to smile about as they prepared for the year's 12th NASCAR Winston Cup Series race.

Busch, who made his series debut in 2000 with Roush, had just gotten the good news: Rubbermaid, the prime sponsor of his No. 97 Ford, had agreed to continue backing the team for another three years.

Elliott was just happy to be back at the track a week after crashing out of The Winston "all-star" race. Elliott's No. 9 Dodge was damaged too badly to complete the special event and he sustained a broken left foot. While doctors said the injury would take about a month to heal, Elliott's driving shoe was equipped with a special orthopedic insole that allowed him to compete in the 600.

"We wanted to be more patient, show some smarts and be up front when it counted. We had a great race car, but having to come from the back, we weren't sure how it was going to work out.

Also grinning like two cats in an aviary, were Jeff Green and Steve Park, who, following the race at Richmond, Va., fell out of favor with their team owners and lost their rides. Green was released by RCR Enterprises because of a public spat with boss Richard Childress but landed a seat in the No. 1 Dale Earnhardt, Inc./Pennzoil Chevrolet. That spot became available when, after seven years at DEI, Steve Park received the pink slip. Park, however, landed on his feet like any agile feline and took over the No. 30 AOL Chevrolet previously driven by Green.

The two drivers who showed up for the Coca-Cola 600 with the biggest smiles, however, had to be Jimmie Johnson and Matt Kenseth. Fresh from winning the 19th version of The Winston, Johnson (sixth in series points) was again ready to challenge

Jimmie Johnson (48) begins his charge from the back of the field alongside Robby Gordon (31) after having to start last due to a pre-race engine change. Robby Gordon also was faced with racing from the back because he missed the pre-race drivers' meeting while returning from the Indianapolis 500 earlier in the day.

the high-banked trioval for his team's co-owners, Rick Hendrick and Jeff Gordon. Kenseth, who finished seventh at Richmond, remained first in NASCAR Winston Cup Series points for the eighth straight week and continued to provide a "ray of hope" for his boss, Jack Roush.

Dale Earnhardt Jr. finished third at Richmond and came into LMS second in points, just 20 behind Kenseth. Busch's eighth-place run at Richmond – which might have had a positive effect on the Rubbermaid folks – advanced to third in points, 167 behind Kenseth and 147 behind Earnhardt, while nipping at Busch's heels were Jeff Gordon, fourth in the standings, and Bobby Labonte, who advanced from 15th to fifth in the standings in just three races.

Though Johnson had dropped from fifth to sixth in points after Richmond, he scored a pair of top-10 finishes at LMS in 2002 and had a good feeling for the track. The point race for the rest of the 10 was also tight. Just 102 markers separated seventh-place Michael Waltrip and 10th-running Sterling Marlin, while Kevin Harvick and Rusty Wallace were sandwiched between in eighth and ninth places.

(Above) Michael Waltrip (15) takes on his new DEI teammate, Jeff Green, driving the Pennzoil machine for the first time, with point leader Matt Kenseth (17) looking for a line on the outside. After leading the most laps in the race, Kenseth was able to finish second, further increasing his lead in the points, while Waltrip just missed a top five, in sixth.

(Left) Steve Park wore a smile at Charlotte after making the jump from DEI to Richard Childress Racing and the AOL car vacated by Jeff Green in a driver switch following the race at Richmond.

(Above) John Andretti's Cheerios Dodge limps to pit road after being caught up in a multi-car incident that started with Ricky Craven's blown engine on lap 264. Andretti was unable to return to action and was listed 39th in his second DNF of the year.

(Below) Ryan Newman holds his own in front of RCR teammates Robby Gordon (31) and Kevin Harvick (29). Pole-winner Newman set the early pace in the race before settling in for a solid fifth place, ending a string of four straight poor finishes.

Although his time and speed of 29.140 seconds and 185.312 mph were nowhere close to the track record (186.414 mph) set by Johnson a year ago, the effort was more then enough to put Ryan Newman on the pole in the No. 12 Penske South/ALLTEL Dodge. It was his third No. 1 start of the year and 10th of his career and fourth for Dodge in 2003.

Elliott Sadler, in the No. 38 Pedigree/M&M's Ford, clocked in second fastest at 184.300 mph, while third through fifth quickest were Mike Skinner, Jeff Gordon and Jack Sprague. Tony Stewart posted his seventh top-10 start of the year in taking the sixth position on the grid, while Joe Nemechek, Dave Blaney, Michael Waltrip and

Johnny Benson filled in the top 10. Hermie Sadler, Brett Bodine and Derrike Cope weren't quick enough to make the 43-car field, while five drivers, Jimmie Johnson among them, had to use provisionals to make the field.

The start of the weekend was made even more difficult for Johnson, who had to start the race in last place because his car underwent an engine change two days before the green flag. That didn't seem to have too much of an effect on the young Californian's morale, however, and he went on to grab his first points-race victory of the year in a race that was shortened by 124 laps and 186 miles because of rain.

Forty-six of the event's 276 laps (including the

first three) were run under the yellow flag. Basically, it was a combination of eight caution flags, precision work by his pit crew and an overwhelming desire to conquer the track that shared his team sponsor's name that led to Johnson's trip into victory lane.

By the time he made his first pit stop on the 54th lap, Johnson had already sawed his way through half the field and was running 20th. Less then 30 laps later he was in 14th place and at the 135-lap mark, he cracked the top 10 and was running seventh.

Johnson's only edgy moment came after he made a planned pit stop on lap 194. Several laps later the spinning car of Ricky Rudd brought out the event's fourth yellow flag, and Johnson could have gone a lap down. He didn't, though, instead remaining in contention. After the fifth caution (laps 223-227) ended, Johnson found himself running in fifth behind leader Bobby Labonte and Kenseth, J. Gordon and Busch.

Two more caution flags and a spate of furiously close racing saw Johnson working his way to the front. When Labonte slipped and went high in turn two on lap 234, Kenseth charged past for the lead,

while Gordon, Busch and Johnson also slipped by the No. 18 Chevrolet.

When Kevin Harvick scraped the wall between turns three and four on the 241st lap, he dumped debris on the track and slowed the event a seventh time. The leaders pitted, Johnson's crew was a tad quicker and he took the lead for the first time on lap 242. He held the point through lap 264, losing

(Above) Dale Jarrett keeps his UPS Ford on track in front of Sterling Marlin. Jarrett's ninth-place finish in the Coca-Cola 600 was welcome relief for the UPS team as their fist top 10 since a win in the second race of the season.

(Left) Running alone in the opening laps of the race, Jimmie Johnson hits his marks in search of the leaders. It took Johnson until lap 242 to reach the front, but from there he led all but one of the remaining laps.

Jimmie Johnson's team makes its second trip to victory lane in as many weeks at the track bearing the name of its sponsor, Lowe's. Including The Winston, Hendrick Motorsports had taken the top spot in four of the last five NASCAR Winston Cup Series events.

it for just one lap while in the pits for a final time and retook the lead on lap 266. Rain started falling eight laps later, and the field was brought back onto pit road under the red flag.

The race came to a halt around 9 p.m., and about 30 minutes later, NASCAR, saying there was no way the track could be dried out in a reasonable amount of time, called the event official.

Johnson became the 11th different winner in 12 races. Kenseth, Labonte, Jimmy Spencer and Newman completed the top five, while Waltrip, Marlin, Gordon, Dale Jarrett and Ward Burton rounded out the top 10 finishers.

"This year, we had a different mindset here," said Johnson, who started on the pole and led the most laps in the 2002 Coca-Cola 600 but finished seventh. "We wanted to be more patient, show some smarts and be up front when it counted. We had a great race car, but having to come from the back, we weren't sure how it was going to work out."

Johnson completed the event in 3 hours 16 minutes and 50 seconds at an average speed of 126.198 mph and carried off $271,900.

"Maybe what we need is some rain-shortened races," quipped the happy winner.

Coca-Cola 600 *final race results*

Fin. Pos.	Start Pos.	Car No.	Driver	Team	Fin. Pos.	Start Pos.	Car No.	Driver	Team
1	37	48	Jimmie Johnson	Lowe's Chevrolet	23	16	54	Todd Bodine	National Guard Ford
2	18	17	Matt Kenseth	DEWALT Power Tools Ford	24	10	10	Johnny Benson	Valvoline Pontiac
3	11	18	Bobby Labonte	Interstate Batteries Chevrolet	25	17	42	Jamie McMurray	Havoline Dodge
4	14	7	Jimmy Spencer	Sirius Satellite Radio Dodge	26	32	9	Bill Elliott	Dodge Dealers/UAW Dodge
5	1	12	Ryan Newman	ALLTEL Dodge	27	13	30	Steve Park	America Online Chevrolet
6	9	15	Michael Waltrip	NAPA Chevrolet	28	30	49	Ken Schrader	Freightline/BAM Racing Dodge
7	36	40	Sterling Marlin	Coors Light Dodge	29	21	6	Mark Martin	Viagra Ford
8	4	24	Jeff Gordon	DuPont Chevrolet	30	31	45	Kyle Petty	Georgia Pacific/Brawny Dodge
9	23	88	Dale Jarrett	UPS Ford	31	43	01	Mike Wallace	U.S. Army Pontiac
10	41	22	Ward Burton	Caterpillar Dodge	32	27	71	Kevin Lepage	Warranty Gold/Pro Motorsports Ford
11	7	25	Joe Nemechek	UAW-Delphi Chevrolet	33	40	21	Ricky Rudd	Motorcraft Ford
12	34	2	Rusty Wallace	Miller Lite Dodge	34	29	14	Larry Foyt	Harrah's Dodge
13	20	29	Kevin Harvick	GM Goodwrench Chevrolet	35	19	41	Casey Mears	Target Dodge
14	8	77	Dave Blaney	Jasper Engines & Transmissions Ford	36	2	38	Elliott Sadler	Pedigree/M&M's Ford
15	12	97	Kurt Busch	Rubbermaid Ford	37	25	74	Tony Raines	BACE Motorsports Chevrolet
16	26	16	Greg Biffle	Grainger Ford	38	33	32	Ricky Craven	Tide Pontiac
17	38	31	Robby Gordon	Cingular Wireless Chevrolet	39	42	43	John Andretti	Cheerios Dodge
18	35	99	Jeff Burton	CITGO Ford	40	6	20	Tony Stewart	Home Depot Chevrolet
19	15	1	Jeff Green	Pennzoil Synthetic Chevrolet	41	24	8	Dale Earnhardt Jr.	Budweiser Chevrolet
20	3	4	Mike Skinner	Kodak Pontiac	42	28	23	Kenny Wallace	Stacker2 Dodge
21	39	5	Terry Labonte	Kellogg's/got milk? Chevrolet	43	22	19	Jeremy Mayfield	Dodge Dealers/UAW Dodge
22	5	0	Jack Sprague	NetZero Pontiac					

MBNA ARMED FORCES FAMILY 400

June 1, 2003

Dating back to 1969, the year Dover (Del.) International Speedway opened and hosted its first NASCAR Winston Cup Series race, only three drivers had won a trio of consecutive races at the exceedingly demanding oval later dubbed the "Monster Mile."

Coincidentally, all three won the series championship at least once. David Pearson (now retired) was the first to capture a "Dover triple" when he won in the fall of 1972 and then both races in 1973. Twenty years later, Rusty Wallace did the same thing by winning the fall 500-miler in 1993 and both events the following year, while Jeff Gordon repeated the pattern in 1995-96.

> "It's a team effort ... If they don't give me a straight arrow, I can't hit the target. They gave me a straight arrow today."

Going into the 13th event on the 2003 NASCAR Winston Cup Series tour, Jimmie Johnson, who won both events at Dover in '02, was on a "high" and was entertaining thoughts of joining the exclusive "three-straight club."

And for good reason: The driver of the No. 48 Lowe's Chevrolet, co-owned by Gordon and Hendrick Motorsports, was on a roll. The 27-year-old speedster had dominated at Lowe's Motor Speedway by winning the May 25 Coca-Cola 600 and The Winston non-points special event the week before. In doing so, he joined Darrell Waltrip (1985), the late Davey Allison ('91), the late Dale Earnhardt ('93) and Gordon ('97) as being the only drivers to sweep both events in the same year.

Add to that fact the Monday leading into the Dover weekend Lowe's Home Improvement Warehouse had signed a five-year extension with Hendrick and Gordon, while Hendrick Motorsports had extended the contracts of Johnson and his crew chief, Chad Knaus, for at least another five seasons.

Jimmie Johnson takes the wheel prior the Armed Forces Family 400 at Dover, focused on his goal of winning three straight at the Monster Mile and continuing a hot streak he began two weeks earlier in Charlotte.

"Really, that's been in the works awhile," Johnson said. "So, we're looking forward to going to Dover, but the mindset is not to let the pressure of trying to win again get to us. Right now, we're just looking for solid finishes every week.

"That's how we're approaching it."

The victory at Lowe's Motor Speedway also moved Johnson up a notch in NASCAR Winston Cup Series points from sixth to fifth with 1,552, putting him 247 behind Matt Kenseth, the leader. Kenseth, who finished second in the Coca-Cola 600, cushioned his advantage over Dale Earnhardt Jr. from 20 points to 160. It marked Kenseth's ninth consecutive week as the points leader and 11th in the top 10.

Earnhardt Jr. stumbled a bit at LMS with a 41st-place finish, leaving him to contend with Gordon, who was just 56 points behind in third place. Kurt Busch dropped from third place in points to fourth, but the spread between himself and Gordon was just eight points. Bobby Labonte, despite a fourth straight top-five finish, dropped to sixth in the standings behind Johnson, while Michael Waltrip, Kevin Harvick, Sterling Marlin and Rusty Wallace all remained in the top 10.

It might have been a bit premature for Ryan Newman to be thinking about winning a second straight $100,000 season-ending prize for notching the most Bud Pole Awards (he took six

No. 1 starting spots in 2002), but the thought had to cross his mind in qualifying for the MBNA Armed Forces Family 400. Newman did it again. With a speed of 158.716 mph, he put the No. 12 Penske South/ALLTEL Dodge on the pole for the fourth time in 2002. It turned out to be a good day for the Mooresville, N.C., operation, as Newman's teammate, Rusty Wallace, was quick enough (157.322 mph) to take the outside front row starting position in the Miller Lite Dodge.

At least in qualifying, Dodge seemed to have the edge, as Jeremy Mayfield was third quickest in the Evernham Motorsports/Dodge Dealers entry. Point leader Kenseth was fourth quickest, in a Ford, Johnson was fifth fastest, and rounding out the top 10 fastest in time trials were Sterling Marlin, Kurt Busch, Earnhardt Jr., Bill Elliott and Johnny Benson.

"It's a team effort," Newman noted. "If they don't give me a straight arrow, I can't hit the target. They gave me a straight arrow today."

(Left) Driver Matt Kenseth (above) and team owner Jack Roush (below) were all business at Dover. Their continued consistency (top 10s in all but two of the season's first 12 events) had them atop the points by 160, and they weren't about to let up. As they packed up to go home, their margin had increased by another 11 points.

(Below) Ryan Newman (12) leads the way for (in order) Matt Kenseth, Joe Nemechek, Jimmie Johnson, Tony Stewart, Rusty Wallace, Ricky Craven and Terry Labonte. Newman spent a good bit of the day out front, leading four times for 162 laps, 95 more than his closest challenger, Stewart.

(Above) Terry Labonte sported a special "Finding Nemo" paint scheme on his Kellogg's Chevrolet at Dover, and he had no problem remembering his way around the one-mile oval. Labonte, who qualified eighth, stayed on the lead lap and picked up his second top-10 finish of the season.

(Right) A NASCAR official (bravely) holds Tony Stewart in his pit stall as a penalty for pitting outside the box. It was deemed his right-front tire was over the line, a call crew chief Greg Zipadelli (far right) felt the need to "discuss." The penalty cost Stewart a lap, which he later made up on the way to a hard-fought, fourth-place finish.

How straight? Put it this way: If Newman had been in an archery contest elimination with William Tell, he would have split the arrow Tell fired to knock the apple off his kid's head!

In a nutshell, the burly Hoosier avoided the "slings and arrows of outrageous fortune" and won the race. It was his second victory of the year and tied him with Roush Racing's Busch as the only other driver to win more than one event in 2003. Newman led four times for 162 of the race's 400 laps and won by staying clear of the trouble caused by various accidents, fending off a dis-

gruntled Tony Stewart and manhandling a car whose power steering "went south" with 180 laps left to go.

"I'm definitely tired, and I'll feel it even more on Monday and maybe Tuesday," Newman said at the end of a long afternoon. "My arms hurt, my back hurts and my neck hurts. I couldn't even scrub (clean off) my tires.

"But we had a fast race car, and I wasn't about to pull into the garage and say, 'That's it, guys.'"

Defending NASCAR Winston Cup champion Stewart, who had seen his fortunes sink as the season progressed, was determined to run strong at Dover. Wallace led the first 41 laps, Newman the next 28 and Stewart got his No. 20 Home Depot Chevrolet underneath Newman on the 70th circuit, in turn one, and led through lap 116 when he pitted under caution. While Stewart gave up the lead, it was for just two laps. When the race went green on lap 20 he was back in the lead, which he held through the 139th circuit when he pitted under the next yellow flag.

That was his undoing. NASCAR deemed the right-front of his car was outside his pit box and penalized him one lap. Newman then took over the No. 1 spot and it was his until caution No. six came out on lap 203. Newman also held off Stewart at the start-finish line – tossing the so-called "gentlemen's agreement" to the wind – and prevented Stewart from getting back on the lead lap.

The driver nicknamed "Smoke" was a bit "put

out" by Newman's faux pas and ran him up the track between the first and second turns. Stewart got back onto the lead lap on the 219th circuit when he passed Johnson and eventually finished fourth. However, he wasn't available for comment after the race.

"If the situation had been reversed, (Stewart) would have done the same thing," Newman later explained. You can give them the lost lap or they can take it. He wasn't in a position to take it, and I wasn't in a position to give it to him.

"I thought it was in my best interest to keep him a lap down."

Soon after Stewart regained his lost lap, smoke began coming from Newman's Dodge. After checking his gages and seeing nothing amiss, he realized it was the power steering pump.

(Above) Johnny Benson's Valvoline Pontiac, shown here in qualifying trim, came to Dover ready to race. Although Benson qualified 30th, he drove a hard race, picking up 25 positions on the day to take fifth in his first top-10 finish of the season.

(Left) Three-time Dover winner Rusty Wallace had his Miller Lite Dodge flying on the Dover concrete as the race got underway. From his front-row starting spot (next to teammate Newman) he jumped to the point immediately and led the first 41 laps, eventually finishing sixth for his fourth top 10 in the last five events.

Jeff Gordon (24) puts the heat on race leader Ryan Newman on the final restart with just six laps to go, with Tony Stewart (20) and Bobby Labonte (18) in third and fourth. Gordon immediately dove to the inside in a bid for the lead, a move Newman successfully blocked to preserve his second win of the season.

Newman hoped the smoke would abate before he became the victim of a black flag and luckily got his wish.

Johnson, Gordon, Bobby Labonte and Kurt Busch all took turns leading chunks of laps as the race wore on, but Newman stayed in contention and ultimately took advantage of the last two caution-flag periods. He was in the lead when the race went green for the final time on lap 394 and held off a challenge from Gordon, who finished

second 0.834-second behind. Labonte got around Stewart to finish third and Johnny Benson drove a strong race to take fifth.

Jimmie Johnson saw his chance for a "Dover triple" disappear when, on the 278th lap, he crashed on the backstretch and ended up with a 38th-place finish.

Newman completed the race in 3 hours, 44 minutes and 31 seconds at an average speed of 106.896 mph and won $199,325.

MBNA Armed Forces Family 400 *final race results*

Fin. Pos.	Start Pos.	Car No.	Driver	Team	Fin. Pos.	Start Pos.	Car No.	Driver	Team
1	1	12	Ryan Newman	ALLTEL Dodge	23	36	23	Kenny Wallace	Stacker2 Dodge
2	9	24	Jeff Gordon	DuPont Chevrolet	24	37	25	Joe Nemechek	UAW-Delphi Chevrolet
3	13	18	Bobby Labonte	Interstate Batteries Chevrolet	25	33	1	Jeff Green	Pennzoil Chevrolet
4	11	20	Tony Stewart	Home Depot Chevrolet	26	25	49	Ken Schrader	BAM Racing Dodge
5	30	10	Johnny Benson	Valvoline Pontiac	27	23	29	Kevin Harvick	GM Goodwrench Chevrolet
6	2	2	Rusty Wallace	Miller Lite Dodge	28	43	14	Larry Foyt	Harrah's Dodge
7	4	17	Matt Kenseth	DeWalt Power Tools Ford	29	31	7	Jimmy Spencer	Sirius Satellite Radio Dodge
8	20	32	Ricky Craven	Tide Pontiac	30	15	16	Greg Biffle	Grainger Ford
9	38	31	Robby Gordon	Cingular Wireless Chevrolet	31	42	74	Tony Raines	America's Second Harvest Chevrolet
10	8	5	Terry Labonte	Kellogg's/"Finding Nemo" Chevrolet	32	10	30	Steve Park	America Online Chevrolet
11	12	8	Dale Earnhardt Jr.	Budweiser Chevrolet	33	17	38	Elliott Sadler	M&M's Ford
12	21	54	Todd Bodine	National Guard Ford	34	40	43	John Andretti	Cheerios Dodge
13	19	42	Jamie McMurray	Havoline Dodge	35	6	40	Sterling Marlin	Coors Light Dodge
14	28	99	Jeff Burton	CITGO Ford	36	35	4	Mike Skinner	Kodak Pontiac
15	7	97	Kurt Busch	Rubbermaid Ford	37	39	22	Ward Burton	Caterpillar Dodge
16	16	15	Michael Waltrip	NAPA Chevrolet	38	5	48	Jimmie Johnson	Lowe's Chevrolet
17	24	21	Ricky Rudd	Motorcraft Ford	39	29	88	Dale Jarrett	UPS Ford
18	32	6	Mark Martin	Viagra Ford	40	22	41	Casey Mears	Target Dodge
19	18	01	Mike Wallace	U.S. Army Pontiac	41	41	0	Jack Sprague	NetZero Hi Speed Pontiac
20	26	77	Dave Blaney	Jasper Engines & Transmissions Ford	42	34	11	Brett Bodine	Hooters Restaurants Ford
21	3	19	Jeremy Mayfield	Dodge Dealers/UAW Dodge	43	27	45	Kyle Petty	Brawny/Georgia Pacific Dodge
22	14	9	Bill Elliott	Dodge Dealers/UAW Dodge					

POCONO 500

June 8, 2003

Tony Stewart runs alone – and away from trouble. The Home Depot team put together a strategic gem in the Pocono 500 and avoided the bad luck that had been living in their camp to grab the defending series champion's first victory of the season.

B enny Parsons, the 1973 NASCAR Winston Cup Series champion, who retired as a driver in 1988 and is now a race broadcaster for NBC-Sports, doesn't have to worry. His unofficially patented nickname, "Mr. Nice Guy," is still safely his.

That's not to say many of today's drivers aren't "nice." They, however, are a bit different. Most are aware of their celebrity status and the accompanying pressure it brings, and guys like Tony Stewart are a lot edgier than drivers from Parsons' generation. Last year, while en route to the NASCAR Winston Cup championship, Stewart let this trait get the better of him and that resulted in conflict with the media and sanctioning body officials.

Through great personal effort, the driver of Joe Gibbs Racing's Home Depot Chevrolet underwent an attitude adjustment during the off-season, and the results of his therapy became evident as the 2003 season began to unfold. After scoring four top-10 finishes in the year's first five events, Stewart's fortunes began to sour. He crashed at Bristol, Tenn., and finished 26th, dropped out of the Texas event with a blown engine (in a backup car after officials confiscated his primary mount), finished 25th at Talladega, Ala., 41st at Fontana, Calif., because of a blown engine, and 41st again at Richmond, Va., after another wreck. Ill fortune continued to plague him at Concord, N.C., and after finishing an unhappy fourth at Dover, Del., he found himself mired 16th in series points by the time he got to Pocono for the June 500-miler.

Through it all, though, the fiery Indiana native somehow managed to stay cool and for the most part keep his emotions in check.

"I think (everyone) expected me to flip out this year the way things have gone, but we're running good ... it was just a matter of time before things turned in our favor."

MONTE CARLO

20

"I think (everyone) expected me to flip out this year the way things have gone, but we're running good," Stewart said. "We're doing everything right; we just haven't had the luck to go with it.

"We're doing everything we can do. It's just a matter of getting luck on our side."

Luck aside, a fourth-place start in the Pocono 500, skill on Stewart's part and a gutsy order from his crew chief Greg "Zippy" Zipadelli to make a late-race pit stop finally turned the tide in Stewart's favor. The victory was his 16th in his 154th series start and ended a 28-race winless streak dating back to Watkins Glen, N.Y., the previous August. It also moved Stewart up to 13th in points.

"We knew in our hearts and minds it was just a matter of time before things turned in our favor." noted the winner.

Going into the Pocono race, Matt Kenseth was firmly in control of the championship standings for the 10th straight week. The Roush Racing Ford pilot, with 1,945 points, was 171 in front of second-place Dale Earnhardt Jr. Yet, Earnhardt, who had climbed from 38th in points after Rockingham, N.C., to second following the event at Talladega, Ala., had never done better points-wise in his career.

Jeff Gordon's runner-up finish at Dover kept him third in points, 187 behind Kenseth and 16 in back of Earnhardt, while Bobby Labonte with 1,716 points was fourth in the standings. Kurt Busch dropped to fifth after Dover, Michael Waltrip climbed from seventh to sixth, and Jimmy Johnson's crash at Dover dropped him from fifth

(Left) Jimmy Spencer prepares to go to work on his "home" track of sorts. Spencer hails from nearby Berwick, Pa., and enjoys a home-state following at Pocono. Unfortunately, an ill-handing Dodge and a broken rear end caused a premature end to his day.

(Below) Casey Atwood gets service on his Mountain Dew Dodge, a third entry from Evernham Motorsports at Pocono. Atwood's first start of the year ended abruptly in a puff of smoke when his engine expired after 77 laps.

A member of Dale Jarrett's UPS crew limbers up with a 22 lb. disk while waiting for his time to scale the wall and go to work.

(Right) Raybestos Rookie contender Jamie McMurray takes a moment to sign a few autographs before making his first big-league start on the tricky three-cornered track in the Pocono Mountains.

(Below Right) Jimmie Johnson (48) leads (in order) Bill Elliott, Tony Stewart, Elliott Sadler and Dale Earnhardt Jr. on lap 17, immediately following the first restart of the race. Johnson, the pole winner, had just taken the point from Elliott, who scraped the wall the next time around and fell from winning contention.

to seventh. Rounding out the top 10 were Rusty Wallace, Kevin Harvick and Robby Gordon, who moved up from 12th to 10th.

While he wasn't at the northeastern Pennsylvania speedway to share the good news, driver Jerry Nadeau appeared to be well on the road to good health. Injured in a bad crash at Richmond, Va., in early May, the Connecticut native was released from a Charlotte rehab facility several days before the Pocono race and was continuing to recover at home.

MB2 Motorsports General Manager Jay Frye, in making the announcement, said Nadeau had overcome "another hurdle" and was making "remarkable progress."

The layout of the 2.5-mile Pocono track – it's a low-banked triangle with sweeping straights and tight turns – make it look like a deceptively simple raceway. Yet many competitors call it a combination superspeedway-road course with a dragstrip's, characteristics and it can be tricky. Even qualifying well is considered quite an accomplishment.

This time around, Johnson, in the No. 48 Lowe's Chevrolet, was the master of time trials and won his fifth career Bud Pole position with a time and speed of 52.741 seconds and 170.645 mph, well below the record of 172.391 mph set by Stewart in July 2000. Johnson's effort, however, was comfortably better than Ryan Newman's second-fastest speed of 170.513 mph.

Bobby Labonte posted his sixth top-10 start of the year by qualifying third, while Stewart's fourth-place effort was the sixth time he cracked the top 10 at Pocono in nine attempts. Earnhardt Jr. and Mark Martin secured the fifth and sixth spots on the starting grid, while seventh through 10th went to Dale Jarrett, Bill Elliott, Elliott Sadler and Casey Atwood.

Robby Gordon, Kenny Wallace, Ken Schrader, Kyle Petty, Mike Skinner, Tony Raines and Larry Foyt used provisionals to make the field, while Derrike Cope and Morgan Shepherd failed to make the 43-car field.

"I heard the Tunnel Turn (second corner) was extremely tricky – and they weren't lying," noted Raybestos Rookie of the Year point leader Jamie McMurray. "Every time you go through there you hold your breath hoping your car will stick."

McMurray's No. 42 Ganassi Racing/Havoline Dodge "stuck" well enough for him to qualify 28th fastest.

The first of five yellow flags encompassing 25 laps came out early (lap 8), the last was displayed late (198), and in between, Stewart never ran outside the top 10. He was comfortable on the three-cornered track, and for a change, things were going his way. It seemed that, at last, somebody else would have to be fingered as the poster child for problematic races.

Stewart came in for a splash of fuel under the first caution and pitted again under green on the 46th circuit while running second and reentered the race in the same spot. He led briefly (two laps) while the event was under its second yellow flag from lap 55 through 61, and paced the field on laps 90 and 91. He repeated the same scenario again, leading laps 126-127 and made another green-flag stop on lap 128.

The third caution, caused by a stalled car in the second corner was brief – laps 154-157 – but it gave Stewart a shot at showing his eventual dominance. He made a quick pit stop, beat Sterling Marlin's Dodge back onto the track and took the lead when Michael Waltrip made his stop on the 156th circuit.

Stewart stretched his lead over Marlin to

almost two seconds when the call that probably played a big role in his victory came under green on the 176th lap when Zipadelli told his driver to come in for a splash of fuel. The stop took just 3.6 seconds, and after four other drivers took turns leading, their cycle of pit stops all worked in Stewart's favor.

"I didn't know what Zippy had in mind," Stewart said about the order to pit while leading the race. "That's not my job. I just turn laps as fast as I can."

When Todd Bodine made his final pit stop on the 190th circuit, he handed the lead – and win – to Stewart.

(Above) Dale Earnhardt Jr. heads back to the action after a sizzling pit stop by his Budweiser crew. Little E, second in points going into the race, remained a contender all day and wound up fourth, but still dropped five points to Kenseth, who came home in third.

(Left) Mark Martin (6) stalks Ward Burton's Caterpillar Dodge through Pocono's six-degree-banked third turn. Burton stayed away from on-track troubles and secured a solid eighth place for his third top 10 of the year, while Martin posted a season-best runner-up finish.

Tony Stewart pits under green at lap 45, his second stop of the day. Brilliant work both on the track and along pit road turned everything in the Home Depot team's direction this day, reversing a bad-luck trend and resulting in the win.

Mark Martin had moved his Ford into second place, but he was 1.56 seconds behind the Home Depot Chevrolet. The race was yellow-flagged again on the 194th lap because of a crash, but the leaders stayed on the track. The race went back to green with just three laps left, but a four-car crash on the backstretch slowed the field with just five miles left. Stewart was home free and led Martin to the yellow-and-checkered flag finish.

Kenseth, Earnhardt Jr. and Newman completed the top five, while Marlin, Terry Labonte, Ward Burton, Elliott Sadler and Ricky Craven filled in the top 10 finishers.

Stewart completed the event in 3 hours, 42 minutes and 24 seconds at an average speed of 134.892 mph. His share of the pot was $214,253.

"It's fun when it works out the way you want it to," beamed Zipadelli.

Pocono 500 *final race results*

Fin. Pos.	Start Pos.	Car No.	Driver	Team		Fin. Pos.	Start Pos.	Car No.	Driver	Team
1	4	20	Tony Stewart	Home Depot Chevrolet		23	21	43	John Andretti	Cheerios Dodge
2	6	6	Mark Martin	Viagra Ford		24	24	10	Johnny Benson	Valvoline Pontiac
3	25	17	Matt Kenseth	DEWALT Power Tools Ford		25	20	29	Kevin Harvick	GM Goodwrench Chevrolet
4	5	8	Dale Earnhardt Jr.	Budweiser Chevrolet		26	22	77	Dave Blaney	Jasper Engines & Transmissions Ford
5	2	12	Ryan Newman	ALLTEL Dodge		27	40	45	Kyle Petty	Georgia Pacific/Brawny Dodge
6	23	40	Sterling Marlin	Coors Light Dodge		28	37	31	Robby Gordon	Cingular Wireless Chevrolet
7	11	5	Terry Labonte	Kellogg's/got milk? Chevrolet		29	38	23	Kenny Wallace	Stacker2 Dodge
8	17	22	Ward Burton	Caterpillar Dodge		30	42	74	Tony Raines	BACE Motorsports Chevrolet
9	9	38	Elliott Sadler	M&M's Ford		31	31	01	Mike Wallace	U.S. Army Pontiac
10	32	32	Ricky Craven	Tide Pontiac		32	28	42	Jamie McMurray	Havoline Dodge
11	14	54	Todd Bodine	National Guard Ford		33	35	1	Jeff Green	Pennzoil Chevrolet
12	1	48	Jimmie Johnson	Lowe's Chevrolet		34	41	4	Mike Skinner	Kodak Pontiac
13	12	24	Jeff Gordon	DuPont Chevrolet		35	36	30	Steve Park	America Online Chevrolet
14	16	99	Jeff Burton	CITGO Ford		36	10	97	Kurt Busch	Rubbermaid Ford
15	33	19	Jeremy Mayfield	Dodge Dealers/UAW Dodge		37	29	21	Ricky Rudd	Motorcraft Ford
16	27	2	Rusty Wallace	Miller Lite Dodge		38	15	25	Joe Nemechek	UAW-Delphi Chevrolet
17	3	18	Bobby Labonte	Interstate Batteries Chevrolet		39	30	7	Jimmy Spencer	Sirius Satellite Radio Dodge
18	13	15	Michael Waltrip	NAPA Chevrolet		40	34	91	Casey Atwood	Mountain Dew Live Wire Dodge
19	8	9	Bill Elliott	Dodge Dealers/UAW Dodge		41	43	14	Larry Foyt	Harrah's Dodge
20	26	16	Greg Biffle	Grainger Ford		42	7	88	Dale Jarrett	UPS Ford
21	19	41	Casey Mears	Target Dodge		43	39	49	Ken Schrader	Blair.com Dodge
22	18	0	Jack Sprague	NetZero Hi Speed Pontiac						

SIRIUS 400

June 15, 2003

Nascar CEO Bill France Sr. effectively curtailed a lot of speculation in January when he told an assemblage of motorsports media members that there would be changes coming in the structure of the schedule that comprises the NASCAR Winston Cup Series, and this "realignment" would possibly take effect as soon as 2004.

By the time the teams got to Michigan International Speedway in mid June for the season's 15th event, possibility had become reality. It had been announced that next year, the "Labor Day" date, officially the province of Darlington (S.C.) Raceway since its opening in 1950, would be moved to California Speedway, giving the Fontana, Calif., superspeedway two series races. The early September Pop Secret Microwave Popcorn 500 would be televised live and would begin at 8 p.m. eastern time, making it the first Sunday night race to be broadcast in prime time.

The Southern 500 at Darlington would move to November, while Darlington's "neighbor," North Carolina Speedway in Rockingham, would retain its early-season NASCAR Winston Cup Series race but would lose its event in the fall.

"Unbelievable ... this is just a one-in-a-million shot to get Ford its 100th anniversary victory today ... It was a wonderful ending ... just perfect."

"To be in the Southern California marketplace twice is a significant deal," NASCAR President Mike Helton said. "It's not a matter of abandoning tradition ... it's a matter of making the most efficient use of the opportunities we have."

There was other news, too, that surrounded the 400-mile event in Michigan. To wit:

The marriage of four-time series champion Jeff Gordon and his estranged wife, Brooke, had ended on June 10. The breakup of the seven-year "storybook" union was in the news for over a year.

John Andretti's stint as the driver of Petty Enterprises' No. 43 Dodge had ended with his

Joe Gibbs Racing teammates Tony Stewart (left) and Bobby Labonte (right) are feeling pretty good at Michigan as they prepare for the Sirius 400. Labonte had already started his weekend off right with his third Bud Pole of the season, while Stewart, fresh off his win at Pocono, would be starting on Labonte's right.

release on June 10. Andretti, with the team since 1998, was replaced at Michigan by Christian Fittipaldi.

There was bad news, too, for driver Mike Skinner. After he failed to get the No. 4 Kodak Films Pontiac into the field for the Sirius 400, the California native got his "walking papers" from Morgan-McClure Motorsports. Skinner had been with the team since the start of the 2002 season.

There wasn't much good news for team owner/driver Brett Bodine, either. On June 14, several days after his backer, Hooters Restaurants, told Bodine it was ending its sponsorship, he crashed his Ford while practicing for

the Sirius 400 and sustained a broken clavicle. Sidelined indefinitely, Bodine prepared a backup car for the race and turned it over to his older brother, Geoffrey.

A day after he finished 11th in the race, Jeff Burton and his team owner, Jack Roush, got the word that CITGO Petroleum had decided to conclude its backing of the No. 99 Ford at the end of the year. A change in marketing strategies, and not Burton's performance, was the reason given for the decision.

Going into the Michigan event, Matt Kenseth began his 12th straight week as the leader in NASCAR Winston Cup Series points. With 2,115 markers versus 1,939 for runner-up Dale Earnhardt Jr., Ford-driving Kenseth had a solid, but not insurmountable, lock on the standings. Earnhardt, who was by no means slacking off, had been second in points for the last seven

(Left, Above) Todd Bodine (left) listens intently while Jeff Green makes a point in the Michigan garage.

(Left, Below) Five-time Michigan winner Rusty Wallace prepares for his day on the two-mile oval. Wallace finished in 12th and remained eighth in the point standings after the race.

Labonte added another feather to his war bonnet June 13 by lapping the two-mile Michigan oval in 37.822 seconds at 190.365 mph to win the Bud Pole. Although not a track record, it was a new speed mark for the June event. It was Labonte's third pole of the year and 24th of his career.

Labonte's Joe Gibbs Racing teammate, Tony Stewart, was second fastest in time trials with a speed of 189.464. It marked the first time the two teammates had shared front-row starts in a race and it was the third time in the least five events that teammates had run one-two in qualifying. Terry Labonte and Joe Nemechek (Hendrick Motorsports) did it at Richmond, Va., while Ryan Newman and Rusty Wallace (Penske Racing) accomplished it at Dover, Del.

"I made a banzai run. We have a good, fast race car that's a lot of fun to drive," the pole winner said. "It's good to come out each weekend and have a shot at the pole."

"I'm still trying to figure out how he does it in qualifying," Stewart added. "He's got something I haven't got."

While it's an accomplishment to start on the front row, it's an even bigger one to finish first on the last lap. In this race that honor went to Busch, who started fourth in Roush Racing's No. 97 Rubbermaid/Sharpie Ford and beat the Bud Pole winner to the checkered flag by 0.774-second.

It was a storybook ending of sorts, as Busch not

(Above) Terry Labonte (5) and Jeff Green (1) lead a pack that includes Bill Elliott (9), Dale Jarrett (88), Todd Bodine (54), Tony Raines (74), Joe Nemechek (25) and Johnny Benson (10). Packs of cars spread across the track are common at Michigan with its smooth and wide racing surface.

(Right) Sterling Marlin had things going his way, leading 102 of the first 158 laps, until a missed shift on the sixth restart of the day sent him drifting backwards to an eventual sixth-place finish.

races and was 57 in front of Jeff Gordon, who had been third in points for three consecutive weeks.

Although his run of five straight top-five finishes came to an end at Pocono, Bobby Labonte held on to fourth place in points, and with 1,828, came to Michigan 287 behind Kenseth but 75 up on fifth place Kurt Busch. Despite finishing 36th at Pocono because of a wreck, Busch held on to a top-five spot in points but had both Michael Waltrip and Jimmie Johnson nipping at his heels. Waltrip (1,745 points) came into Michigan sixth in points while Johnson was seventh with 1,738.

Rusty Wallace and Kevin Harvick went into the Pocono event eighth and ninth in points, respectively, and emerged from it with no change in status. Sterling Marlin, with 1,623 points, moved back up to 10th in points from 11th. Marlin, however, was only 21 points in front of 11th-place Mark Martin.

only won one for "Gipper" Roush, but he also made the FoMoCo folks in nearby Dearborn quite happy in the process. Ford Motor Co. was capping off a week marking the centennial of its founding and Busch put the icing on its cake. He also enhanced the speedway's so-called reputation as a "Ford track" – and for good reason. In the 68 NASCAR Winston Cup Series events contested at MIS since its opening in 1969, Ford products had been victorious in 37 – a finishing percentage of 54.4.

"We've been racing Fords for 36 years. It's really awesome to have this kind of result," exulted team owner Jack Roush.

From his starting spot on the outside of the second row, Busch had to watch as Gordon, B. Labonte, Marlin and Stewart took turns leading laps and setting up a final duel for the victory. But a combination of the setup on the Las Vegas native's car and a series of short sprints interrupted by caution flags turned the tide in Busch's favor. While MIS is known as a track that's conducive to long green-flag runs, Busch and his crew chief, Jimmy Fennig, gambled and prepared their car for short sprints around the bottom groove. Gordon and Labonte didn't, and it worked against them.

The race was slowed nine times for 41 of its 200 circuits, and the last four cautions occurred within the last 42 laps. Busch took the lead for the final time with 24 laps to go, and when the race went green for good on lap 196, Labonte and Gordon were able to close in on Busch, but he had just enough to hold them off.

(Above) Tony Stewart (20) takes control of the race in the early going followed by Jeff Gordon (24) and Ryan Newman (12), with Kurt Busch looking to make his challenge on the inside. Stewart led the event on nine different occasions for 51 laps, while Busch took the point just once – and he never gave it up.

(Below) Brothers Kenny Wallace (23) and Mike Wallace (01) team up on Dale Jarrett's inside. Mike Wallace was making his first start in the U.S. Army Pontiac in place of the departed Mike Skinner and finished 23rd, besting younger brother Kenny by two positions.

Crew chief Jimmy Fennig pumps his fist in celebration as his driver, Kurt Busch, takes the checkered flag, his third of the season. Fennig's gamble to give the Rubbermaid/Sharpie Ford a setup for short runs paid off big as the final four cautions flew over the last 42 laps.

Gordon finished third, Matt Kenseth (a Busch teammate) was fifth, and Michael Waltrip was fourth. Sterling Marlin led 106 laps but missed a shift on a restart and settled for sixth. Earnhardt Jr. and Stewart were seventh and eighth, Martin (another Roush driver) was ninth, and T. Labonte was 10th.

"Unbelievable ... this is just a one-in-a-million shot to get Ford its 100th anniversary victory today," Busch said. "It was a wonderful ending ... just perfect.

"Today we had a setup that was able to prevail on shorter runs. That's the way the race came to us."

Busch finished up in 3 hours, 2 minutes and 54 seconds at an average speed of 131.219 mph and won $172,650.

Sirius 400 *final race results*

Fin. Pos.	Start Pos.	Car No.	Driver	Team	Fin. Pos.	Start Pos.	Car No.	Driver	Team
1	4	97	Kurt Busch	Rubbermaid/Sharpie Ford	23	34	01	Mike Wallace	U.S. Army Pontiac
2	1	18	Bobby Labonte	Interstate Batteries/The Hulk Chevrolet	24	16	9	Bill Elliott	Dodge Dealers/UAW Dodge
3	6	24	Jeff Gordon	DuPont Chevrolet	25	24	23	Kenny Wallace	Stacker2 Dodge
4	21	17	Matt Kenseth	DEWALT Power Tools Ford	26	26	10	Johnny Benson	Valvoline Pontiac
5	9	15	Michael Waltrip	NAPA Chevrolet	27	33	30	Steve Park	America Online Chevrolet
6	30	40	Sterling Marlin	Coors Light Dodge	28	13	1	Jeff Green	Pennzoil Chevrolet
7	3	8	Dale Earnhardt Jr.	Budweiser Chevrolet	29	40	7	Jimmy Spencer	Sirius Satellite Radio Dodge
8	2	20	Tony Stewart	The Home Depot Chevrolet	30	31	22	Ward Burton	Caterpillar Dodge
9	15	6	Mark Martin	Viagra Ford	31	29	16	Greg Biffle	Grainger Ford
10	5	5	Terry Labonte	Kellogg's/got milk? Chevrolet	32	25	88	Dale Jarrett	UPS Ford
11	23	99	Jeff Burton	CITGO Ford	33	43	74	Tony Raines	BACE Motorsports Chevrolet
12	17	2	Rusty Wallace	Miller Lite Dodge	34	42	45	Kyle Petty	Georgia Pacific Dodge
13	20	19	Jeremy Mayfield	Dodge Dealers/UAW Dodge	35	36	43	Christian Fittipaldi	Cheerios Dodge
14	39	42	Jamie McMurray	Havoline Dodge	36	18	02	Hermie Sadler	Total Non-Stop Action Wrestling Chevrole
15	37	32	Ricky Craven	Tide Pontiac	37	41	54	Todd Bodine	National Guard Ford
16	11	48	Jimmie Johnson	Lowe's Chevrolet	38	38	77	Dave Blaney	Jasper Engines & Transmissions Ford
17	7	38	Elliott Sadler	M&M's Ford	39	27	11	Geoffrey Bodine	Hooters Restaurants Ford
18	10	29	Kevin Harvick	GM Goodwrench Chevrolet	40	35	37	Derrike Cope	GBROnline.com/Friendly's Chevrolet
19	14	0	Jack Sprague	NetZero Hi Speed Pontiac	41	8	12	Ryan Newman	ALLTEL Dodge
20	22	41	Casey Mears	Target Dodge	42	28	49	Ken Schrader	BLAIR.com Dodge
21	12	25	Joe Nemechek	UAW-Delphi Chevrolet	43	32	21	Ricky Rudd	Motorcraft Ford
22	19	31	Robby Gordon	Cingular Wireless Chevrolet					

DODGE/
SAVE MART 350

June 22, 2003

Usually when the teams of the NASCAR Winston Cup Series make the annual trek westward to California in mid-June to go up against Infineon Raceway, they are totally preoccupied.

The oval track-directed racers have to pit their skills against the twists and turns of the 10-turn, two-mile road course in Sonoma, Calif. They have little else on their minds – except perhaps a bit of quick sightseeing and a good meal at one of the many fine restaurants in the San Francisco area or the "wine country" of the NAPA Valley. The track still commonly called

The U.S. Army crew services their Pontiac with road-racer Boris Said at the controls. Said, who posted a track-record lap to win the Bud Pole for the Dodge/Save Mart 350, led only the first lap of the race, but still came away with a strong sixth-place finish.

"I understood exactly what the rules were and took advantage of it ... I knew if we could get track position we'd be very hard to beat."

"Sonoma" is a challenge, as it's a radical change from Michigan and Pocono, the two venues that precede it on the schedule and even differs from Watkins Glen International, the other series road course in central western New York state.

This year, though, there was plenty to talk about as the teams readied for the Dodge/Save Mart 350. Four days before the race the "mother of all announcements" was made at the stock exchange in New York City which turned all recent rumors and bits of speculation into fact: Nextel Communications Inc. of Reston, Va. – one of the nation's largest wireless service providers – would assume prime sponsorship of NASCAR's flagship racing division beginning in 2004.

Nextel President and CEO Tim Donahue was on hand for the occasion along with NASCAR Chairman Bill France Jr. and a host of NASCAR and Nextel executives. He called the agreement "one of the most significant moments" in his company's history, noting, "it's like joining one of the most passionate families in America."

The NASCAR-Nextel joint announcement unofficially also signaled the end of a 33-year relationship between the race sanctioning body and the

NASCAR Winston Cup Series

R.J. Reynolds Tobacco Co., of Winston-Salem, N.C. Reynolds and its Winston brand first began sponsoring what became the NASCAR Winston Cup Series in 1971 with a point fund worth $100,000. That figure grew by millions of dollars over the years, but market forces and other considerations dictated that RJR bring its involvement to a close.

"My dad (NASCAR founder Bill France Sr.) believed RJR's commitment to NASCAR would bring us to new heights and make us a national sport," France Jr. said. "Today, NASCAR takes another giant step for the future of the sport.

"It is truly a historical moment."

The agreement called for Nextel to commit itself to NASCAR for 10 years and assume responsibility for the series' huge point fund, support the annual "all-star" non-points event for the top drivers and host the year-end awards banquet in New York City.

"I hope this is a lifetime arrangement," Donahue said. "We think we're going to be able to demonstrate to NASCAR and its fans that we're going to be a great partner."

Major changes aside, it was still business as usual for the teams as they got ready for the California road race. After the early-May race under the lights at Richmond, Va., Roush Racing

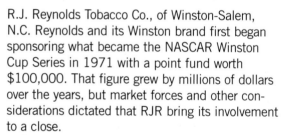

(Far Left) Ron Fellows, who regularly shows up at NASCAR Winston Cup Series road-course events, was on tap at Sonoma to drive the Pennzoil Chevrolet in place of Jeff Green. Fellows had a fine effort, qualifying third fastest and leading twice for 21 laps before taking seventh in the final rundown.

(Left, Above) Boris Said (left) got plenty of attention from the press at Sonoma after his pole-winning run, and he also became the subject of some good-natured kidding when crew members donned their Said-look-alike hairdos.

(Left Below) Bill Elliott (9) works his way toward the leaders ahead of Jeff Burton (99). Elliott, who started 12th, was solid on the twisty course and posted a very fine fourth-place finish, while Burton had problems and fell to 38th.

(Above) At lap 39, the leader board shows Robby Gordon ahead of Kevin Harvick, Ron Fellows, Jeff Gordon and Boris Said as competitors snake their way through Infineon Raceway's second turn.

(Right) Tony Stewart (20) leads Jimmie Johnson (48), Ryan Newman (12), Bobby Labonte (18) and Dale Jarrett (88) up the hill and through turn two. Of the group, Ryan Newman fared best with a fifth place in only his second start at Sonoma.

driver Matt Kenseth edged to a 20-point lead over DEI's Dale Earnhardt Jr. in the NASCAR Winston Cup Series standings. By the time they got to Sonoma Kenseth had stretched his advantage to 185 points. Overall, Kenseth had registered a series-high 13 finishes in the top 10, in 15 starts, to build the healthy advantage.

Always a threat, Jeff Gordon, who finished third

at Michigan, held onto third place in points for the fourth consecutive week and six of the last seven and was 223 markers behind Kenseth going into Sonoma. Bobby Labonte started on the pole at MIS, finished second to Kurt Busch and remained fourth in the points chase with 1,998. While a series-leading third victory of the season was a feather in Busch's cap, he didn't gain enough points to move out of fifth place, but was 33 in front of sixth-place Michael Waltrip, who arrived in California with 1,900.

Jimmie Johnson and Rusty Wallace – seventh and eighth in points going into Michigan – emerged in the same spots, while Sterling Marlin and Mark Martin each moved up one position. Marlin was 10th, but a sixth-place showing at MIS moved him up to ninth. Martin finished ninth at Michigan and cracked the top 10 in points for the first time since a slide that began after the year's third race in Nevada. With 1,740 points, he was 535 behind the leader.

One of the most interesting aspects of a NASCAR Winston Cup Series road race is the influx of left-right specialists or so-called "hired guns." At Infineon Raceway, the contingent was

led by Canadian Ron Fellows, who subbed for Jeff Green in the No. 1 Pennzoil Chevrolet, and Boris Said, who filled in for the injured Jerry Nadeau, in the No. 01 U.S. Army Pontiac. Scott Pruett was entered in a Chip Ganassi Racing Dodge and P.J. Jones took over for Larry Foyt in the No. 14 Harrah's Dodge.

When all was "said and done," it was SCCA Trans-Am champion Said being "all that he could be" and on the Bud Pole after making a track record run of 76.552 seconds at 93.620 mph. Robby Gordon, who cut his racing teeth on desert-based off road courses, was second quickest at 93.262 mph, in the RCR Enterprises/ Cingular Wireless Chevrolet.

Fellows – considered by many to be the nation's best road racer – was third quickest in time trials. Teammates Kenseth and Busch were fourth and fifth in the starting lineup. Completing the top 10 in qualifying were Kevin Harvick, Rusty Wallace, Jeff Gordon, Ricky Rudd and Tony Stewart.

"Someday I would like people to point to me and say, 'That NASCAR Winston Cup driver is also a pretty good road racer,'" Said noted. "My goal is to be a full-time NASCAR Winston Cup driver, and I'm not giving up on that."

Four drivers – Brandon Ash, Jim Inglebright, P.J. Jones and Paul Menard – weren't quick enough to make the 43-car field.

In the race itself, all bets were off during the final nail-biting 18 circuits in the 110-lap contest. The question was: Would Gordon win the race or would he have to settle for second place?

The answer was both. Robby Gordon slid into the lead on lap 80 and led the final 31 laps around the serpentine course to beat Jeff Gordon by 0.533-second at the finish. The victory was R. Gordon's second in the series (his first came at New Hampshire in November 2001), while the outcome advanced J. Gordon to second in division points. R. Gordon led three times for 81 laps and was definitely the man to beat. The trouble was not even his namesake could get around the road-racing veteran, and once he took the lead from Johnny Benson, R. Gordon was unstoppable.

The win, though, was controversial. Several drivers accused Gordon of violating the so-called "gentlemen's agreement," which says that while

(Top) A two-time winner at Infineon Raceway, Rusty Wallace muscles his Miller Lite Dodge through the esses ahead of road-course ace Scott Pruett, driving this event for Chip Ganassi Racing.

(Above) Kevin Harvick showed surprising prowess on the road course and might have had a chance to win, but a sly move by teammate Robby Gordon eventually led to a third-place result.

(Far Left) Ron Fellows (1) shows the way in front of three-time Sonoma winner Jeff Gordon (24) and Boris Said (01). The DuPont driver was unable to lead during the event, but remained near the front of the pack throughout most of the race.

Jeff Gordon (24) tries to chase down Robby Gordon (31) over the event's final laps, but Robby was having none of that this day. The Cingular driver stayed out front for the final 31 trips around the 10-turn track and gained his second career NASCAR Winston Cup Series victory.

it's legal to pass somebody when the caution flag is waved – and you're en route to the start-finish line – you back off and don't do it.

R. Gordon, however, motored on past his RCR teammate, Harvick, when the yellow flag came out on lap 72. In doing so, he picked up a valuable racing position, which some though contributed heavily to his victory.

"It was good, hard racing except for the chicken move under the yellow," said Harvick, who finished third.

"Anybody who races back under the caution like that, I don't know where his mind is," J. Gordon added. "What he did, especially to his teammate, is ridiculous."

R. Gordon stood his ground, though, and was having none of that. He said that during a pre-race drivers' meeting he asked three times about racing back to the line and was told there was no rule against it.

"I understood exactly what the rules were and took advantage of it," he said. "I knew if we could get track position we'd be very hard to beat."

Bill Elliott and Ryan Newman rounded out the top five finishers, while pole-winner Said was sixth. Fellows took seventh, Wallace was eighth, Bobby Labonte ninth and Jeremy Mayfield 10th.

Gordon completed the event in 2 hours, 57 minutes and 55 seconds at an average speed of 73.821 mph and won $204,512. He also gave RCR Enterprises its 74th NASCAR Winston Cup Series victory but just its third on a road course.

Dodge/Save Mart 350 *final race results*

Fin. Pos.	Start Pos.	Car No.	Driver	Team	Fin. Pos.	Start Pos.	Car No.	Driver	Team
1	2	31	Robby Gordon	Cingular Wireless Chevrolet	23	22	54	Todd Bodine	National Guard Ford
2	8	24	Jeff Gordon	DuPont Chevrolet	24	36	4	Johnny Miller	Kodak Pontiac
3	6	29	Kevin Harvick	GM Goodwrench Chevrolet	25	23	5	Terry Labonte	Kellogg's/got milk? Chevrolet
4	12	9	Bill Elliott	Dodge Dealers/UAW Dodge	26	33	41	Casey Mears	Target Dodge
5	13	12	Ryan Newman	ALLTEL Dodge	27	35	45	Kyle Petty	Georgia Pacific/Brawny Dodge
6	1	01	Boris Said	U.S. Army Pontiac	28	5	97	Kurt Busch	Rubbermaid Ford
7	3	1	Ron Fellows	Pennzoil Chevrolet	29	30	23	Kenny Wallace	Stacker2 Dodge
8	7	2	Rusty Wallace	Miller Lite Dodge	30	25	10	Johnny Benson	Valvoline Pontiac
9	14	18	Bobby Labonte	Interstate Batteries Chevrolet	31	34	74	Tony Raines	BACE Motorsports Chevrolet
10	31	19	Jeremy Mayfield	Dodge Dealers/UAW Dodge	32	15	77	Dave Blaney	Jasper Engines & Transmissions Ford
11	11	8	Dale Earnhardt Jr.	Budweiser Chevrolet	33	42	49	Ken Schrader	AT&T Dodge
12	10	20	Tony Stewart	Home Depot Chevrolet	34	18	09	Scott Pruett	Target Dodge
13	20	15	Michael Waltrip	NAPA Chevrolet	35	21	25	Joe Nemechek	UAW-Delphi Chevrolet
14	4	17	Matt Kenseth	DEWALT Power Tools Ford	36	39	7	Jimmy Spencer	Sirius Satellite Radio Dodge
15	9	21	Ricky Rudd	Motorcraft Ford	37	32	16	Greg Biffle	Grainger Ford
16	19	22	Ward Burton	Caterpillar Dodge	38	16	99	Jeff Burton	CITGO Ford
17	37	48	Jimmie Johnson	Lowe's Chevrolet	39	28	0	Jack Sprague	NetZero Hi Speed Pontiac
18	27	40	Sterling Marlin	Coors Light Dodge	40	41	43	Christian Fittipaldi	Cheerios Dodge
19	17	6	Mark Martin	Viagra Ford	41	40	30	Steve Park	America Online Chevrolet
20	26	42	Jamie McMurray	Havoline Dodge	42	29	88	Dale Jarrett	UPS Ford
21	38	32	Ricky Craven	Tide Pontiac	43	43	66	Hideo Fukuyama	Kikkoman Ford
22	24	38	Elliott Sadler	M&M's Ford					

PEPSI 400

July 5, 2003

Finishing ninth in the Dodge/Save Mart 350 at Infineon Raceway, where 43 cars started the race, may have educed elation in someone who had stood a good chance of not making the field in the first place.

For a driver of Bobby Labonte's caliber, though, a top-10 finish may have been just "acceptable." It was a lot better than finishing 40th - or worse - but it certainly wasn't very newsworthy or uplifting.

Therefore, it had to be a boost for the 39-year-old native Texan when four days after the California race it was announced that Labonte had signed a new contract with Joe Gibbs Racing of Huntersville, N.C., which would keep him behind the wheel of the No. 18 Interstate Batteries Chevrolet through 2008. In a sense, it was a reaffirmation of faith in the driver by the team owner. Labonte joined the team in 1995 and won the 2000 NASCAR Winston Cup Series championship. After a mediocre 2002 season, he bounced back, won at Atlanta this past March and was fourth in series points going into the Pepsi 400 at Daytona International Speedway.

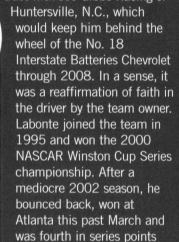

"You probably have to pinch me right now. I feel numb ... I don't feel like I've won a NASCAR Winston Cup Series race yet or been at Daytona in victory lane."

"I feel great that I know where I am going to be driving for quite a few more years," Labonte said.

In other news heading into the Independence Day weekend 400-mile night race at Daytona, the question of the future of the series' annual "all-star" race, known since its inception 19 years ago as The Winston, was answered: The race would be run a 20th time. With the R.J. Reynolds Tobacco Co. bowing out as the series' prime sponsor at the end of the year to be replaced by Nextel Communications beginning in 2004, the fate of the event had been up in the air.

"Yes, there will be a race," NASCAR Chief Operating Office George Pyne said. "It's likely to

The all-Richard Childress Racing front row of Steve Park (30) and Kevin Harvick (29) prepare to lead the field to the green flag for the Saturday-night running of the Pepsi 400. Park's lap at 184.752 mph put the AOL Chevrolet on the pole for the second consecutive time at Daytona.

be called the NASCAR Nextel All-Star race, or something like that."

Also, with the last three NASCAR Winston Cup Series races showing definite ratings gains, the Fox network ended its half of the broadcast season (NBC would take over starting with the Pepsi 400) with a 5.8 rating. The figure was impressive considering the effect the war in Iraq had on sports television viewership. And, too, the 5.8 average rating beat not only the NBA regular season (2.6) but also topped broadcast coverage of the NBA Playoffs (4.8), the NCCA Tournament (5.0) and PGA golf (3.3/all networks).

Life was also still treating Matt Kenseth and his No. 17 Roush Racing Ford team well. Even though the Cambridge, Wis., driver finished a mediocre 14th in the Dodge/Save Mart 350 at Sonoma, Calif., - it marked just the third time in the season he finished out of the top 10 - he lost just 11 points and still retained a healthy advantage in the race for the 2003 NASCAR Winston Cup championship.

The big change was who was nipping at his heels. Jeff Gordon's runner-up finish at Sonoma moved him up a notch in the points chase into second, while Dale Earnhardt Jr. was bumped from second to third. Pointswise, it was Kenseth with 2,396, Gordon with 2,222 and Earnhardt Jr.

with just two points less than the Hendrick Motorsports driver.

Bobby Labonte remained fourth in the standings with 2,1356 points, putting him 260 behind the leader. Michael Waltrip moved from sixth to fifth, with 2,024 points, knocking Kurt Busch down one spot in the process. Jimmie Johnson and Rusty Wallace came to Florida, still seventh and eighth in points, respectively, while a third-place finish in California moved Kevin Harvick from 11th into ninth. Sterling Marlin, with three top-seven finishes in the last four races, finished 18th at Sonoma and fell from ninth to 10th in points.

"I'm not even looking at the points. As a matter of fact, I stopped doing that awhile ago," noted defending series champion Tony Stewart, who ranked 11th in the standings after finishing 10th in California. "We just need to go out, race hard and win races. You do that, and the points take care of themselves.

"I said that last year when I was running for the championship, and I'm saying it now."

Steve Park's lap of 48.714 seconds at 184.752 mph in the No. 30 AOL Chevrolet marked the third straight Bud Pole Award for Richard Childress Racing at Daytona, as well as Park's fourth career pole win and second in 2003. Park was just a tad quicker than his teammate, Kevin Harvick, whose speed of 184.642 mph, put the No. 29 GM Goodwrench Chevrolet on the outside front row. It was also the second consecutive No. 1 start for the car, as Park's predecessor, Jeff Green, put it on the pole for the Daytona 500.

"The team had the confidence that this car would qualify well, so we worked on getting it into race trim," Park said. "I have all the confidence in the world in all of the guys. When they say something they mean it, and they said it (the car) had a lot more than it did."

The efforts by Park and Harvick relegated Jeff Gordon, who held the fastest lap for about two hours, back to the third row next to Sterling Marlin.

(Left) Jeff Gordon (24), Jimmy Spencer (7) and Greg Biffle (16) hook up in a tight draft up the middle with Mike Wallace (01) and Ricky Craven (32) on the outside and Todd Bodine (54) and Bill Elliott (9) taking the low line. Biffle, in his second ever NASCAR Winston Cup Series start at Daytona, went to school on the veterans before taking the lead for the final 21 laps.

(Below Left) DEI teammates Michael Waltrip (15) and Dale Earnhardt Jr. (8) did not enjoy their usual success at the track they've dominated of late. Although both drivers managed to get out front and lead in the race, Earnhardt had to "settle" for seventh, while Waltrip drifted back to 11th at the finish.

Dale Earnhardt, Inc., drivers Dale Earnhardt Jr. and Michael Waltrip secured the fifth and sixth starting spots. Ken Schrader and Jamie McMurray were seventh and eighth quickest in qualifying, while Elliott Sadler and Jeremy Mayfield rounded out the top 10.

Kerry Earnhardt, Shane Hmiel, Christian Fittipaldi and Tony Raines were bumped from the field, while Park and Harvick became the fourth set of teammates to notch a race start's front row in 2003.

Just suppose Gomer Pyle, the naive country boy from Mayberry, N.C., had been calling the final laps of the Pepsi 400 over the public address system. His listeners undoubtedly would have been treated to at least one "goll-ee!" with an accompanying "shazaam!" as Raybestos Rookie of the Year contender Greg Biffle crossed the finish line a whopping 4.102 seconds ahead of Roush Racing teammate Jeff Burton to score his first series win.

Two more facts would have amazed the fictional Pyle, too. First, the driver of the Grainger Ford became the first series rookie to take his initial win at Daytona International Speedway in the so-called "modern era" (1972 forward). Second, he joined Bobby Hamilton, Harvick, Terry Labonte, Mark Martin and Ken Schrader as winners of races in NASCAR's three main divisions, Winston Cup, Busch and Craftsman Truck Series.

Biffle also broke the stranglehold DEI drivers Earnhardt Jr. and Waltrip had on restrictor-plate races at Daytona and Talladega, Ala. Going into the Pepsi 400, Waltrip had won the last two

Bobby Labonte (18) harasses Greg Biffle (16) over the final laps of the event. Labonte's Chevrolet showed great strength but ran dry of fuel just short of the finish. Biffle was equally fast but able to make it to the checkers to pick up his first NASCAR Winston Cup Series win in his 23rd career start.

Daytona races and Earnhardt the previous four in Alabama. In this event, though, strategy and fuel conservation beat horsepower and experience and Biffle triumphed.

"You probably have to pinch me right now. I feel numb," Biffle said. "I don't feel like I've won a NASCAR Winston Cup Series race yet or been at Daytona in victory lane."

Just before the second yellow-flag period ended on lap 80 of 160, Biffle pitted for a quick gulp of gas, which meant he would have to make just one more pit stop. Earnhardt Jr. and Waltrip, running first and second, chose to remain on the track. This, in effect, threw them both out of sequence. The upshot was that Biffle took the lead with 21

laps left and motored away from everybody else.

"Coming down pit road to get that extra fuel really worked out," Biffle, a former NASCAR Busch Series and NASCAR Craftsman Truck Series champion, noted. "It made sense. It wasn't crazy strategy or anything like that."

Ricky Rudd, his Wood Brothers Ford powered by a Roush engine, finished third, Terry Labonte was fourth, and his brother, Bobby, who dogged Biffle for the win, ran out of gas on the last lap and finished fifth. Earnhardt and Waltrip ended up seventh and 11th, respectively.

Biffle's biggest victory came at the end of a 2-hour-24-minute-29-second run at an average speed of 166.109 mph and was worth $187,975.

Pepsi 400 *final race results*

Fin. Pos.	Start Pos.	Car No.	Driver	Team	Fin. Pos.	Start Pos.	Car No.	Driver	Team
1	30	16	Greg Biffle	Grainger Ford	23	42	45	Kyle Petty	Georgia Pacific/Brawny Dodge
2	36	99	Jeff Burton	CITGO Ford	24	9	38	Elliott Sadler	M&M's Ford
3	27	21	Ricky Rudd	Motorcraft Ford	25	12	41	Casey Mears	Target Dodge
4	25	5	Terry Labonte	Kellogg's/got milk? Chevrolet	26	32	80	Mike Bliss	Advair Chevrolet
5	15	18	Bobby Labonte	Interstate Batteries Chevrolet	27	22	10	Johnny Benson	Valvoline Pontiac
6	37	17	Matt Kenseth	Smirnoff Ice Triple Black/DeWalt Ford	28	38	2	Rusty Wallace	Miller Lite Dodge
7	5	8	Dale Earnhardt Jr.	Budweiser Chevrolet	29	34	1	Jeff Green	Pennzoil Synthetic Chevrolet
8	10	19	Jeremy Mayfield	Dodge Dealers/UAW Dodge	30	28	22	Ward Burton	Caterpillar Dodge
9	2	29	Kevin Harvick	GM Goodwrench Chevrolet	31	35	0	Jack Sprague	NetZero Hi Speed Pontiac
10	16	88	Dale Jarrett	UPS Ford	32	21	60	David Green	Haas Automation Chevrolet
11	6	15	Michael Waltrip	NAPA Chevrolet	33	43	4	Stacy Compton	Kodak/Pirates of the Caribbean Pontiac
12	40	7	Jimmy Spencer	Sirius Satellite Radio Dodge	34	26	14	Larry Foyt	Harrah's Dodge
13	41	54	Todd Bodine	National Guard Ford	35	39	77	Dave Blaney	Jasper Engines & Transmissions Ford
14	3	24	Jeff Gordon	DuPont/Pepsi Chevrolet	36	31	97	Kurt Busch	Irwin/Lenox/Rubbermaid Ford
15	29	23	Kenny Wallace	Stacker2/YJ Stinger Dodge	37	8	42	Jamie McMurray	Havoline/Terminator 3 Dodge
16	14	9	Bill Elliott	Dodge Dealers/UAW Dodge	38	20	25	Joe Nemechek	UAW-Delphi Chevrolet
17	19	09	Buckshot Jones	Miccosukee Resorts Dodge	39	1	30	Steve Park	America Online Chevrolet
18	11	48	Jimmie Johnson	Lowe's Chevrolet	40	18	31	Robby Gordon	Cingular Wireless Chevrolet
19	4	40	Sterling Marlin	Coors Light Dodge	41	7	49	Ken Schrader	1-800-Call AT&T Dodge
20	33	6	Mark Martin	Viagra Ford	42	23	01	Mike Wallace	U.S. Army Pontiac
21	13	20	Tony Stewart	The Home Depot Chevrolet	43	17	32	Ricky Craven	Tide Pontiac
22	24	12	Ryan Newman	ALLTEL Dodge					

TROPICANA 400

July 13, 2003

As he prepared himself for the Tropicana 400 – the 18th stop of the year on the NASCAR Winston Cup Series annual national trek – Kevin Harvick appeared to be living up to his nickname.

The driver of Richard Childress' No. 29 GM Goodwrench Chevrolet really was "Happy."

And for good reason: Continuing his dramatic turnaround from the 2002 season when he was 30th in the series standings at this point in the season, Harvick, by virtue of a ninth-place finish in the Pepsi 400, had moved up a spot in points from ninth to eighth. Now, he was heading to a track that had become a second home of sorts. Chicagoland opened in 2001 and Harvick had won both 400-mile races contested at the still-new 1.5-mile oval.

"I wish I knew why; then I wouldn't tell anybody," Harvick joked about his success in the heart of the Midwest. "No, it's just one of those places where something clicks with the way I drive.

"When we unloaded the first time, it fit my driving style for whatever reason."

Harvick might have been in a tad better mood leaving Daytona Beach than several other competitors, who were penalized by NASCAR for various infractions discovered at the Pepsi 400. An unapproved carburetor modification was found on Michael Waltrip's No. 15 Dale Earnhardt, Inc. Chevrolet, and crew chief Richard "Slugger" Labbe was socked with a $25,000 fine. Both Waltrip and his team owner, Teresa Earnhardt, were docked 25 championship points, and Labbe's wallet was lightened up another $500 for an unapproved roof strip on the car.

Waltrip, however, left Daytona still fifth in points. With 2,159, he was 137 behind fourth-place Bobby Labonte and 392 behind leader Matt Kenseth.

"Last year we had it all. We just didn't put it together at the end. This year, fortunately, we were able to put it all together for the end."

The field of 43 is lined up along Chicagoland Speedway's pit road awaiting the start of the third annual Tropicana 400.

(Left) Jamie McMurray (42) takes the wide line through Chicagoland's 18-degree banks flanked by fellow rookie contender Greg Biffle in the Grainger Ford. McMurray was best of the freshman class, staying among the leaders throughout the day before taking a top-10 finish in eighth.

(Right) Jeff Gordon brings the DuPont Monte Carlo back to pit road after a strong run in Bud Pole qualifying. Gordon's speed was just short of that posted by Tony Stewart but was still fast enough to land the outside of the front row for the start of the race.

The No. 45 Petty Enterprises Dodge was caught with unapproved weight-jacking bolts, something that cost crew chief Steven Lane $25,000. Additionally, Kyle Petty, the driver, and the listed car owner, Pattie Petty, each forfeited 15 championship points.

The ever-vigilant inspection corps also caught up with the No. 4 Morgan-McClure Motorsports Pontiac. The offending piece was an unapproved fuel-cell container modification that cost crew chief Chris Carrier $25,000 and 25 points each for driver Stacy Compton and owner Larry McClure.

And since he sacked driver Mike Skinner in mid-June, McClure, through a series of "auditions," had been busy trying to find a steady driver for his Kodak-sponsored entries. Compton drove the car to a 33rd-place finish at Daytona, and Johnny Sauter was scheduled for the ride at Chicago.

As he approached the season's halfway point, Matt Kenseth was clearly in the catbird seat. His sixth-place run in the Pepsi 400 even more cemented his lock on the points chase, as it was the 14th time he'd finished in the top 10. The effort allowed the driver of Roush Racing's No. 17

DeWalt Power Tools Ford to increase his lead in points over Dale Earnhardt Jr. by six. The race also marked the 14th consecutive week, dating back to Atlanta, he'd held first place in points. At this juncture in 2002, he was running eighth.

Earnhardt Jr., with 2,371 points to 2,551 for Kenseth, certainly wasn't slacking off. Finishing seventh in Daytona moved him back into second in points, a spot held by Jeff Gordon the week before. Now he was 23 points in front of Gordon and just 180 behind Kenseth.

Jimmie Johnson was disappointed over finishing 18th in the Pepsi 400 but the effort was good enough to move him up a spot in points to sixth, supplanting Kurt Busch in the process. With 2,079 points, he was in front of Busch by just 12, who was only 18 points up on Harvick.

Rusty Wallace finished 28th at Daytona and that cost him one spot in the top 10. Although he was ninth in points with 2,019, he was still within striking distance of the trio in front of him and was 21 points in front of 10th place Sterling Marlin.

Tony Stewart certainly made up for lost time on July 11 when he ended a spate of 33 races dating back to Aug. 2, 2002, with a No. 1 start. The No. 20 Joe Gibbs Racing/Home Depot Chevrolet driver

scorched the pavement with a record-setting lap of 29.223 seconds at 184.786 mph to win the Bud Pole position. In doing so, he broke Todd Bodine's old record of 183.713 mph recorded two years ago.

Jeff Gordon's speed of 184.445 mph was plenty fast enough for a second-place start, while the next four fastest drivers – Bill Elliott, Casey Mears, Jeremy Mayfield and Jimmie Johnson – also broke the old track record. Greg Biffle, Elliott Sadler, Dave Blaney and Jamie McMurray rounded out the top 10 qualifiers. Ricky Rudd, Kenny Wallace, T. Bodine, Mike Wallace, Kyle Petty, Christian Fittipaldi and Ken Schrader used provisionals to make the field and one driver, Jason Keller, was sent packing.

Rain delayed qualifying for about two hours, making it appears as though Stewart and the others were trying to make up for lost time. "The biggest thing was the condition with the amount of rubber on the track we had to deal with after the rain," Stewart explained. "It changed around just a little bit, but for the most part it was a good solid run."

Stewart also adroitly and with characteristic aplomb deflected rumors that he would be leaving Joe Gibbs Racing when his contract with the

(Left) Ryan Newman's ALLTEL crew provides fresh rubber and as much fuel as they can squeeze into the Penske Dodge on a stop under green. Newman made his last stop of the day on lap 198, took the lead 11 laps later and went the rest of the way to take the win.

(Below) Point leader Matt Kenseth (17) runs alongside two-time defending event champion Kevin Harvick (29) in their race for position. Harvick was plenty fast in his bid for a Chicagoland hat trick, but the fuel tank in his GM Goodwrench Chevrolet went dry two laps short of the finish.

former NFL head coach expired at the end of next year. He did, however, verify as true that his contract with JGR is up at the conclusion of the 2004 season.

"You know why I don't say anything about it? It's because I don't read the papers anymore," Stewart said. "I use them to light my fireplace in the winter."

Stewart's feisty spirit almost paid off with a victory at Chicagoland. He led the first 60 laps (plus 20 more) and was consistently two-tenths of a second faster than everyone else. But after finishing second to Penske Racing South driver Ryan Newman – who recorded his third win of the year – Stewart, still in a good mood, said that minor miscalculations and getting caught in traffic prevented him from winning.

"I think we had the fastest car today," he said. "It was just scenarios where we got caught back in the pack and the leaders were able to get away from us. I'd be happier if I was in victory lane, but I've had a doggone good weekend, and I'm pretty happy with it all."

Newman inherited the lead for

the first time late in the 267-lap race – on lap 190 – when McMurray made a green-flag pit stop. Newman and Harvick made their stops under the green eight laps later, and that passed the lead to Johnson, who was in front of Jeff Gordon, McMurray, Newman, Stewart and Jeff Burton once the pit stops were completed.

When the fifth of seven yellow flags was displayed on lap 208, several of the leaders pitted again – but not Newman and Harvick. Gordon led one lap (209), but when the race went green on lap 213, Newman was in command for good.

Harvick grabbed second place from Waltrip under green on the 225th lap and closed to within a quarter-second of Newman. Then two laps from the finish Harvick's hopes for a third Chicagoland victory literally dried up when he ran out of fuel. That passed second place to Stewart, who could get no closer than 2.633 seconds to the winner. Johnson, Gordon and Waltrip completed the top

five, while Harvick ended up a lap down in 17th place.

"You've got to have everything in the equation to be able to sit where I am right now," said Newman, who started 12th and led twice for 67 laps. "You cant just have a good race car or good pit stops. You've got to have it all.

"Last year we had it all. We just didn't put it together at the end. This year, fortunately, we were able to put it all together for the end."

Newman finished in just 45 seconds under three hours at an average speed of 134.059 mph. His win was worth $191,000.

Tropicana 400 *final race results*

Fin. Pos.	Start Pos.	Car No.	Driver	Team
1	14	12	Ryan Newman	ALLTEL Dodge
2	1	20	Tony Stewart	Home Depot Chevrolet
3	6	48	Jimmie Johnson	Lowe's Chevrolet
4	2	24	Jeff Gordon	DuPont Chevrolet
5	12	15	Michael Waltrip	NAPA Chevrolet
6	27	99	Jeff Burton	CITGO Ford
7	35	31	Robby Gordon	Cingular Wireless Chevrolet
8	10	42	Jamie McMurray	Havoline Dodge
9	8	38	Elliott Sadler	M&M's Ford
10	5	19	Jeremy Mayfield	Dodge Dealers/UAW Dodge
11	3	9	Bill Elliott	Dodge Dealers/UAW Dodge
12	24	17	Matt Kenseth	DEWALT Power Tools Ford
13	37	21	Ricky Rudd	Motorcraft Ford
14	13	6	Mark Martin	Viagra Ford
15	28	5	Terry Labonte	got milk?/Kellogg's Chevrolet
16	15	1	Jeff Green	Pennzoil Synthetic Chevrolet
17	11	29	Kevin Harvick	GM Goodwrench Chevrolet
18	36	10	Johnny Benson	Valvoline Pontiac
19	30	22	Ward Burton	Caterpillar Dodge
20	7	16	Greg Biffle	Grainger Ford
21	19	40	Sterling Marlin	Coors Light Dodge
22	29	74	Tony Raines	BACE Motorsports Chevrolet
23	21	7	Jimmy Spencer	Sirius Satellite Radio Dodge
24	38	23	Kenny Wallace	Stacker2 Dodge
25	26	32	Ricky Craven	Tide Pontiac
26	23	30	Steve Park	America Online Chevrolet
27	41	45	Kyle Petty	Georgia Pacific/Brawny Dodge
28	43	49	Ken Schrader	AT&T Dodge
29	42	43	Christian Fittipaldi	Cheerios Dodge
30	33	88	Dale Jarrett	UPS Ford
31	9	77	Dave Blaney	Jasper Engines & Transmissions Ford
32	22	2	Rusty Wallace	Miller Lite Dodge
33	39	54	Todd Bodine	National Guard Ford
34	4	41	Casey Mears	FujiFilm/Target Dodge
35	20	4	Johnny Sauter	Kodak Pontiac
36	18	18	Bobby Labonte	Interstate Batteries Chevrolet
37	40	01	Mike Wallace	USG Sheetrock Pontiac
38	16	8	Dale Earnhardt Jr.	Budweiser Chevrolet
39	32	97	Kurt Busch	IRWIN/LENOX/Rubbermaid Ford
40	34	0	Jack Sprague	NetZero Hi Speed Pontiac
41	31	14	Larry Foyt	Harrah's Dodge
42	17	25	Joe Nemechek	UAW-Delphi Chevrolet
43	25	37	Derrike Cope	GBROnline.com Chevrolet

The new racing surface at Bob Bahre's New Hampshire International Speedway seemed to have pl— grip, but that didn't stop John Andretti, driving the NetZero Pontiac for the first time after Jack Spra— release, from spinning after contact with Jimmy Spencer's Sirius Dodge in the opening laps.

NEW ENGLAND 300

July 20, 2003

Two things brought a bit of cheer to the competitors of the NASCAR Winston Cup Series as they made their 19th stop of the season in picturesque New England at Bob Bahre's creation nestled in lovely Loudon, N.H.

First, Bahre had completely repaved his 1.058-mile low-banked oval, and from all indications, he got it right.

And second, Jerry Nadeau, himself a native New Englander, dropped in for a visit.

Basically, the track had been the target of criticism almost from the time it opened in 1990 and then after the first NASCAR Winston Cup Series race there three years later.

Some said the asphalt surface was too rough and broke up too easily. Other complained there was just one poorly defined racing "groove" and others called for a complete redesign. After Bahre — who was personally well liked by almost everyone in racing — tried several things, he finally opted for a complete repaving job in mid-April.

His method, was, in a word, "exotic." Bahre bought asphalt mined in Trinidad (a West Indies island off the coast of Venezuela), which was then shipped to Germany for processing and finally mixed with an aggregate in the United States.

"I thought everything worked out well," Bahre said after the New England 300 was run. "It (asphalt) had plenty of time to cure, so we're very pleased with it. I think it's going to be fine for quite a few years. It's so hard it's not going to wear hardly at all."

Nadeau, who showed up at NHIS two days before the event, made his first appearance at a race track since his accident at Richmond, Va. After undergoing an extensive rehabilitation process, the Connecticut-born driver had reduced

"It's taken me a few years of running here to get used to it. I'm very excited and proud to win on such a technical track, a flat short track like this."

his physical therapy sessions from five days a week to three and had even run a few Go-Kart races near his home in North Carolina. He also said no one was pressuring him to get back into MB2 Motorsports' U.S. Army-sponsored Pontiacs.

"I can't tell you it's going to happen next week or the week after," he said. "A doctor can't schedule or plan when you're going to come back. Last week I ran the Go-Kart and it felt like I never left.

"When I knew I could move my arms and legs, and when I got back in that Go-Kart, I knew right then and there I was going to come back."

After losing his ride in the No. 43 Cheerios/Petty Enterprises Dodge in June, John Andretti, on July 16, was named to replace Jack Sprague in the CNC Racing/NetZero Pontiac. Sprague had experienced a lackluster season and team owner Gene Haas decided Andretti would be a better fit.

It was also announced on July 16 that NASCAR had fined Kevin Harvick's crew chief, Todd Berrier, $25,000 for breaking the rules the week before at Chicagoland Speedway. During a pre-race inspection, an unapproved "travel-limiting device" was found on the rear suspension of the No. 29 RCR Enterprises Chevrolet. Harvick was fined 25 driver points while Richard Childress lost 25 car owner points, as well.

For the first time in its 20-year history, Morgan-McClure Motorsports had entered two drivers in the same race. Larry McClure, still on a campaign to find a replacement for Mike Skinner in the No 4 Kodak Pontiac, entered Johnny Sauter in that car while bringing another mount for David Reutimann. Unfortunately, the weather threw a monkey wrench into McClure's plan – Bud Pole qualifying was rained out – and Reutimann had to watch the event from the sidelines.

No time trials meant that the field lined up for the race according to car owner points, and that automatically put Matt Kenseth on the pole. With 2,768 points, Kenseth entered the Chicago event

(Left) Jerry Nadeau lifted everyone's spirits at New Hampshire, especially those of his MB2/U.S. Army team, by returning to the track for the first time since his accident at Richmond in early May.

(Below) Dale Jarrett (88) leads Mark Martin (6) and Greg Biffle (16) in a short parade of Fords. Jarrett picked up a much-needed top-10 finish, his fifth in the season's first 19 events.

(Above) Greg Biffle (16) become a Ford sandwich between the Chevrolets of Jeff Green (1) and Tony Stewart (20). Biffle bested his veteran counterparts this day and also took the top spot among rookies in 10th.

(Right) Steve Park had a strong showing in the AOL Monte Carlo, joining his Richard Childress Racing teammates in the final top 10. Park took eighth, with RCR drivers Robby Gordon finishing fifth and Kevin Harvick in second.

with a point lead of 180 over then-second place Dale Earnhardt Jr. and departed it 165 markers in front of Jeff Gordon, who had bumped Earnhardt back to third. Kenseth's consistency had kept him in the lead for 15 consecutive weeks and in the top 10 in points for 17 weeks in a row.

Earnhardt Jr. crashed at Chicago, finishing 38th, and it marked the first time in the last six races he'd finished outside the top 11. That put him 93 points behind Gordon and 258 in back of Kenseth.

Bobby Labonte fared not much better than Earnhardt at Chicago – he crashed and finished 36th – marking only the second time in the last 10 events that he had finished outside the top 10. He, however, retained his fourth-place spot in points and went into New Hampshire with 2,351.

Michael Waltrip's fifth-place showing in the Tropicana 400 gave him his fourth consecutive top-15 finish and second fifth-place effort in the last four races. He remained in the top five in points for the third consecutive week and had not dropped out of the top 10 since the season started in February.

Jimmie Johnson snapped a run of five straight races without a top-10 finish by snaring fourth at Chicago, which kept him sixth in the championship standings, while Kevin Harvick – even with the loss of points because of the technical infraction – moved to seventh from eighth in points.

Tony Stewart's second-place finish at Chicago shot him from 11th to eighth in points with 2,129, while Kurt Busch dropped from seventh to ninth. Sterling Marlin, with 2,098 markers, kept 10th place in the standings for the third straight race, but the next five drivers in the ranks were all within 75 points of catching up.

At least from a fan perspective, Bob Bahre's massive improvement paid off. There may have been 12 caution flags for 63 of the event's 300 laps, but there was also plenty of good solid racing that was highlighted by 14 lead changes among nine drivers.

It also had to be a time of mixed emotions for team owner Rick Hendrick. While one of his most promising drivers, Jimmie Johnson, was able to easily move through the field and collect his second win of the year, his "star" performer, Jeff Gordon, who was a favorite to win, left the track bitterly disappointed.

(Above) Jeff Gordon waits for tires and fuel on a busy pit road under caution. Gordon led on five occasions and appeared to be the man to beat until his car's handling deteriorated in the closing stages of the race.

(Left) Matt Kenseth (17) leads the way for Terry Labonte (5) and Todd Bodine (54). Kenseth started on the pole and led just the first lap after the field was set according to points, but he hung near the front all day and picked up a third-place finish, padding his lead in the standings.

Johnson led just twice for 58 laps, but once he passed Ryan Newman with 37 laps to go, the event was his. Johnson surprised not only the full grandstands with an upset victory, but he surprised himself, too.

"I never thought it would happen to me, winning on a flat track," he said. "It's taken me a few years of running here to get used to it. I'm very excited and proud to win on such a technical track, a flat short track like this.

"I was able to stay patient and not hurt my race car, not wear the brakes out and not cause problems."

Johnson, along with Harvick and Kenseth (who finished second and third), all made crucial pit stops before the event's last yellow flag came out on lap 233, and that put them in a dominant position. Johnson moved into second place on lap 245 and then began his winning pursuit. When the checkered flag came out, he was almost 1.6

Jimmie Johnson (48) and Kevin Harvick (29) make a drag strip out of New Hampshire's frontstretch as they fight for track position. Both drivers were fast all day on the flat New England oval and captured the top two spots at the conclusion of the race.

seconds in front of the runner-up. Ryan Newman and Robby Gordon rounded out the top five, while Earnhardt Jr., Dale Jarrett, Steve Park, Jeff Burton and Greg Biffle completed the top 10.

But what happened to four-time NASCAR Winston Cup Series champion J. Gordon, who led more than anyone else – five times for 133 laps? His fate was perplexing, but it appeared after he pitted on lap 235 under the final yellow, his effort fell apart. He'd led the previous 26 laps, but by

the time his teammate was en route to victory, he was heading toward a 24th-place finish, the final driver to complete every lap.

"The cautions didn't fall right for us," J. Gordon said. "I don't know if the tires killed it or something broke. I really don't know what happened. I'm completely in shock."

Johnson finished the race in 3 hours, 16 minutes and 29 seconds at an average speed of 96.924 mph and won $200,225.

New England 300 *final race results*

Fin. Pos.	Start Pos.	Car No.	Driver	Team	Fin. Pos.	Start Pos.	Car No.	Driver	Team
1	6	48	Jimmie Johnson	Lowe's Chevrolet	23	41	4	Johnny Sauter	Kodak Easy Share Pontiac
2	7	29	Kevin Harvick	GM Goodwrench Chevrolet	24	2	24	Jeff Gordon	DuPont Chevrolet
3	1	17	Matt Kenseth	DEWALT Power Tools Ford	25	21	22	Ward Burton	Caterpillar Dodge
4	16	12	Ryan Newman	ALLTEL Dodge	26	26	10	Johnny Benson	Valvoline Pontiac
5	15	31	Robby Gordon	Cingular Wireless Chevrolet	27	18	38	Elliott Sadler	M&M's Ford
6	3	8	Dale Earnhardt Jr.	Budweiser Chevrolet	28	5	15	Michael Waltrip	NAPA Chevrolet
7	29	88	Dale Jarrett	UPS Ford	29	24	25	Joe Nemechek	UAW-Delphi Chevrolet
8	34	30	Steve Park	America Online Chevrolet	30	30	1	Jeff Green	Pennzoil Chevrolet
9	13	99	Jeff Burton	CITGO/Bassmaster Classic Ford	31	19	9	Bill Elliott	Dodge Dealers/UAW Dodge
10	20	16	Greg Biffle	Grainger Ford	32	36	45	Kyle Petty	Georgia Pacific/Brawny Dodge
11	9	97	Kurt Busch	Rubbermaid Ford	33	40	74	Tony Raines	BACE Motorsports Chevrolet
12	23	21	Ricky Rudd	Motorcraft Ford	34	25	19	Jeremy Mayfield	Dodge Dealers/UAW Dodge
13	27	77	Dave Blaney	Jasper Engines & Transmissions Ford	35	42	37	Derrike Cope	Friendly's Chevrolet
14	4	18	Bobby Labonte	Interstate Batteries Chevrolet	36	38	49	Ken Schrader	AT&T Dodge
15	31	7	Jimmy Spencer	Sirius Satellite Radio Dodge	37	37	43	Christian Fittipaldi	Cheerios Dodge
16	35	41	Casey Mears	Target Dodge	38	28	23	Kenny Wallace	Stacker2/YJStinger Dodge
17	11	2	Rusty Wallace	Miller Lite Dodge	39	10	40	Sterling Marlin	Coors Light Dodge
18	12	6	Mark Martin	Viagra Ford	40	22	42	Jamie McMurray	Havoline Dodge
19	32	54	Todd Bodine	National Guard Ford	41	39	0	John Andretti	NetZero Hi Speed Pontiac
20	14	5	Terry Labonte	Kellogg's/got milk? Chevrolet	42	33	01	Mike Wallace	U.S. Army Pontiac
21	17	32	Ricky Craven	Tide Pontiac	43	43	89	Morgan Shepherd	Racing for Jesus/Red Line Oil Ford
22	8	20	Tony Stewart	Home Depot Chevrolet					

RACE

PENNSYLVANIA 500

July 27, 2003

Ryan Newman lights up the tires in a celebratory burnout after taking his series-leading fourth win of the season. He also collected his fifth Bud Pole of the year to lead that category as well.

On Jan. 20, 1981, Ronald Reagan took the oath of office as the 40th president of the United States. A little over two months later, he barely survived an assassin's bullet.

Later that year, Pac-Man was introduced, sparking a video-game revolution, MTV aired its first telecast and the wedding of Great Britain's Prince Charles to Diana Spencer was watched on TV by millions of viewers.

Nine days before Reagan began his first of two terms as the country's leader, a young race driver from Chesapeake, Va., who ran his first NASCAR Winston Cup Series race in 1975, was about to begin a historical ride that would stretch over the next 22 years. Ricky Rudd made his debut in the No. 88 DiGard/Gatorade Chevrolet in the Winston Western 500 at Riverside (Calif.) International Raceway. He started third, completed 98 of 119 laps and finished 19th because of engine failure.

"... (Going the distance on fuel) was a gamble our team was willing to take. ... It was just a matter of going for the gutsy call."

— Ryan Newman

For Rudd, it was the beginning of an amazing record, which would culminate at Pocono Raceway with 700 consecutive series starts.

That's 700 races without an interruption because of sickness, injury or being without a job.

Even the legendary Richard Petty never made it past 656 races in a row. And with luck on his side, four-time series champion Jeff Gordon won't hit the 700 mark until halfway through the 2013 season!

"There have been quite a few injuries along the way, but I was fortunate none were serious enough that I couldn't get in the car," Rudd said while being honored a day before he started 27th at Pocono in the No. 21 Wood Brothers/Motorcraft Ford. "There are no guarantees you'll reach 700 ... but it looks like it's here."

With the season just past its midpoint, things at the rumor mill were already starting to crank up. One target was the Mooresville, N.C.-based Robert Yates Racing team, which fields Fords for drivers Dale Jarrett and Elliott Sadler. The team owner was surprised to hear that a Charlotte TV station reported he was considering merging his operation with another team or selling it outright. Jarrett, who was in the midst of a winless streak, was also the target of speculation.

"Absolutely not," Yates said. "I love what I do (and) I haven't talked to anybody about anything like that. I hate when our performance is bad, but we have all the faith we'll learn a lot and get out of this slump."

Jarrett was even more succinct: "I ain't going anywhere. That's all I've got to say."

The racing community was saddened, on July 23, by the passing of Robert G. "Bob" Latford, 67, after a lengthy illness. Latford was recognized as the mastermind behind the points system, which, since 1975, has been used to determine the NASCAR Winston Cup Series championship. He was born in England, moved to Daytona Beach at a young age where he sold race programs at the old Beach and Road Course and embarked on a public relations career in the sport that spanned 50 years.

Will NASCAR's top series expand again and add events down the road? Perhaps in years to come, but certainly not in 2004, said NASCAR President

Mike Helton. "We said earlier this year that we won't be increasing the number of races in 2004," Helton noted. "And to the best of my knowledge, that has not changed."

Something else that didn't change going into the Pennsylvania 500 at Pocono was Matt Kenseth's lock on NASCAR Winston Cup Series points. His third-place finish in the New England 300 at New Hampshire International Raceway extended his points lead to the largest advantage he's yet enjoyed. Ranked first for the 16th consecutive week, he held a lead of 234 points over Jeff Gordon, easily topping his previous best lead of 185 points over Dale Earnhardt Jr. following the Michigan race.

Gordon's disastrous 24th-place finish at New Hampshire was costly. Though still ranked second, he came into Pocono 234 points behind the leader (2,848-2,614), a loss of 69 points in one week.

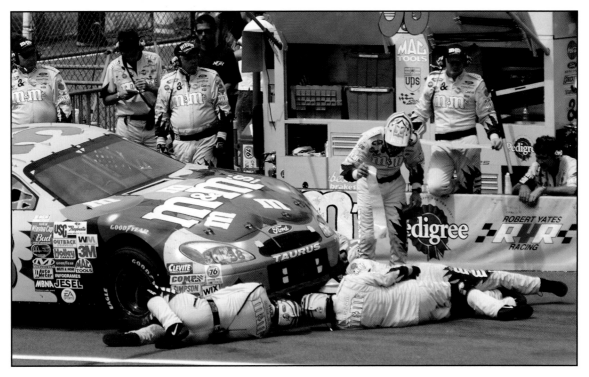

Earnhardt Jr., (third in points) and Bobby Labonte (fourth) remained "static" in the standings from the last race, but Jimmie Johnson, who became the third three-time race winner of the year, advanced a spot in points to fifth, while knocking Michael Waltrip down to sixth. Earnhardt's sixth-place run at New Hampshire was his best showing since finishing fourth at Pocono five races ago. Labonte's 14th-place showing in the New Hampshire 300 was just his third finish outside the top 10 in the previous 11 events but his second in a row.

Kevin Harvick (2,316 points) matched his season-best performance – second at Talladega, Ala. – when he finished as the runner-up in New Hampshire, and that kept him seventh in the standings for the second straight week. Kurt Busch, by finishing 11th at New Hampshire, moved up a spot in points to eighth, knocking defending series champion Tony Stewart from eighth to ninth in the process.

Jeff Burton made the most significant move of anyone in the top-10 list by getting onto it. Following a ninth-place run in Loudon, he jumped

from 13th to 10th in points and went into Pocono with 2,200 markers, 648 behind the leader.

While it was well off the track record of 172.391 mph, established by Stewart in July 2000, Ryan Newman's lap at 170.358 mph (52.830 seconds) in the No. 12 Penske Racing South/ALLTEL Dodge was more than enough to secure the Bud Pole position for the Pennsylvania 500. The best anyone else could muster was a speed of 169.821 mph, which put Johnson's No. 48 Lowe's Chevrolet next to Newman on the starting grid

"I don't think it's much as an advantage for me as it is for the team," Newman said of winning his fifth Bud Pole Award of the year. "The team gets so much of a confidence booster. It pumps them up and gives them a great outlook for the day."

Newman was the only driver to crack the 170 mph mark in time trials. Like Johnson, Elliott Sadler exceeded 169 mph, while Bobby Labonte (168.932) and John Andretti (168.925) were the fourth- and fifth-quickest in the lineup. Completing the top 10 were Terry Labonte, Rusty Wallace, Jarrett, Kenseth and Casey Mears.

Time was on Newman's side in qualifying and timing paid off for the Indiana native two days later when he led three times for 88 laps and won his fourth race of the year and fifth overall. From the pole, he paced the first 31 laps but had to pit because of a flat tire. Others had to make green-flag stops, too, however, and he was right back in front on lap 38, leading through the 50th circuit on the three-cornered track.

The eventual victor made another stop under the first caution (laps 50-53) and was running ninth when the race went green. He'd moved up to fourth by the 77th lap, thanks to another caution, and when the leaders pitted on the 106th lap, under green, Newman's crew changed four tires while most everyone else got just two.

That put Newman back a bit in the field, but it was a crucial move that played heavily on the race's outcome. When the engine in Stewart's Chevrolet let go on the 154th lap, the yellow flag flew a sixth time and the leaders pitted again for fuel and rubber. This time, most of the cars got new tires all the way around while the Newman crew opted for just two.

(Above) Terry Labonte brings the Kellogg's Chevrolet in for service under green-flag conditions. Although Labonte was unable to lead during the 200-lap event, he ran a smart race that turned his sixth-place qualifying effort into a fifth-place finish for the team that was definitely gaining momentum.

(Left) Dale Earnhardt Jr. lays the "horn" on Ryan Newman. Earnhardt Jr. took the point for 25 laps near the race's three-quarter mark, but couldn't outfox Newman and eventually settled for third at the finish.

Newman's ALLTEL crew pits their driver under the first caution at lap 50. Newman took four tires when the rest of the leaders took just two and dropped to ninth on the restart. Ironically the apparent gaffe ultimately set the winning strategy.

That did the trick. Newman took the lead on lap 157 and led the rest of the way (44 laps) to beat Busch by 0.307-second in front of about 100,000 fans. Earnhardt Jr., Michael Waltrip and Terry Labonte were third through fifth, while Jeff Burton, Joe Nemechek, Todd Bodine, Dave Blaney and Sterling Martin completed the top 10.

"It's just being in the right position at the right time," said Matt Borland, Newman's crew chief. "Things shook out for us to take on two tires at the end. I screwed up on the first stop (on the first caution). We put four on, everybody else took two or none and we got killed. So from there on out, we started playing a different strategy."

Newman, who won $180,575, took 3 hours, 54 minutes and 55 seconds to go from green to checkered, but his average speed was slowed to 127.705 mph because of eight caution flags for 36 laps.

The day could have gone better for "Iron Man" Rudd. He started 27th, went to the garage with a blown engine in his Wood Brothers Ford on the 122nd lap and finished 39th.

"I just wish the outcome would have turned out a little different, and it would be something we'd remember 700 by," he said. "We'll remember it, but not in a real super-positive way."

Pennsylvania 500 *final race results*

Fin. Pos.	Start Pos.	Car No.	Driver	Team	Fin. Pos.	Start Pos.	Car No.	Driver	Team
1	1	12	Ryan Newman	ALLTEL Dodge	23	40	01	Mike Wallace	U.S. Army Pontiac
2	13	97	Kurt Busch	Rubbermaid Ford	24	36	43	Christian Fittipaldi	Cheerios Dodge
3	18	8	Dale Earnhardt Jr.	Budweiser Chevrolet	25	16	30	Steve Park	America Online Chevrolet
4	17	15	Michael Waltrip	NAPA Chevrolet	26	34	49	Ken Schrader	AT&T Dodge
5	6	5	Terry Labonte	Kellogg's/got milk? Chevrolet	27	24	16	Greg Biffle	Grainger Ford
6	19	99	Jeff Burton	CITGO Ford	28	12	42	Jamie McMurray	Havoline Dodge
7	26	25	Joe Nemechek	UAW-Delphi Chevrolet	29	43	50	Larry Foyt	Harrah's Dodge
8	23	54	Todd Bodine	National Guard Ford	30	4	18	Bobby Labonte	Interstate Batteries Chevrolet
9	22	77	Dave Blaney	Jasper Engines & Transmissions Ford	31	39	1	Jeff Green	Pennzoil Chevrolet
10	20	40	Sterling Marlin	Coors Light Dodge	32	28	23	Kenny Wallace	Stacker2 Dodge
11	7	2	Rusty Wallace	Miller Lite Dodge	33	5	0	John Andretti	NetZero Hi Speed Pontiac
12	31	29	Kevin Harvick	GM Goodwrench Chevrolet	34	35	45	Kyle Petty	Georgia Pacific Dodge
13	9	17	Matt Kenseth	DEWALT Power Tools Ford	35	10	41	Casey Mears	Target Dodge
14	3	38	Elliott Sadler	M&M's Ford	36	25	24	Jeff Gordon	DuPont Chevrolet
15	2	48	Jimmie Johnson	Lowe's Chevrolet	37	33	20	Tony Stewart	Home Depot Chevrolet
16	30	74	Tony Raines	BACE Motorsports Chevrolet	38	15	19	Jeremy Mayfield	Dodge Dealers/UAW Dodge
17	11	9	Bill Elliott	Dodge Dealers/UAW Dodge	39	27	21	Ricky Rudd	Motorcraft Ford
18	37	31	Robby Gordon	Cingular Wireless Chevrolet	40	32	32	Ricky Craven	Tide Pontiac
19	38	22	Ward Burton	Caterpillar Dodge	41	14	6	Mark Martin	Viagra Ford
20	29	10	Johnny Benson	Valvoline Pontiac	42	41	37	Derrike Cope	Friendly's Chevrolet
21	8	88	Dale Jarrett	UPS Ford	43	42	89	Morgan Shepherd	Racing for Jesus Ford
22	21	7	Jimmy Spencer	Sirius Satellite Radio Dodge					

BRICKYARD 400

August 3, 2003

When you talk about the most venerated oval race track in the world – one that rests upon a history dating back to 1909 – one decade may not seem like much. But to the competitors of the NASCAR Winston Cup Series, the 10th annual Brickyard 400 at Indianapolis Motor Speedway was definitely a milestone.

In "NASCAR years," the 400-mile, 160-lap event had, by 2003, become something of a tradition. When Jeff Gordon beat 42 other drivers to win the first Brickyard 400 in 1994, the stock cars they drove were somewhat gaudy, loud and exotic to the packed grandstands more accustomed to open-wheel competition.

Gordon went on to win the race two more times, Dale Jarrett scored twice, and by the time Bill Elliott earned the honor of kissing the "yard of bricks" last year NASCAR and Indy had become as intimately entwined as coffee and cream or Mom and apple pie.

"I really can't put it all into words. I really don't know how I feel yet. But I know I feel good. I can tell you that much."

With Matt Kenseth firmly ensconced at the top of the point standings it was hard to pick a favorite to win at Indy, but several drivers went into the event breathing a bit easier. The day before the race, Sterling Marlin announced he'd signed a contract extension with Chip Ganassi Racing and would be driving the team's Dodges for at least another year. Jarrett, whose future had recently been the subject of speculation, said in no uncertain terms he was staying put with Robert Yates Racing and sponsor UPS.

"I'm at Robert Yates Racing, I intend to be (there) for quite awhile, and UPS is going to be the sponsor," Jarrett said. "We haven't been exactly happy with our performance, but that's no reason to quit, and we're not quitters."

In a related announcement, Ford Motor Co. signed five year-deals with Yates and two other

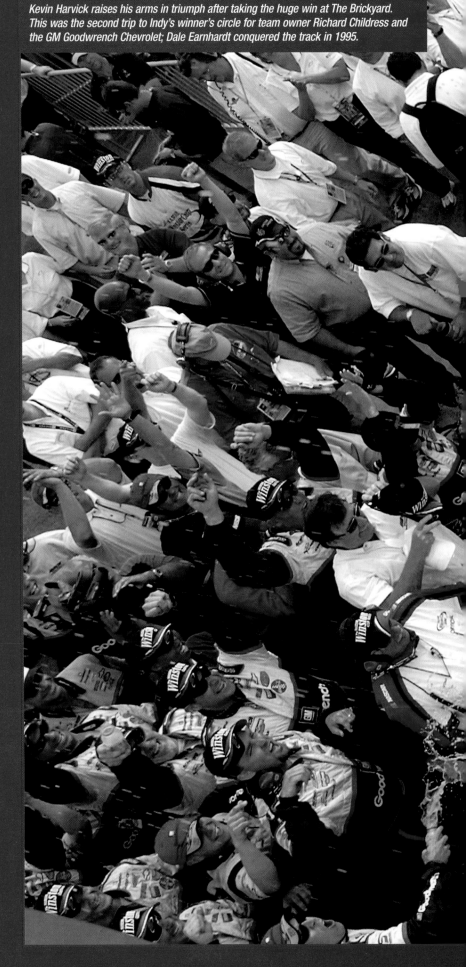

Kevin Harvick raises his arms in triumph after taking the huge win at The Brickyard. This was the second trip to Indy's winner's circle for team owner Richard Childress and the GM Goodwrench Chevrolet; Dale Earnhardt conquered the track in 1995.

failure), but he was only two points behind Johnson (2,547-2,545).

Michael Waltrip's strong fourth-place run at Pocono was his best showing since finishing third at Las Vegas in March, and that kept him ranked sixth in points. Heading into Indy, he was just seven points behind Labonte and nine behind Johnson. Kevin Harvick – thanks to finishing 12th at Pocono – stayed seventh in points for the third consecutive race and in the top 10 for the 17th straight week.

Kurt Busch, who had finished 28th or worse in three of the last four starts, rebounded to finish second at Pocono. That kept him running eighth in points and just 25 markers behind Harvick. The

(Left, Above) Kevin Harvick's Monte Carlo rolls through famed Gasoline Alley on the way to its No. 1 starting slot for the Brickyard 400. Harvick shattered Tony Stewart's old track record by 1.383 miles per hour and won his first Bud Pole of the season.

(Left, Below) Elliott Sadler (left) and Tony Stewart have a good laugh during pre-race cere-monies at Indy. They would start together on the eighth row but finish far apart as Sadler blew an engine at lap 107, while Stewart led the most laps but finished 12th.

teams that field Fords for eight drivers and kept them under contract through at least 2007. Ford also unveiled its new-design Taurus for 2004, although NASCAR yet had not approved the car.

Kenseth's 13th-place finish at Pocono in the Roush Racing/DeWalt Tools Ford didn't really hurt his lead in points. He arrived in Pennsylvania 234 markers in front of Jeff Gordon and left it 232 points in front of Dale Earnhardt Jr., who had bumped Gordon back to third. Earnhardt's third-place showing at Pocono was his third top-10 finish in the last four races and fifth in the last seven.

Gordon, with 2,669 points, was just 308 behind the leader and 122 points in front of his team-mate, Jimmie Johnson, who had moved up a notch from fifth to fourth. Bobby Labonte's seven-week reign at No. 4 in the NASCAR top 10 came to an end with a 30th-place finish at Pocono (engine

A crowd estimated at 300,000 – the largest on the NASCAR Winston Cup Series schedule – enjoys a beautiful afternoon in Speedway, Indiana.

biggest beneficiary of the "points parade" was the Pocono winner, Ryan Newman. His series-leading fourth victory moved him into the top 10 (he was 13th) for just the second time of the season.

Busch's Roush Racing teammate, Jeff Burton, recorded his fourth consecutive top-10 finish at Pocono (he finished sixth) and stayed 10th in points for the second straight week. With 2,355 points, he was only eight behind Newman. The "light at the end of the tunnel," was a bit dim, as he trailed Kenseth by 644 markers.

An excellent run around the Brickyard in Bud Pole qualifying was just the tonic for "Happy" Harvick and team owner Richard Childress, but it

was a lousy break for Ken Schrader and his bosses at BAM Racing, who were striving to keep up with the circuit's better funded operations. In a sport where "cold" can be the "hot ticket," Harvick was the "coolest" cat on the track.

In essence, Harvick made his run for the pole earlier in the session under a friendly cloud cover that cooled the speedway's surface and improved tire traction. Harvick not only put the No. 29 GM Goodwrench Chevrolet on the pole, he did it at a record stock car speed of 184.343 mph. That was almost one and a half miles per hour quicker than the old record of 182.960 mph, set a year ago by Tony Stewart, and it was comfortably better than Newman's second-quickest speed of 184.237. In fact, the top 11 qualifiers all eclipsed Stewart's mark.

Bill Elliott, Ward Burton and Waltrip qualified third through fifth quickest, while Busch, Joe Nemechek, Bobby Labonte, Johnson and Jeremy Mayfield completed the fastest 10 qualifiers. Nine drivers didn't make the cut. One was Schrader, who ended a streak of 579 consecutive starts dating back to November 1984.

"The first year I raced here the sun came out,

the track got hot and the guys at the end of qualifying didn't have a chance," Harvick noted. "You
can't get any better track position than where we
are, and that is such a critical element on this
race track.

"I was fortunate enough to get an early draw,
and that is such a critical element on this race
track. When you start up front, it usually makes
your day – if nothing goes wrong."

This time around, everything went just right for
the California native, the 13th Bud Pole winner of

the year. Harvick led the first 17 laps and, most
important, the final 16. His fourth career NASCAR
Winston Cup Series win came at the expense of
Kenseth, who was a distant second, 2.758 seconds behind the winner.

"I can't believe this. I don't even know if I can
explain it. This is awesome," said Harvick, who
carted off a whopping purse of $418,253.

"I really can't put it all into words. I really don't
know how I feel yet. But I know I feel good. I can
tell you that much."

Although Harvick lost his initial lead when
Elliott caught and passed him, he never strayed
that far out of the top 10. Five caution flags for
25 laps broke up the on-track action, but Harvick
wasn't really affected. He was near the leader on
each green-flag restart. In fact, when the fourth
caution flag came out on lap 139, McMurray and
Harvick chose to stay on the track and were running one-two at the green flag on lap 145.

*(Above) Matt Kenseth arrives in
his pit with the crew already in
motion. The team made their
bid for victory with a two-tire
stop under caution late in the
race, a decision that nearly got
them the win.*

*(Left) Joe Nemechek gives
Johnny Benson's Valvoline
Pontiac a little nudge as they
race down the frontstretch.
Nemechek later left the race
with accident damage, while
Benson, who started 40th, fin-
ished 13th.*

*(Far Left, Above) The skyline of
nearby downtown Indianapolis
sets the backdrop between
turns one and two.*

*(Left, Below) Defending
Brickyard 400 champion Bill
Elliott charges off the turn in
front of Dave Blaney's Jasper
Ford. Elliott took an early lead
from his third-place starting
spot, struggled some in the
middle of the event and climbed
back to fifth at the finish.*

Kevin Harvick (29) and Jamie McMurray (42) race for the lead with Matt Kenseth lurking behind. Harvick and McMurray stayed out on the fourth caution and led the field on the restart with Kenseth in third, and the three drivers settled the finish among themselves.

It was then that Harvick dove underneath McMurray, who was trapped behind a lapped car. A multicar incident slowed the race a final time on the 149th circuit, but it didn't mean much to the winner, who retained control of the race. Just before the event ended, Kenseth got the better of McMurray, who ended up in third place. Jeff Gordon and Elliott rounded out the top five, while Robby Gordon, Busch, Jimmy Spencer, Mark Martin and Rusty Wallace completed the top 10.

"We said all weekend that we needed to make sure we put ourselves in position," Harvick added. "Fortunately, our car was by far the best it had been all day. Track position worked itself out perfect. All the pit stops were good (and) came at the right time with the yellows.

"Everything just clicked."

Harvick completed the 10th annual Brickyard 400 in 2 hours, 58 minutes and 22 seconds at an average speed of 134.554 mph.

Brickyard 400 *final race results*

Fin. Pos.	Start Pos.	Car No.	Driver	Team	Fin. Pos.	Start Pos.	Car No.	Driver	Team
1	1	29	Kevin Harvick	GM Goodwrench Chevrolet	23	31	54	Todd Bodine	National Guard Ford
2	17	17	Matt Kenseth	Smirnoff Ice Triple Black/DeWalt Ford	24	29	23	Kenny Wallace	Stacker2 Dodge
3	22	42	Jamie McMurray	Havoline Dodge	25	33	74	Tony Raines	Aaron's Dream Machine Chevrolet
4	19	24	Jeff Gordon	DuPont Chevrolet	26	4	22	Ward Burton	Caterpillar Dodge
5	3	9	Bill Elliott	Dodge Dealers/UAW Dodge	27	37	99	Jeff Burton	CITGO Ford
6	13	31	Robby Gordon	Cingular Wireless Chevrolet	28	20	77	Dave Blaney	Jasper Engines & Transmissions Ford
7	6	97	Kurt Busch	Rubbermaid Ford	29	28	41	Casey Mears	Target Dodge
8	32	7	Jimmy Spencer	Sirius Satellite Radio Dodge	30	21	57	Kevin Lepage	CLR Ford
9	25	6	Mark Martin	Viagra Ford	31	27	91	Casey Atwood	Evernham Motorsports Dodge
10	14	2	Rusty Wallace	Miller Lite Dodge	32	42	14	Larry Foyt	Harrah's Dodge
11	2	12	Ryan Newman	ALLTEL Dodge	33	26	0	Jason Leffler	NetZero Hi Speed Pontiac
12	15	20	Tony Stewart	Home Depot Chevrolet	34	12	40	Sterling Marlin	Coors Light Dodge
13	40	10	Johnny Benson	Valvoline Pontiac	35	24	01	Mike Skinner	U.S. Army Pontiac
14	36	8	Dale Earnhardt Jr.	Budweiser Chevrolet	36	43	37	Derrike Cope	Friendly's Chevrolet
15	23	30	Steve Park	America Online Chevrolet	37	7	25	Joe Nemechek	UAW-Delphi Chevrolet
16	5	15	Michael Waltrip	NAPA Chevrolet	38	39	21	Ricky Rudd	Rent-A-Center/Motorcraft/USAF Ford
17	35	32	Ricky Craven	Tide Pontiac	39	34	88	Dale Jarrett	UPS Ford
18	9	48	Jimmie Johnson	Lowe's Chevrolet	40	41	45	Kyle Petty	Georgia Pacific Dodge
19	38	5	Terry Labonte	Kellogg's/got milk? Chevrolet	41	10	19	Jeremy Mayfield	Dodge Dealers/UAW Dodge
20	30	1	Jeff Green	Pennzoil Chevrolet	42	16	38	Elliott Sadler	Pedigree Ford
21	18	16	Greg Biffle	Grainger Ford	43	11	81	John Andretti	Kraft 100th Anniversary Chevrolet
22	8	18	Bobby Labonte	Interstate Batteries Chevrolet					

SIRIUS AT THE GLEN

August 10, 2003

With 21 of 36 NASCAR Winston Cup Series races tucked into the annals of motorsports, Matt Kenseth's chances of securing the 2003 division championship appeared to be improving with each lap completed.

True, there were still 15 events remaining as the circuit's competitors prepared to take on the challenging 2.45-mile Watkins Glen International road course nestled in New York state's scenic Finger Lakes region, and anything could happen. Yet, the driver of Roush Racing's No. 17 DeWalt Power Tools Ford was continuing to run consistently well as the season wound on. He'd kept a tenacious grip on the lead in series points for 18 consecutive weeks and, going into The Glen, he was the only driver to have scored 16 top-10 finishes in 21 events.

Kenseth's second-place finish to Brickyard 400 winner Kevin Harvick was his best effort since another runner-up result in May at Lowe's Motor Speedway. One result was that he padded his lead in points to the largest advantage he'd yet enjoyed – 286 over No. 2 runner Dale Earnhardt Jr. and 318 in front of third-running Jeff Gordon.

"We're in a really great position right now," Kenseth said. "But it's certainly not one we couldn't mess up and throw away if we're not real careful. There's a lot of racing left."

Another perhaps unintended result was an increased scrutiny of the NASCAR Winston Cup points system itself. In effect since 1975, the way of determining the season champion emphasized consistent "up-front" finishes more than just race victories. So while Kenseth had won just one race since February, he was far ahead of four-time victor Ryan Newman, who was ninth in the standings.

"I don't think we had the best car today. We just drove (with) a good smart strategy, and they made some good calls on pit lane."

Robby Gordon drives to his second road-course win of the season in a three-year-old chassis of his design that he brought with him to Richard Childress Racing.

NASCAR. *Winston Cup Series* ™

AR Winston Cup Se

Hence, it was considered newsworthy when NASCAR Chairman Bill France said in a newspaper interview published a day after the Sirius at The Glen that before the year was out he would recommend changes to the system to "spice up our show and make it better." France didn't offer any specifics such as giving the race winner more points, but he was thinking about a "modification to the distribution of points."

"Whoever is our champion needs to be able to pass muster with the media and public at large," he said. "They have to come down at the end of the day and be accepted and not be somebody who just backed into it. So far we've been able to do that (but) if it appears that trend is not holding true to form, we'll try to figure out what to do to fix it, tweak it and change (it) around a little bit."

With 2,866 points to 3,152 for Kenseth, Earnhardt Jr. kept the No. 2 spot in points, even though he finished 14th in the Brickyard 400. It also marked his 15th consecutive week in the top three, but his cushion over third-running Jeff Gordon was just 34 points (2,866-2,834). Gordon had trailed Earnhardt by 76 markers going into Indy, but he cut the deficit by more than half by virtue of a fourth-place finish in the Brickyard 400.

Jimmie Johnson's 18th-place run at the track in Speedway, Ind., was good enough to keep him at fourth place in the standings for the second consecutive week. He was, however, 176 points behind Gordon, his co-driver at Hendrick Motorsports. Michael Waltrip came home 16th at Indy, but the effort was good enough to improve him one position to No. 5, while knocking Bobby Labonte back to sixth.

Kevin Harvick, who finished the Brickyard 400 in the same position he started it – first – became the 15th different winner in 21 races. Although he remained seventh in points for the third

(Above) Rounding Watkins Glen's turn 11, the starting field rolls down the frontstretch prepared to take the green flag for 90 laps of road-course action. Watkins Glen International is the only track on the schedule where pit road is on the drivers' right, creating a unique challenge for drivers and crews.

(Left) Another unique aspect of the twisty track in upper New York State is this additional platform for spotters at the far end of the track, a technically difficult section that is hard for the regular spotters to see from the frontstretch towers.

(Right) Jimmie Johnson slings his Lowe's Chevrolet through a hard left-hander in search of the leaders. Johnson had a good day, fighting to fourth at the finish after having to start near the back of the field due to a pre-race engine change.

(Below) Christian Fittipaldi tags the foam-padded wall after he and Steve Park tangled in turn 11. The padded blow gave Fittipaldi's team a chance to repair the damage and return their driver to action. He finished the event, 10 laps down in 40th.

(Below Right) Jimmy Spencer spins in the first turn at lap 59 but is able to keep the car out of the way of Boris Said (01) and Todd Bodine (54). Spencer recovered without bringing out the yellow flag and finished on the lead lap.

straight week, he made some gains on the drivers in front of him. He arrived at The Glen 19 points behind Labonte, 30 in back of Waltrip and 33 in arrears of Johnson.

Kurt Busch, Newman and Rusty Wallace were eighth through 10th in points leaving Indy, with Wallace cracking the top 10 after being 11th the previous three weeks.

If Jeff Gordon had turned his No 24 Hendrick Motorsports/DuPont Chevrolet over to Sean Penn, while crew chief Robbie Loomis had handed Judge Reinhold the crew chief's hat, Bud Pole qualifying for the year's second road race could have been called Fast Times at Watkins Glen.

It was, however, Gordon, who charged around the serpentine road course in 70.798 seconds at 124.580 mph to set a course record in notching

the No. 1 starting position for the race. In doing so, he eclipsed Dale Jarrett's mark of 71.884 seconds at 122.698 mph, set two years ago. It was Gordon's second pole of the year and 44th of his career.

Gordon's effort was also comfortably quicker than that of rookie candidate Greg Biffle, who toured the track at 124.497 mph. Mark Martin was third fastest and, in fact, the top 17 qualifiers all exceeded Jarrett's old mark. Unfortunately for Jarrett, he wasn't among them.

"We're about a second faster than last year," Gordon said. "We've made a lot of gains. I think another reason we're so fast is the temperatures. They were perfect for fast speeds."

Six so-called road-course "ringers" made the field for the 90-lap contest, among them Ron

Fellows, P.J. Jones, Scott Pruett and Boris Said. The four drivers who failed to make the race were Larry Foyt, Scott Maxwell, Joe Varde and an unlucky Ken Schrader.

From green flag to checkered, the Sirius at The Glen took 2 hours, 26 minutes and 17 seconds to complete. In between, there were eight lead changes among as many drivers, six caution-flag periods for 14 laps, and several unhappy competitors. Mark Martin, who started third, never led a lap and finished 10th, said, "we are the most unluckiest team out here." Others, however, would have disputed that claim.

Sterling Marlin's Coors Light Dodge lasted one lap before losing its engine, defending champion Tony Stewart started fourth, overshot his pit on a stop and finished 11th, and Jeff Gordon was the victim of two mishaps. He got hit by rookie Greg Biffle on the first lap and an accident one lap from

the finish when he ran out of gas and got tagged by Harvick took him out for good.

When everything calmed down, it was Robby Gordon popping champagne and swapping hats for the photographers in victory lane. The driver of Richard Childress Racing's Cingular Wireless Chevrolet had taken the lead for the first – and only – time on lap 61 and cruised to a 1.335-second victory over Pruett, who drove a Target-sponsored Dodge owned by Chip Ganassi.

It was the second straight win for Childress' team, its third of the year, as well as the second of the season for Gordon. His first came in June at Infineon Raceway, the series' only other road course. Also, Gordon won in a car that originally belonged to him when he had his own team three years ago. When he signed on with RCR, he signed the car over to the team.

"We handed it over to RCR at the beginning of

(Above) Scott Pruett (39), driving a fourth entry from Chip Ganassi Racing, charges through the first turn ahead of Kevin Harvick's GM Goodwrench Chevrolet. Pruett sliced through the field from the 29th starting spot to take the point on lap 24, then stayed among the leaders before finishing runner-up to Robby Gordon. Harvick continued to show promise on the road courses, adding a fifth place to his third-place finish at Infineon Raceway in June.

(Left) Dale Earnhardt Jr. showed road-course competitiveness by leading 11 laps in the middle portion of the event and taking a strong, third place at the finish line.

Robby Gordon shows the way for (in order) Ryan Newman, Boris Said, Ward Burton and pole-winner Jeff Gordon. R. Gordon took the lead for the first time on lap 61, largely due to a heads-up call from crew chief Kevin Hamlin, and led the final 30 circuits for his second win of the season, the third of his NASCAR Winston Cup Series career.

the season because we felt it was a design that was good for road racing," Gordon explained. "I had a chassis designed for us. RCR put one of their big motors in it and put a good body on it, and it's been to victory lane now twice."

The winner's big break came on the 52nd lap when a tire on Rusty Wallace's Dodge locked up and the car slipped off the track right in front of Gordon. Crew chief Kevin Hamlin then quickly ordered Gordon to pit before the fifth caution

period went into effect. It meant he got the eventual jump on everyone else. By the time the other front-runners had made their stops, Gordon had taken the lead and would not be passed.

"I'll be honest," Gordon said. "I don't think we had the best car today. We just drove (with) a good smart strategy, and they made some good calls on pit lane."

Gordon's average speed was 90.441 mph and he won $156,752.

Sirius At The Glen *final race results*

Fin. Pos.	Start Pos.	Car No.	Driver	Team	Fin. Pos.	Start Pos.	Car No.	Driver	Team
1	14	31	Robby Gordon	Cingular Wireless Chevrolet	23	39	7	Jimmy Spencer	Sirius Satellite Radio Dodge
2	28	39	Scott Pruett	Target Dodge	24	33	4	P.J. Jones	Kodak Perfect Touch Pontiac
3	6	8	Dale Earnhardt Jr.	Budweiser Chevrolet	25	16	77	Dave Blaney	Jasper Engines & Transmissions Ford
4	20	48	Jimmie Johnson	Lowe's Chevrolet	26	41	30	Steve Park	America Online Chevrolet
5	11	29	Kevin Harvick	GM Goodwrench Chevrolet	27	27	10	Johnny Benson	Valvoline Pontiac
6	22	22	Ward Burton	Caterpillar Dodge	28	38	32	Ricky Craven	Tide Pontiac
7	30	88	Dale Jarrett	UPS Ford	29	43	33	Paul Menard	Menards/Turtle Wax Chevrolet
8	7	17	Matt Kenseth	DEWALT Power Tools Ford	30	2	16	Greg Biffle	Grainger Ford
9	13	12	Ryan Newman	ALLTEL Dodge	31	23	99	Jeff Burton	CITGO Ford
10	3	6	Mark Martin	Viagra Ford	32	12	41	Casey Mears	Target Dodge
11	4	20	Tony Stewart	Home Depot Chevrolet	33	1	24	Jeff Gordon	DuPont Chevrolet
12	8	97	Kurt Busch	Rubbermaid/Sharpie Ford	34	35	23	Kenny Wallace	Stacker2 Dodge
13	34	15	Michael Waltrip	NAPA Chevrolet	35	17	54	Todd Bodine	National Guard/Subway Ford
14	9	18	Bobby Labonte	Interstate Batteries Chevrolet	36	32	04	Johnny Miller	Kodak Easy Share Pontiac
15	24	38	Elliott Sadler	M&M's Ford	37	5	2	Rusty Wallace	Miller Lite Dodge
16	40	19	Jeremy Mayfield	Dodge Dealers/UAW Dodge	38	18	1	Ron Fellows	Pennzoil Chevrolet
17	21	25	Joe Nemechek	UAW-Delphi Chevrolet	39	10	01	Boris Said	USG Sheetrock Pontiac
18	19	5	Terry Labonte	Kellogg's/got milk? Chevrolet	40	36	44	Christian Fittipaldi	New York Yankees Dodge
19	15	0	John Andretti	NetZero Hi Speed Pontiac	41	42	74	Tony Raines	BACE Motorsports Chevrolet
20	25	9	Bill Elliott	Dodge Dealers/UAW Dodge	42	31	45	Kyle Petty	Georgia Pacific/Brawny Dodge
21	26	21	Ricky Rudd	Air Force/Motorcraft Ford	43	37	40	Sterling Marlin	Coors Light Dodge
22	29	42	Jamie McMurray	Havoline Dodge					

Dale Earnhardt Jr. sits in his pit after a collision with Rusty Wallace near the entrance of pit road. Wallace had decided not to pit under caution and darted back toward the racing surface, colliding with Earnhardt's Budweiser Chevrolet.

GFS MARKETPLACE 400

August 17, 2003

To paraphrase the ageless motto of the United States Postal Service: Neither rain, nor sleet nor gloom of night .... or a massive power blackout that affected 50 million people in parts of the Northeast, Midwest and Canada kept the warriors of the NASCAR Winston Cup Series from their assigned task – putting on the 23rd event of the 2003 season.

Three days before the running of the GFS Marketplace 400, a breakdown of the power grid that provides a quarter of the nation with electricity crashed. While the outage lasted just a day or less, people living in places like New York City, Cleveland and Detroit were literally in the dark. Although MIS, located about 70 miles west of the Motor City, "went black" for less than 60 seconds, the surrounding area was affected. Race fans and competitors had to hustle a bit to find things like flashlights, batteries and candles, as well as eateries that were able to provide food.

"It was just kind of wait and see. I wanted to run down Kurt, but I wanted to save fuel."

However, by the time practice and qualifying was scheduled to start, things were back to normal, and the "Big Blackout of '03" became fodder for future "I was there when ..." stories.

A few days before, though, Dale Earnhardt Jr. "lit up" the rumor mill when he publicly said he had not signed a contract extension with Dale Earnhardt Inc., as had been announced by DEI at the start of the season. He said he'd had thoughts of becoming a "free agent" if certain unspecified differences involving himself and the team founded by his late father were not resolved. He added, though, he had no plans to go elsewhere.

"I'm looking forward to fixing the contract like I want it and just being patient and making sure everything is where I want it to be," he said. "I don't want to get into a hurry and sign a contract that doesn't have everything I feel like I have a right to.

Bobby Labonte (18) sets the early pace in front of (in order) Jimmie Johnson, Kevin Harvick and Ryan Newman following the first of eight cautions in the race. Labonte completed a Bud Pole sweep at Michigan but suffered engine failure past the midpoint of the race. Johnson took the lap-leader bonus, but a late-race stop for fuel dropped him to 27th place at the end.

"My mind and heart is on driving the (No.) 8 car and it always has been. But I want to get what I feel like I deserve."

Things got a lot brighter for NASCAR on Aug. 15 when its officials and those of Sunoco Inc. of Philadelphia announced the petroleum refiner would, beginning in 2004, become the official fuel supplier of the sanctioning body's three major divisions and had inked a 10-year contract. A search had been ongoing for a company to replace ConocoPhillips, which said it would leave racing to pursue other marketing opportunities.

Under the agreement, Sunoco – the world's largest supplier of racing fuel – would provide free gasoline to NASCAR's Winston Cup, Busch and Craftsman Truck Series. Sunoco products, at the time of the announcement, were used by 30 race

sanctioning groups and were found at 400 race tracks, including 80 percent of the speedways that hosted the NASCAR Dodge Weekly Series.

ConocoPhillips, under the names Unocal, Union 76 and Pure Oil had been a part of NASCAR competition since the early 1950s.

After finishing eighth in the Sirius at The Glen, the week before the 400-miler at Michigan, Matt Kenseth, the leader in the race for the championship, lost 28 points to Earnhardt Jr., who had finished third in his best-ever showing on a road course. Yet, Kenseth and his Roush Racing team didn't seem overly concerned, since Kenseth's cushion over Earnhardt was a healthy 258 points (3,194-3,036). Kenseth had been a poor qualifier at Michigan – 20th or worse in eight starts – but the race itself was another matter. He'd racked up

(Above) Ken Schrader (49) leads Robby Gordon (31) and Christian Fittipaldi (43) around Michigan's upper groove. Schrader came from the 30th starting spot and, with the help of good pit strategy, handed BAM racing its best finish of the year in eighth.

(Right) Kevin Harvick (29) takes the green flag on the race's third restart in front of (in order) Terry Labonte, Ryan Newman and Tony Stewart, with Elliott Sadler, Ricky Rudd and Jeff Gordon a lap down on the inside.

and finished 33rd. While still third in points with 2,898, he now trailed Kenseth by 396 and dropped to 198 behind Earnhardt. Gordon, however, had proven to be a strong runner at MIS with 14 top-five finishes in 21 starts that included victories in 1998 and 2001.

Jimmie Johnson, by finishing fourth at The Glen, retained his fourth-place spot in points and moved to within 82 of Gordon. Kevin Harvick made the biggest jump in the top 10 in points, advancing from seventh to fifth thanks to a fifth-place run at The Glen. It marked Harvick's 19th week in the top 10 and seventh in a row. Also, he was only 38 points behind Johnson.

Michael Waltrip finished 13th at The Glen and dropped from fifth to sixth in the standings. But with 2,777 points he was just one marker behind Harvick. Bobby Labonte, with 2,768 points, fell from sixth to seventh. It was the third straight week he'd lost points positions, but he was just nine behind Waltrip and 10 in back of Harvick.

Kurt Busch and Ryan Newman entered Michigan in the same spots in points they were in prior to The Glen – eighth and ninth – while Robby Gordon, who'd won on the road course, advanced from 11th to 10th, displacing Rusty Wallace in the process. Busch may have had the best reason to feel optimistic about the Irish Hills track. He'd qualified fourth in June and went on to win the race.

three top-five finishes in his last four starts, including a win in June 2002.

Earnhardt had been a strong qualifier at MIS, starting among the top seven in six of the last seven races. During that run, he also captured two Bud Poles.

Jeff Gordon's string of successes at Watkins Glen – he'd won four of its previous six races – came to a halt on Aug. 22 when he got into two accidents

In Bud Pole qualifying for the GFS Marketplace 400, Bobby Labonte certainly didn't come near the track record of 191.149 mph, set by Earnhardt Jr. in August 2000, but his lap at 190.240 was good enough to put him on the pole for the race. While the track had sufficient electrical power (it was just outside the area affected by the blackout), race control went to backup generators to avoid any possible problem.

Except for a two-hour rain delay, qualifying went off trouble free, and Labonte took his fourth pole at the track in 23 races. It was also the first time since Bill Elliott did it in 1988 that a driver had won both MIS poles in the same year. Labonte was the only driver to exceed 190 mph. Newman mustered a speed of 189.929 mph, which was good enough for a second-place start.

"I like coming here. It's one of my favorite tracks," Labonte said. "The guys gave me a good car today. I just felt really comfortable with it. At the speeds we run here, if the car starts twitching, you're in lots of trouble."

Robby Gordon was third quickest in qualifying, Kevin Lepage was fourth, while Terry Labonte was fifth. Rounding out the top 10 were Jason Leffler, Christian Fittipaldi, Jeff Burton, Dave Blaney and Jimmy Spencer. One driver, Stacy Compton, failed to make the 43-car field.

In June at MIS, Busch was in high spirits, especially after winning the race and helping Ford Motor Co. celebrate its 100th birthday. Newman, on the other hand, dropped out of the event and left the track early.

This time around, Newman and his Penske Dodge team played the "fuel-mileage card" to their advantage and landed in victory lane. Busch, seemingly on his way to a second straight win, ran out of gas with three laps left, pitted on the next-to-last circuit and ended up finishing 18th. Worse, he came out second best in a post-race physical confrontation with his old nemesis, Jimmy Spencer, and had to go to the infield medical center for wounds suffered in the argument.

The race was slowed by eight yellow-flag periods for 46 laps. On the seventh (laps 135-138), the lead-lap drivers, including Busch, pitted for fuel and on the green, Harvick was leading and Busch was running eighth. The race was slowed again on the 142nd lap, and just before the green flag on lap 150, the leaders, including Newman but excepting Busch, made a final stop. That put Spencer in the lead, but he was quickly dispatched by Busch, who sailed away.

That's when Newman put his foot on the accelerator and, forgetting fuel mileage, charged after

the leader. On lap 198, Busch faded and Newman headed toward the win, beating runner-up Harvick by 1.652 seconds.

"It was just kind of wait and see. I wanted to run down Kurt, but I wanted to save fuel," said Newman, who, via radio, actually asked his crew chief if it was OK to forget about fuel efficiency.

(Above) Ryan Newman (12) looks for racing room down low to challenge Matt Kenseth (17) and Jeff Burton (99), with Christian Fittipaldi running next to the wall. Consistent Kenseth grabbed another top 10, this time in ninth, while Newman drove to his series-leading fifth win of the season.

(Left) Jimmy Spencer (7) leads on the final restart followed by Kurt Busch and Dale Jarrett with 50 laps remaining. Busch immediately passed Spencer, yielded briefly to Jarrett, and then assumed control of the race before running out of fuel three laps from the finish.

"It doesn't matter how much (gas) we had left. We made it to the end."

Tony Stewart, Greg Biffle and Steve Park completed the top five in a race that lasted 3 hours, 8 minutes and 31 seconds and saw Newman win at an average speed of 127.310 mph.

Bad blood had existed between Busch and Spencer for almost two years. After another on-track clash, it came to a head when words were exchanged in the garage. Spencer then "popped" Busch, and both drivers got an invitation to the NASCAR trailer.

GFS Marketplace 400 *final race results*

Fin. Pos.	Start Pos.	Car No.	Driver	Team	Fin. Pos.	Start Pos.	Car No.	Driver	Team
1	2	12	Ryan Newman	ALLTEL Dodge	23	29	88	Dale Jarrett	UPS Ford
2	11	29	Kevin Harvick	GM Goodwrench Chevrolet	24	24	74	Tony Raines	GFS Marketplace Chevrolet
3	23	20	Tony Stewart	Home Depot Chevrolet	25	9	77	Dave Blaney	Jasper Engines & Transmissions Ford
4	12	16	Greg Biffle	Grainger Ford	26	10	7	Jimmy Spencer	Sirius Satellite Radio Dodge
5	18	30	Steve Park	America Online Chevrolet	27	15	48	Jimmie Johnson	Lowe's Chevrolet
6	3	31	Robby Gordon	Cingular Wireless Chevrolet	28	40	19	Jeremy Mayfield	Dodge Dealers/UAW Dodge
7	13	15	Michael Waltrip	NAPA Chevrolet	29	27	21	Ricky Rudd	Motorcraft Ford
8	30	49	Ken Schrader	SEM Products/Color Horizons Dodge	30	21	24	Jeff Gordon	DuPont Chevrolet
9	33	17	Matt Kenseth	DEWALT Power Tools Ford	31	4	57	Kevin Lepage	CLR Ford
10	35	10	Johnny Benson	Valvoline Pontiac	32	19	8	Dale Earnhardt Jr.	Budweiser Chevrolet
11	8	99	Jeff Burton	CITGO Ford	33	7	43	Christian Fittipaldi	Cheerios Dodge
12	17	38	Elliott Sadler	M&M's Ford	34	43	37	Derrike Cope	Friendly's Chevrolet
13	5	5	Terry Labonte	Kellogg's/got milk? Chevrolet	35	6	0	Jason Leffler	NetZero Hi Speed Pontiac
14	22	22	Ward Burton	Caterpillar Dodge	36	26	42	Jamie McMurray	Havoline Dodge
15	32	9	Bill Elliott	Dodge Dealers/UAW Dodge	37	1	18	Bobby Labonte	Interstate Batteries Chevrolet
16	36	45	Kyle Petty	Georgia Pacific Dodge	38	31	2	Rusty Wallace	Miller Lite Dodge
17	37	6	Mark Martin	Viagra Ford	39	14	50	Larry Foyt	Harrah's Dodge
18	20	97	Kurt Busch	Rubbermaid Ford	40	39	32	Ricky Craven	Tide Pontiac
19	38	40	Sterling Marlin	Coors Light Dodge	41	16	41	Casey Mears	Target Dodge
20	25	25	Joe Nemechek	UAW-Delphi Chevrolet	42	28	23	Kenny Wallace	Stacker2 Dodge
21	34	1	Jeff Green	Pennzoil Chevrolet	43	41	54	Todd Bodine	National Guard Ford
22	42	01	Mike Skinner	U.S. Army Pontiac					

RACE

SHARPIE 400

August 23, 2003

There's an old racing adage that says when a driver falls out of favor with the public, the best way he can get it back on his side is to win.

Kurt Busch tried his best to prove that maxim true Saturday night in eastern Tennessee when he led the final 121 laps of the Sharpie 500 and won not only his second straight race at Bristol Motor Speedway, but also his fourth of the 2003 campaign. While the win could not be called "popular" with many of the 165,000 fans that packed the grandstands to capacity, Busch at least redeemed himself in the eyes of his teammates at Roush Racing.

A long-simmering feud with Jimmy Spencer had come to a head the week before at Michigan International Speedway. After the race, the two drivers confronted each other in the garage area. Words were exchanged, and Spencer lost his cool and assaulted Busch. NASCAR found fault with both men. Officials placed Busch on probation for the rest of the year and fined Spencer $25,000, barred him from racing at Bristol and also placed him on probation through Dec. 31.

"I hate it that Jimmy is not here this weekend ... He's a tough competitor, just as I am, especially at this place."

"Both of them had been involved in this conflict ever since it started at Phoenix (Ariz.) in 2001, I guess, so neither of them are scot-free of the whole deal," NASCAR President Mike Helton explained. "Michigan was not the first time the two characters in this episode had locked horns.

"... So we reacted specifically on what Jimmy did, but we certainly felt like Kurt was part of this whole episode."

At Bristol, Busch tried hard to concentrate on the job at hand in a 500-lap event slowed a record-tying 20 times for 119 laps. In fact, he later apologized for making contact with "native son" Sterling Marlin and bringing out the 17th yellow when Marlin went into the wall. Busch was

Michael Waltrip goes for a spin in turns three and four as Robby Gordon tries to squeeze past on the inside. Rusty Wallace, however, was not that lucky and hit Waltrip hard as the NAPA Chevrolet slid to the apron. Both Waltrip and Wallace were done for the night.

NASCAR Winston Cup Series

warned by NASCAR to be careful and from then on, he was. His frontstretch pass of Kevin Harvick on lap 380 was clean and he held the point for the rest of the night.

As far as NASCAR Winston Cup Series points were concerned, there were no radical changes among the top 10 drivers after they left the sweeping wide turns of the two-mile Michigan track for the high banks of the Bristol "bullring." Matt Kenseth finished ninth at MIS and widened the gap between himself and his closest pursuers, who had struggled throughout the day. Kenseth's effort, coupled with a 32nd-place finish by Dale Earnhardt Jr. and a 30th-place showing by Jeff Gordon, increased his points advantage to 329 over the former and 461 over the latter. With 3,432 points in his pocket, Kenseth enjoyed his largest lead yet.

Despite an accident and tire problems at MIS, Earnhardt Jr. remained the No. 2 runner in points for the fourth straight week. Still, a net loss of 71 points was hard to take. Gordon had problems at MIS right off the bat and never got them resolved. His finish was his third of 30th or worse in the last four races. While he remained No. 3 in points, he fell 461 behind the leader.

At MIS, Harvick finished second best to winner Ryan Newman, marking his third consecutive top-five finish and fourth in the previous five events. Pointswise, he moved up a notch from fifth to fourth, a ranking that matched his season best. His good fortune along with Gordon's lousy luck separated the two by just 18 points going into Bristol.

Michael Waltrip also moved up the points ladder from sixth to fifth, and it was a seventh-place run

As daylight fades to night, Jeff Gordon stretches an early lead in front of a capacity crowd of 165,000 at Bristol Motor Speedway. Gordon led a total of three times during the evening for 176 laps, besting all drivers in that category.

(Above) In the Hendrick Motorsports camp, Jimmie Johnson (left) and crew chief Chad Knaus (right) discuss matters with teammate/car owner Jeff Gordon. Gordon, who had finished 24th or worse in four of the last five races, was hoping to turn things around after winning his third Bud Pole of the season.

(Above Right) On the track, Johnson (48) and Gordon (24) run together as Dale Earnhardt Jr. drifts dangerously close to the wall. Earnhardt avoided catastrophe and finished ninth, while Johnson grabbed his sixth top five of the season.

(Right) Bill Elliott, showing front-end damage from an earlier confrontation, brings Elliott Sadler (38) and Johnny Benson (10) through the first turn under caution while Ricky Craven and Mike Skinner head toward the exit of pit road. The 10th of a record-tying 20 cautions flew just past the mid-point of the race, at lap 256.

in the Irish Hills that helped. It was his 23rd consecutive week in the NASCAR top 10, and he and sixth-place Jimmie Johnson remained the only drivers to be so ranked for the entire season. Johnson, however, dropped from fourth in the points race to sixth after a disappointing finish at MIS. There, he led the most laps and was looking at victory. But a late-race fuel stop dropped him to 27th in the final rundown. It was his worst finish in the last 10 races.

The "bad news bear" kept chasing Bobby Labonte, too. His 37th-place finish at Michigan, because of engine problems, was the sixth straight time the 2000 NASCAR Winston Cup champion had finished 14th or worse. While he remained seventh in points (2,825), Ryan Newman, No. 8 on the list, closed to nine points behind Labonte, while ninth-ranked Kurt Busch (2,810) was just 15 behind the Gibbs driver.

Newman's win at Michigan was his series-

leading fifth of the year. That allowed him to move up a notch from ninth to eighth, which matched his season best ranking he achieved after the event at Texas. Busch's travails at MIS dropped him to ninth in the standings and he found himself just 33 points ahead of Robby Gordon, who jumped from 16th in points to 10th – a remarkable move.

"I've still got hope (for another championship), but it's a long shot," Jeff Gordon said after whipping his No. 24 Hendrick Motorsports/DuPont Chevrolet around the Bristol half-miler in 15.038 seconds at 127.597 mph to win his third Bud Pole position of the season. "I tell the crew to stay focused and keep trying to win races. That's all we can control right now – and recently we haven't been doing a very good job of that."

Gordon broke Rusty Wallace's event-qualifying record speed of 125.447 mph, set three years ago. It was his 45th career pole and first since August at Watkins Glen, N.Y. Mark Martin set the second-fastest time – 15.039 seconds at 127.588 mph – and in all, the top 34 qualifiers all exceeded Wallace's old mark.

Waltrip, Mike Skinner and Busch were third through fifth quickest, while Newman, Ted Musgrave (substituting for the sidelined Spencer), Ricky Rudd, Earnhardt Jr. and Kenseth completed the top 10. Billy Bigley Jr., Derrike Cope and Hermie Sadler failed to gain a berth in the starting field, while Morgan Shepherd withdrew his entry.

Qualifying was delayed by rain about an hour,

and Gordon was the 16th driver to make a run. He was less than optimistic about his chances for an up-front start and hence was pleasantly surprised at the outcome.

"The whole day has been really great for us," he said, "but I didn't think that was my best lap. When the rain came, I thought for sure somebody was going to beat us."

When the green flag dropped, Gordon sped off and led the first 66 laps before pitting under the

(Above) Rusty Wallace emerges from his battered Miller Lite Dodge after hard contact with Michael Waltrip that brought out the fourth caution on lap 90. Wallace, a nine-time Bristol winner, was listed last on the final rundown.

(Left) Matt Kenseth (17) holds the bottom line ahead of Dale Jarrett, with the damaged Dodge of Casey Mears giving way on the outside. Kenseth recovered from a flat tire and avoided further trouble in the accident-filled race to finish solidly in fourth. Jarrett, although he sustained damage, soldiered to a seventh-place, lead-lap result.

second yellow and ceding the front spot to Jeff Green. Gordon also led laps 83-162 and 193-225 and successfully survived the first 18 yellow-flag periods. His luck ran out, though, on lap 445. When he slowed down to avoid a car with a flat tire, he was tagged by Kenseth and spun out of the race.

Two laps after the incident with Marlin, Busch made the night's crucial move and was 0.818-second in front of Harvick at the end. Jamie McMurray, Kenseth and Johnson were third through fifth, and Newman, Dale Jarrett, Ricky Craven, Earnhardt Jr. and Jeremy Mayfield completed the top 10.

"I hate it that Jimmy is not here this weekend," Busch said, as he attempted to bring the Michigan incident to a close. "He's a tough competitor, just as I am, especially at this place. I hate it for the Spencer fans, for both our sponsors and teams that Jimmy and I finished the day the way we did last Sunday.

"It's a shame for all of us that NASCAR was left with no choice but to impose the penalties it did. As for my part, I'm sorry I had anything to do with it."

Busch completed the event in 3 hours, 26 minutes and 32 seconds at an average speed of 77.421 mph and won $237,565.

Sharpie 500 *final race results*

Fin. Pos.	Start Pos.	Car No.	Driver	Team	Fin. Pos.	Start Pos.	Car No.	Driver	Team
1	5	97	Kurt Busch	Sharpie/Rubbermaid Ford	23	18	20	Tony Stewart	Home Depot Chevrolet
2	23	29	Kevin Harvick	GM Goodwrench Chevrolet	24	28	27	Scott Wimmer	YJ Stinger Chevrolet
3	31	42	Jamie McMurray	Havoline Dodge	25	21	4	Johnny Sauter	Kodak Pontiac
4	10	17	Matt Kenseth	DEWALT Power Tools Ford	26	30	0	Jason Leffler	NetZero Hi Speed Pontiac
5	16	48	Jimmie Johnson	Lowe's Chevrolet	27	19	18	Bobby Labonte	Interstate Batteries Chevrolet
6	6	12	Ryan Newman	ALLTEL Dodge	28	1	24	Jeff Gordon	DuPont Chevrolet
7	27	88	Dale Jarrett	UPS Ford	29	35	30	Steve Park	America Online Chevrolet
8	14	32	Ricky Craven	Tide Pontiac	30	15	77	Dave Blaney	1st TN Bank/Jasper Powered Ford
9	9	8	Dale Earnhardt Jr.	Budweiser Chevrolet	31	7	7	Ted Musgrave	Sirius Satellite Radio Dodge
10	29	19	Jeremy Mayfield	Dodge Dealers/UAW Dodge	32	37	99	Jeff Burton	CITGO Ford
11	13	5	Terry Labonte	Kellogg's/got milk? Chevrolet	33	8	21	Ricky Rudd	Motorcraft Ford
12	26	49	Ken Schrader	SEM Color Horizons Dodge	34	42	45	Kyle Petty	Georgia Pacific Dodge
13	24	22	Ward Burton	Caterpillar Dodge	35	22	31	Robby Gordon	Cingular Wireless Chevrolet
14	32	10	Johnny Benson	Valvoline Pontiac	36	2	6	Mark Martin	Viagra Ford
15	11	23	Kenny Wallace	Stacker2 Dodge	37	40	54	Todd Bodine	National Guard Ford
16	25	9	Bill Elliott	Dodge Dealers/UAW Dodge	38	17	38	Elliott Sadler	Combos Ford
17	36	40	Sterling Marlin	Coors Light Dodge	39	33	50	Larry Foyt	Harrah's Dodge
18	4	01	Mike Skinner	U.S. Army Pontiac	40	39	1	Jeff Green	Pennzoil Chevrolet
19	38	25	Joe Nemechek	UAW-Delphi Chevrolet	41	43	43	Christian Fittipaldi	Cheerios Heart Health Dodge
20	12	74	Tony Raines	BACE Motorsports Chevrolet	42	3	15	Michael Waltrip	NAPA Chevrolet
21	41	41	Casey Mears	Target Dodge	43	20	2	Rusty Wallace	Miller Lite Dodge
22	34	16	Greg Biffle	Grainger Ford					

MOUNTAIN DEW SOUTHERN 500

August 31, 2003

S torybook finishes" in NASCAR Winston Cup Series races: Over the long history of the sport there have been more than a few but not so many that the term itself had degenerated into just another tired cliché.

Two come to mind. For example, there was July 4, 1984 at Daytona Beach, Fla., when Richard Petty took advantage of a late-race mistake by Cale Yarborough and crossed the line to win the Firecracker (Pepsi) 400. Not only was it the "King's" historic 200th series victory, but he also accomplished it with one of his political heroes in the audience – President Ronald Reagan.

Flash ahead to Feb. 15, 1998, also at Daytona International Speedway. After 19 attempts – several of them heartbreaking – the 20th was the charm for seven-time NASCAR Winston Cup champion Dale Earnhardt. After winning about everything possible at the speedway except NASCAR's most prestigious race, Earnhardt sailed across the finish line to capture the Daytona 500. Coincidentally, it was also a great way for NASCAR to kick off its 50th anniversary celebration as well as the 40th for the track itself.

Though some future historians may dispute it, Terry Labonte's victory in the Mountain Dew Southern 500 may well fall into the "storybook" category.

On the plus side, the reasons are evident: First, this 54th annual version of the "Labor Day" Southern 500 was the last. As part of its "realignment," NASCAR and International Speedway Corp. (the track's owner) had decided to move the early-September race date to another of its race courses in Fontana, Calif., beginning in 2004, while rescheduling the Southern 500 for November.

> "I've won some big races, but this is the biggest one ... It's nice to end the losing streak from hell. I'm glad it's over."

Ricky Rudd (21) scoots away from his pit stall barely ahead of Ken Schrader (49), while Kyle Petty's crew finishes up on the Georgia-Pacific Dodge. Pit road was a busy place during the Mountain Dew Southern 500, with 10 yellow flags displayed over the 367-lap event.

NASCAR.
Winston Cup
Series

Next, Labonte made his NASCAR Winston Cup Series debut in this event on Sept. 4, 1978, and he finished an impressive fourth behind established winners Cale Yarborough, Darrell Waltrip and Petty. Next, Labonte returned to the track two years later and bested established Darlington master David Pearson. The Southern 500 was Labonte's first career victory.

And finally: In driving Hendrick Motorsports' No. 5 Kellogg's/got milk? Chevrolet to his 22nd career victory, the Corpus Christi, Texas, native ended a 156-race winless streak dating back March 1999 at, of all places Texas Motor Speedway. Also, he moved up a notch in the points from 12th to 11th.

So much for the critical historians of years to come!

"I've won some big races, but this is the biggest one," said the two-time series champion. "It's nice to end the losing streak from hell. I'm glad it's over."

Steady though he was, the elder Labonte wasn't really in the spotlight after finishing 11th in the Sharpie 500 in Bristol, Tenn. Rather, the man still in the limelight was Matt Kenseth. He finished fourth at Bristol and left the track with 3,592 points – 351 more than points runner-up Dale Earnhardt Jr. Kenseth extended his dominance in points to 21 consecutive weeks, and he was the only driver to score 19 top-10 finishes in the year's first 24 races, four more than Earnhardt.

Earnhardt Jr. finished ninth at Bristol and although he lost 93 points to Kenseth in the last two races, he remained comfortably in second place in points, with 113 more than Kevin Harvick. In seven races at Darlington, Earnhardt led in just three but he did finish sixth in this year's spring event there.

Harvick, in one of RCR Enterprises' trio of Chevrolets, had a good night at Bristol, finishing second to Ford-driving Kurt Busch. It was his fifth top-five finish in the last

(Upper Left) Jimmy Spencer answers questions from members of the motorsports press in the Darlington garage. Spencer, who returned to the tour at Darlington after serving a one-race suspension, crashed in qualifying and had to start a backup car in 38th.

(Middle Left) Jeremy Mayfield relaxes on pit road prior to the start of Sunday's race. Mayfield, who has had some strong runs at Darlington, picked up a season-best sixth-place finish at the conclusion of the event, one spot behind his Evernham Motorsports teammate, Bill Elliott.

(Below Left) This fan likely speaks for all 75,000 in attendance, urging the competitors on as the action gets underway.

Jamie McMurray's Havoline crew hustles through a four-tire stop under caution. The crew put McMurray on the track in first during the ninth caution of the day, a lead he held for 21 laps between yellow-flag periods. The Havoline driver eventually finished fourth and increased his lead over Greg Biffle in a tight battle for rookie honors.

six events, and in just three races, he went from seventh to third in points. At this point a year ago, he was 19th in points. Harvick, however, said he would have been happier if he'd beaten Busch in Tennessee!

Jimmie Johnson's fifth-place effort at Bristol was particularly beneficial, as he jumped from sixth to fourth in NASCAR Winston Cup Series points and provided a needed boost for the Hendrick Motorsports conglomerate. Johnson headed to the "Track Too Tough To Tame" with 10 finishes in the top 10 and a record showing he'd been in the top 10 in points since the year's first event at Daytona Beach, Fla. In just three races at Darlington, he finished 10th or better twice.

Johnson's mentor and co-car owner, Jeff Gordon, left Bristol still under a cloud of despond. A disappointing 28th-place finish at Bristol dropped him from third to fifth in points. He'd finished 24th or worse in five of the last six events and lost 367 points to Kenseth in the process. With 3,060 points, he trailed the leader 532 and the runner-up by 181. On the bright side, though, Gordon headed to the egg-shaped Darlington track

with a record of 14 top-10 finishes there, including six victories.

Busch put aside his problems related to his run-in with Jimmy Spencer at Michigan when he won the Sharpie 500 at Bristol. The victory also shot him from ninth to sixth in points heading into Darlington, just 70 behind Johnson and 19 in front of Ryan Newman. His Darlington record included a second-place showing in this past spring's race.

The only driver to win five races in 2003, Ryan Newman jumped up a spot in points – eighth to seventh – largely because of a sixth-place run at Bristol. With 2,971 markers, he was just 11 in front of Michael Waltrip, who because of a 42nd-place finish at Bristol, dropped from fifth to eighth in the standings. A poor finish there (27th) dropped Bobby Labonte from seventh to ninth in points, while Robby Gordon remained in 10th place, 757 points in arrears of Kenseth.

If either Newman or Johnson had any thoughts of Darlington Raceway being difficult to negotiate, they put them aside in Bud Pole qualifying. Newman took the No. 1 starting spot – also his

Elliott Sadler and Bobby Labonte were the fourth- and fifth-quickest qualifiers, while Matt Kenseth, Mark Martin, Ricky Craven, Greg Biffle and Dave Blaney completed the top 10. Larry Foyt failed to make the field, while Jimmy Spencer, making his comeback from a one-race suspension, crashed during qualifying. Eighth quickest in a pre-qualifying practice session, Spencer had to go to a backup car and start 38th in the race.

"I was trying to sit on the pole, and that's what happens here. You sit on the wall instead," Spencer quipped.

sixth Bud Pole Award of the year – with a 29.090-second lap at a speed of 169.048 mph. Johnson's time and speed of 29.122 seconds and 168.862 mph put him second on the starting grid. He ran just a tad quicker than T. Labonte, who notched spot No. 3 at 168.538, claiming his first top-10 start at Darlington since this race in 1996.

"It is a tough track, no doubt," Newman said. "But a good driver should be able to adapt to any situation."

"It was a good run for us," Labonte noted. "It was just typical Darlington. You make two or three runs and hope you can get it right."

The final Labor Day Southern 500 was just like so many others over the years. It was hot and humid, and the race was interrupted 10 times for 55 laps, mostly for accidents and fender-benders. The race winner ran in the front most of the afternoon but had to wait until later in the day to make the move that counted.

When Robbie Gordon banged into the wall on the 332nd circuit and brought out the final yellow flag, the leaders dove into the pits for tires and a splash of fuel. Labonte came in third and about 13 seconds later beat Jamie McMurray and Harvick onto the track, taking the lead for the first

(Above) In the move that really counted, Labonte beats Kevin Harvick and Jimmie Johnson off pit road during the day's final caution, giving the Kellogg's driver the lead for the first - and last - time during the race.

(Right) Contrary to contemporary celebrations, Terry Labonte takes a traditional victory lap with checkered flag in hand. It was Labonte's second such souvenir from the Southern 500 and the last to be displayed at Darlington on Labor Day weekend.

time. He then put enough space – as well as the lapped cars of Newman and Earnhardt Jr. – between himself and Harvick to pace the final 33 laps and beat Harvick to the win by 1.651 seconds.

Newman led more times and laps – five for 120 – but fell victim to his own mistake and ended up 18 laps down in 23rd. During a routine pit stop, he accidentally hit the "kill switch" (a toggle that cuts all electrical power off). By the time he and his crew figured the problem out, it was too late.

Labonte celebrated his victory by going back to his short-track "roots." Instead of doing the now familiar "donut" in front of the crowd, he drove to the start-finish line and accepted the checkered flag from starter Jimmy Howell. Labonte, in a "wave" to tradition, then toured the track, waving flag in hand.

"I'm too old to do donuts," Labonte said. "I think they're goofy looking, anyway."

Labonte completed the Southern 500 in 4 hours, 9 minutes and 7 seconds at an average speed of 120.744 mph and won $204,736.

Mountain Dew Southern 500 *final race results*

Fin. Pos.	Start Pos.	Car No.	Driver	Team
1	3	5	Terry Labonte	Kellogg's/got milk? Chevrolet
2	18	29	Kevin Harvick	GM Goodwrench Chevrolet
3	2	48	Jimmie Johnson	Lowe's Chevrolet
4	17	42	Jamie McMurray	Havoline Dodge
5	22	9	Bill Elliott	Dodge Dealers/UAW Dodge
6	15	19	Jeremy Mayfield	Dodge Dealers/UAW Dodge
7	5	18	Bobby Labonte	Interstate Batteries Chevrolet
8	8	32	Ricky Craven	Give Kids the World/Tide Pontiac
9	4	38	Elliott Sadler	M&Ms Ford
10	9	16	Greg Biffle	Grainger Ford
11	28	99	Jeff Burton	CITGO Ford
12	20	20	Tony Stewart	Home Depot Chevrolet
13	31	97	Kurt Busch	Rubbermaid/Sharpie Ford
14	6	17	Matt Kenseth	Smirnoff Ice Triple Black/DEWALT Ford
15	41	4	Kevin Lepage	Kodak Pontiac
16	30	21	Ricky Rudd	Motorcraft Ford
17	27	54	Todd Bodine	National Guard Ford
18	35	1	Jeff Green	Pennzoil Chevrolet
19	29	22	Ward Burton	Caterpillar Dodge
20	32	30	Steve Park	America Online Chevrolet
21	26	25	Joe Nemechek	UAW-Delphi Chevrolet
22	38	7	Jimmy Spencer	Sirius Satellite Radio Dodge
23	1	12	Ryan Newman	ALLTEL Dodge
24	24	23	Kenny Wallace	Stacker2 Dodge
25	12	8	Dale Earnhardt Jr.	Budweiser Chevrolet
26	36	0	Jason Leffler	NetZero Pontiac
27	40	45	Kyle Petty	Georgia Pacific Dodge
28	25	31	Robby Gordon	Cingular Wireless Chevrolet
29	16	01	Mike Skinner	U.S. Army Pontiac
30	10	77	Dave Blaney	Jasper Engines & Transmissions Ford
31	13	40	Sterling Marlin	Coors Light Dodge
32	14	24	Jeff Gordon	DuPont Chevrolet
33	7	6	Mark Martin	Viagra Ford
34	19	88	Dale Jarrett	UPS Ford
35	21	41	Casey Mears	Target Dodge
36	34	2	Rusty Wallace	Miller Lite Dodge
37	37	15	Michael Waltrip	NAPA Chevrolet
38	39	49	Ken Schrader	1-800-CallATT Dodge
39	42	37	Derrike Cope	Friendly's/SP Films Chevrolet
40	11	10	Johnny Benson	Valvoline Pontiac
41	43	02	Hermie Sadler	goteamva.com Pontiac
42	33	74	Tony Raines	BACE Motorsports Chevrolet
43	23	43	Christian Fittipaldi	Cheerios Dodge

CHEVY ROCK & ROLL 400

September 6, 2003

By the time the NASCAR Winston Cup Series left Darlington (S.C.) Raceway and prepared to "go under the lights" in Richmond, Va., the chefs of fate were beginning to add ingredients to the cauldron that held the "silly season stew."

Who would be in what car in 2004? Would drivers whose jobs were in doubt have a ride following the year's last race? Would teams whose sponsorships were in doubt have the necessary finances to keep competing, and would anyone be leaving the series at the end of 2003?

"We unloaded this race car and we struggled quite a bit. To fight back and make the changes that they made overnight, the guys did an awesome job."

— Ryan Newman

One driver who didn't have to worry about a secure future was Tony Stewart. Another who would become an unemployment statistic by season's end was Joe Nemechek. Two days before he ran the Aug. 31 event at Darlington, Stewart announced he had "re-upped" with Joe Gibbs Racing and had agreed to stay with the team through 2009. Sponsorship pressures had a lot to do with Nemechek being replaced in Hendrick Motorsports' No. 25 Chevrolet, in 2004, by NASCAR Busch Series rookie Brian Vickers, who was not yet 20 years old.

Stewart said the main reason he decided to stick with Gibbs and reject "a lot of generous offers" was the people on the No. 20 team. Included were team owner Joe Gibbs and crew chief Greg "Zippy" Zipadelli.

"Joe and Zippy, that's what it boiled down to," Stewart said. "I had everything, and I was comparing apples to apples and oranges. But the part where people are involved, you can't put a price tag on that. It came down to Joe's patience and Zippy's patience, and their consideration of questions that we had."

An estimated 105,000 fans encircle the three-quarter-mile Richmond oval for Saturday night short-track racing, NASCAR Winston Cup Series style.

According to Hendrick, the United Auto Workers (UAW) was ending its co-sponsorship of the No. 25 team, and the only way to get a replacement – in this case GMAC Financial Services – was to bring in a younger driver. Vickers, who had won two NASCAR Busch Series races for Hendrick, was the logical choice.

"It's just unfortunate circumstances, but I'll rebound from it," Nemechek, 39, said Sept. 5. "Rick Hendrick is doing everything he can to help me land in a good quality ride for next year."

Something else had also been settled between Darlington and Richmond. NASCAR released its 2004 NASCAR Winston Cup Series schedule, and as expected, there were no big surprises. The season would begin Feb. 15 in Daytona Beach, Fla., and end Nov. 21 in Homestead, Fla. California Speedway would host its second of two annual races on Sept. 5, with Darlington, S.C.'s second event set for Nov. 14. Also, the annual non-points "all-star" event – renamed the NASCAR NEXTEL All-Star Challenge – would run again at Lowe's Motor Speedway.

With a 14th-place finish in the Mountain Dew Southern 500, Matt Kenseth further strengthened his grip on the lead in points toward the championship. Although the Roush Racing Ford driver had snapped a streak of four straight top-10 finishes, with 3,718 points, he was comfortably in front of No. 2 points man Dale Earnhardt Jr. Kenseth, to date, had spent 22 consecutive weeks in the lead and had been in the top 10 for 24 of 25.

Earnhardt Jr. finished 25th at Darlington and lost 38 points to Kenseth. But with 3,329 points he remained second in the running for the sixth consecutive week and among the top three for 19 weeks in a row. Obviously, Kevin Harvick was in a better mood than Earnhardt after Darlington, as he finished second to winner Terry Labonte for his third consecutive runner-up finish and fifth top five in a row. While he trailed Kenseth by 415 points, he was 26 behind Earnhardt.

Jimmie Johnson and his "boss," Jeff Gordon, went into Darlington ranked fourth and fifth in points, respectively, and left the same way. Johnson's third-place effort in South Carolina was his third top-five showing in the last four races.

Tony Stewart (20) makes a hard right to get out of his pit stall, sandwiched between those of Johnny Benson (10) and Jeremy Mayfield (19). The three drivers had very different Richmond experiences: Stewart spun a few times and lost laps before finishing down in the order; Mayfield climbed steadily from 23rd at the start to a strong second place at the finish; while Benson finished the night right where he started, in ninth.

(Above) Tony Stewart (20), Kurt Busch (97) and Matt Kenseth (17) chase Jimmie Johnson and the Lowe's Chevrolet through Richmond's 14-degree-banked turns. Kenseth was the only one of the group to work his way into the top 10 at the end, allowing him to further pad his lead in the point standings.

(Below) Dale Earnhardt Jr. pokes the nose of his Budweiser Chevrolet under-neath Jeff Gordon's DuPont Monte Carlo in their on-track duel for the lead. The two drivers swapped the point back and forth three times during the second half of the event before Newman took control.

With 3,233 points, he was 70 in back of Harvick, and only he and Michael Waltrip had been ranked in the top 10 in points for all 25 race weeks contested.

Four-time champion Gordon was unable to break out of his depressing slump at Darlington, where he finished 32nd for his fourth straight showing of 28th or worse. He maintained his

No. 5 points ranking for the second straight week and had been in the top five in points for 18 consecutive weeks. With 3,127 markers, he trailed Johnson by 106 and was just 13 up on sixth-place man Kurt Busch.

Coming off his fourth victory of the year at Bristol, Tenn., Busch finished 13th at Darlington to remain sixth in points for the second week in

a row. Heartened, he was looking to get back in the top five in the title race since being ranked fifth following his win at Michigan in June.

Seemingly on a winning tear of late, Ryan Newman finished 23rd at Darlington for just his second sub-top-10 showing in the last eight races. The finish, his worst since a 41st at Michigan in June, did not knock him out of seventh in points, and he headed to Richmond with 3,075 points, just 39 behind Busch.

Bobby Labonte snapped out of a seven-race slump with a seventh-place effort at Darlington and moved from ninth to eighth in the standings. It was his first top-10 performance since a fifth at Daytona Beach in July, and he was just 22 points behind Newman.

A 37th-place showing at Darlington dropped Waltrip from eighth to ninth in points, while defending NASCAR Winston Cup champion Tony Stewart used a 12th-place run in the Southern 500 to move back into the NASCAR top 10 after a one-month absence.

Mike Skinner, subbing for the recovering Jerry Nadeau, in the MB2/U.S. Army Pontiac, won the Bud Pole by lapping the 0.75-mile Richmond track in 21.464 seconds at 125.792 mph. Skinner's rock 'n' rollin' road to the front row might have been a precursor for how the event itself would shake out. In a practice session the day before the event, he hit the frontstretch wall and destroyed his car. Then, in a backup Pontiac, Skinner turned the session's second-quickest time

and he went on to win the pole. But in the following practice session, Skinner slammed the first-turn wall and crumbled that car.

"This is just my luck," said Skinner, who would start the event last in a backup for the backup. "We're running out of cars."

Skinner said he had no idea why he crashed the first time, but oil on the track caused the second wreck, ironically sending him into the wall at the same spot where Nadeau crashed in May. Skinner, however, hit the new SAFER "soft wall" barrier and walked away without a scratch.

Skinner's sixth career Bud Pole came at the expense of rookie Greg Biffle. The Roush Racing Ford driver recorded a time and speed of 21.489 seconds at 125.646 mph for a second-place start, ahead of fellow Roush driver Mark Martin, who was third quickest. Ryan Newman was fourth fastest, in a Dodge, while Sterling Marlin, also in a Dodge, was the No. 5 qualifier.

While several other drivers chose to "rock on" behind him, the steady Newman took the lead on lap 277 of 400, after the ninth of 14 yellow flags, and, never pitting again, kept the lead from that point on.

The real fireworks came just a few laps from the finish and then in a post-race confrontation involving Harvick, Ricky Rudd and their crews. With seven laps left, just after the 13th yellow, Harvick, who had been pursuing Newman, spun in the first turn and brought out the last caution flag. Rudd – who said he thought Harvick had braked

Kevin Harvick was anything but happy at the conclusion of the race, feeling as though Ricky Rudd caused him to spin in the final laps. After pulling alongside Rudd's Motorcraft Ford on pit road, Harvick climbed out of his Chevrolet and left his impression of the incident on Rudd's hood.

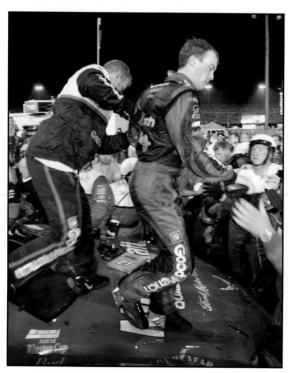

Ryan Newman (12) works to the inside of pole-winner Mike Skinner, driving the U.S. Army Pontiac, with Kevin Harvick checking the action from behind. Newman led one lap in the early going and then took over for good before the three-quarter mark, leading the final 124 circuits to gain his sixth win of the year, his fourth in the last nine races.

too hard – went on to finish third, behind the winner and runner-up Jeremy Mayfield.

Harvick, knocked back to 16th at the finish as the last driver on the lead lap, drove up to Rudd's car on pit road and the confrontation began. Angry words were exchanged and Harvick and a couple of his crewman did a Mexican hat dance on Rudd's car.

"I drove by it. I don't know (what happened), and I don't care," Newman said of the Harvick-Rudd clash. "My front bumper is clean. I don't care about anyone else's."

Newman won his first short-track race by averaging 94.945 mph in 3 hours, 9 minutes and 35 seconds. His 0.159-second margin of victory was worth $160,970.

Chevy Rock & Roll 400 *final race results*

Fin. Pos.	Start Pos.	Car No.	Driver	Team	Fin. Pos.	Start Pos.	Car No.	Driver	Team
1	4	12	Ryan Newman	ALLTEL Dodge	23	34	23	Kenny Wallace	Stacker2 Dodge
2	23	19	Jeremy Mayfield	Dodge Dealers/UAW Dodge	24	25	97	Kurt Busch	Rubbermaid Ford
3	19	21	Ricky Rudd	Motorcraft Ford	25	27	49	Ken Schrader	BAM Racing Dodge
4	7	99	Jeff Burton	CITGO Ford	26	11	25	Joe Nemechek	UAW-Delphi Chevrolet
5	17	2	Rusty Wallace	Miller Lite Dodge	27	14	20	Tony Stewart	Home Depot Chevrolet
6	16	18	Bobby Labonte	Interstate Batteries Chevrolet	28	40	0	Jason Leffler	NetZero Pontiac
7	18	17	Matt Kenseth	Smirnoff Ice Triple Black/DEWALT Ford	29	21	31	Robby Gordon	Cingular Wireless Chevrolet
8	32	5	Terry Labonte	Kellogg's/got milk? Chevrolet	30	35	32	Ricky Craven	Tide Pontiac
9	9	10	Johnny Benson	Valvoline Pontiac	31	39	30	Steve Park	America Online Chevrolet
10	5	24	Jeff Gordon	DuPont Chevrolet	32	33	15	Michael Waltrip	NAPA Chevrolet
11	26	48	Jimmie Johnson	Lowe's Chevrolet	33	38	77	Dave Blaney	Jasper Engines & Transmissions Ford
12	42	09	Mike Wallace	Miccosukee Resorts Dodge	34	10	45	Kyle Petty	Georgia Pacific Dodge
13	3	6	Mark Martin	Viagra Ford	35	20	74	Tony Raines	BACE Motorsports Chevrolet
14	24	1	John Andretti	Pennzoil Chevrolet	36	22	7	Jimmy Spencer	Sirius Satellite Radio Dodge
15	8	22	Ward Burton	Caterpillar Dodge	37	15	9	Bill Elliott	Dodge Dealers/UAW Dodge
16	28	29	Kevin Harvick	GM Goodwrench Chevrolet	38	36	4	Johnny Sauter	Kodak Easy Share Pontiac
17	13	8	Dale Earnhardt Jr.	Budweiser Chevrolet	39	30	38	Elliott Sadler	M&M's Ford
18	1	01	Mike Skinner	U.S. Army Pontiac	40	43	02	Hermie Sadler	VCU Rams/Dollar Tree Chevrolet
19	29	42	Jamie McMurray	Havoline Dodge	41	31	41	Casey Mears	Target Dodge
20	2	16	Greg Biffle	Grainger Ford	42	12	54	Todd Bodine	National Guard Ford
21	37	88	Dale Jarrett	UPS Ford	43	41	43	Christian Fittipaldi	Cheerios Heart Health Dodge
22	6	40	Sterling Marlin	Coors Light Dodge					

SYLVANIA 300

September 14, 2003

Mostly everyone heading into New Hampshire International Speedway for the NASCAR Winston Cup Series' 27th event of the season was expecting another "good" race on a much improved track surface. Hardly anyone anticipated a surprise announcement made the day before the running of the 317.4-mile contest: William C. "Bill Jr." France, 70, was stepping down as the race sanctioning body's supreme leader and had named his son, Brian Z. France, 37, as his replacement.

"I am happy to announce the appointment of Brian France as the chief executive officer and chairman of the board of NASCAR," France said in a formal news conference the following Monday. "Brian has worked long and hard for the opportunity, just as I had when I took over the reins from my father. He has earned his chance, and I know how important that is to him and me."

NASCAR was founded in 1948 by William H.G. France, who was its top executive until he stepped down in favor of his son in 1972. In recent years, France Jr. had ceded portions of his responsibilities to others, most recently naming Mike Helton as NASCAR President in 2000.

"This," noted Brian France, "is a great day for me, and I don't take that lightly. I do share the vision, beliefs and traditions of my father and his father before him, that above all the sport has to continue to grow and get better."

Following a post-race altercation at Richmond, Va., the week before that involved driver Kevin Harvick and several members of his crew and the crew of driver Ricky Rudd, several severe fines were handed out, generally for "actions

"... Once everybody got strung out, we started passing some guys and before we knew it we were in second. So it was meant to be."

Jimmie Johnson's third win of the year didn't come without some contact, evidenced here by a few "donuts" left on the side of the Lowe's Chevrolet by other competitors. The victory also completed a season sweep at New Hampshire by the young driver from Hendrick Motorsports.

detrimental to stock car racing." Harvick, who lost his temper, was fined $35,000 and placed on probation for the rest of the year. His crew chief, Todd Berrier, was fined $10,000 for failing to control the actions of his teammates. Four other RCR Enterprises crewmen were fined and either suspended from competition for a week or placed on probation, and Rudd's crew chief, Pat Tryson, was fined $5,000 for use of naughty language.

The changing of the guard in Daytona Beach had little impact on Matt Kenseth's total domination of the run for the championship. With a seventh-place run at Richmond, the DeWalt Tools Ford driver continued to solidify his No. 1 ranking, which he'd held for 23 consecutive weeks. He gained 29 points on No. 2 pointsman Dale Earnhardt Jr. and 23 on "Happy" Harvick, leading them by 418 and 441 points, respectively.

Earnhardt Jr.'s spate of poor fortunes continued at Virginia's capital city speedway. A 17th-place

finish marked the third time in the last four races he'd been unable to muster a finish in the top 15. He, however, remained second in points (3,446) for a seventh consecutive week.

Harvick's accident in the "Rock & Roll" 400 at Richmond resulted in a 16th-place finish, his worst in the last eight times at bat. But with 3,423 points he was still third in the standings. Also, he led 23 laps in the race, good for five bonus points, and it was the fourth consecutive event in which he'd paced at least one circuit.

Jimmie Johnson went into Richmond fourth in points and emerged in the same spot. He'd been ranked in the top five in points for seven of the last eight weeks and headed to New Hampshire just 60 points behind Harvick. He also led 58 laps in winning the July event at Loudon.

Jeff Gordon, who had struggled in his previous four races with finishes of 28th or worse, snapped that drought with a 10th-place effort at Richmond.

(Below) Roush Racing teammates Mark Martin (6) and Kurt Busch (97) attack New Hampshire's relatively flat banks while jockeying for track position. Busch managed to pull off a 15th-place finish, which brought him even in the point standings with Bobby Labonte, who finished one spot behind Busch, in 16th.

(Right) Matt Kenseth (17) runs in front of Kurt Busch (97) and Mike Skinner (01), with Scott Wimmer, making his second start in the YJ Stinger Chevrolet, and Jeremy Mayfield trailing behind. Kenseth did what he needed to do at New Hampshire: He led once for two laps to pick up five bonus points and posted another top-10 finish, this time in seventh.

(Below Right) The ALLTEL crew goes to work on Newman's Dodge at the far end of pit road. Newman's team selected the advantageous pit position by virtue of winning the Bud Pole, Newman's seventh of the season.

It was his 12th top-10 showing of the season but just his second in the previous eight events. He, however, stayed at fifth in the standings and headed to New Hampshire trailing Johnson by 92 points. Gordon has had mixed results at the New England oval but does lead everyone else there with three Bud Poles and eight top-five finishes.

Ryan Newman again did car owner Roger Penske proud by winning the Chevy Rock & Roll 400 for a series-leading six victories in 2003. The win moved him up a spot in points from seventh, to his highest ranking of the season. In a nine-race stretch, dating back to Chicago in mid-July,

Newman had registered seven top-10 finishes, including four victories to jump from 16th in points to sixth. With 3,255 points, he was just 16 behind Gordon.

Circumstances continued to look up for Bobby Labonte as he worked on erasing a recent slump. His sixth-place run at Richmond was his second straight top-10 finish, his efforts coming on the heels of a seven-race stretch in which he was 22nd or worse five times. In moving up a spot from eighth to seventh in championship standings, he was only 47 points behind Newman and 63 behind Gordon.

Kurt Busch's 24th-place finish at Richmond proved costly, as he fell two spots in points from sixth to eighth. On the up side, he's been in the NASCAR top 10 for 25 of 26 weeks, including 22 in a row. With 3,205 points he left Virginia 659 points behind leader Kenseth but 123 ahead of the ninth-place runner, Terry Labonte.

Bobby's older brother has not only "got milk?" but he must have been ingesting large quantities of the lactic fluid. An eighth-place run in Virginia – his fourth consecutive top-15 finish – saw him jump from 11th to ninth in points. Michael Waltrip, conversely, finished a dismal 32nd at ISC's Virginia facility and slid one position in the markers from ninth to 10th. But with 3,079 points he was just three behind T. Labonte as they

readied for Bob Bahre's Sylvania 300.

If Jerry Seinfeld had been in the pits at New Hampshire scouting for the autograph of the Bud Pole position winner, undoubtedly he would have approached the No. 1 qualifier for the Sylvania 300 and, notebook in hand, would have broken the ice with, "Hello, Newman."

But the Penske Dodge driver's season record seventh Bud Pole was no laughing matter. He toured the track at a record 133.357 mph and left everyone else scrambling for second place. Newman's speed was over a mile an hour faster than the old record established in this race last year – by Newman!

Terry Labonte's speed of 132.780 mph also eclipsed the former mark of 132.241 mph, but Jaime McMurray's third-place effort – 132.131 mph – fell a bit short. Greg Biffle (131.989) was fourth fastest in time trials while Michael Waltrip was fifth at 131.906.

"We knew we had a fast car because this is the car we had here last when we won," Newman said. "It's a good car, no doubt. It's another dot on the resume.

"I enjoy qualifying because I get to out there and attack the race track one on one – just me vs. the track – and I don't have to worry about anything else out there."

Waltrip and Earnhardt Jr. were the fifth- and

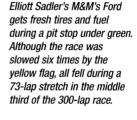

Elliott Sadler's M&M's Ford gets fresh tires and fuel during a pit stop under green. Although the race was slowed six times by the yellow flag, all fell during a 73-lap stretch in the middle third of the 300-lap race.

Jimmie Johnson (48) and Ward Burton, in the Caterpillar Dodge, leave little negotiating room as they race together, with Ricky Rudd bearing down on them from behind. A few laps later, Johnson and Burton tangled, sending Burton into the wall. Rudd stayed as close as he could to Johnson and eventually finished second, although he was more than six seconds behind at the checkers.

the year, Johnson became the first series driver to sweep both events at the track in the same season. He took the lead from Robby Gordon with seven laps left and outran runner-up Rudd by a whopping 6.240 seconds.

To do so, the Lowe's Chevrolet driver had to endure a bit of adversity. During the first of six yellow flags for 38 laps, on lap 127, J. Gordon attempted to cut through Waltrip's pit stall at the same moment Waltrip was trying to make his stop. The two cars collided and Gordon's went into Johnson's stall striking three of his crewmen. Luckily, all three escaped with minor bruises. After getting checked out at the infield medical center, they returned to whip off excellent pit stops that contributed to their driver's victory.

Except for that incident and another involving driver Ward Burton that brought out the

sixth-fastest qualifiers, and Jeff Gordon, Johnson and Sterling Marlin completed the top 10 on the starting grid.

In winning his second straight NASCAR Winston Cup Series race at New Hampshire, and third of

second yellow on lap 148, Johnson was able to stay in control and carry the day.

Johnson completed the event in 2 hours, 58 minutes and 41 seconds at an average speed of 106.580 mph and won $200,225.

Sylvania 300 *final race results*

Fin. Pos.	Start Pos.	Car No.	Driver	Team	Fin. Pos.	Start Pos.	Car No.	Driver	Team
1	8	48	Jimmie Johnson	Lowe's Chevrolet	23	34	7	Jimmy Spencer	Sirius Satellite Radio Dodge
2	31	21	Ricky Rudd	Motorcraft Ford	24	35	27	Scott Wimmer	YJ Stinger Chevrolet
3	25	25	Joe Nemechek	UAW-Delphi Chevrolet	25	22	10	Johnny Benson	Valvoline Pontiac
4	12	9	Bill Elliott	Dodge Dealers/UAW Dodge	26	5	15	Michael Waltrip	NAPA Chevrolet
5	6	8	Dale Earnhardt Jr.	Budweiser Chevrolet	27	41	0	Jason Leffler	NetZero Pontiac
6	11	2	Rusty Wallace	Miller Lite Dodge	28	33	6	Mark Martin	Viagra Ford
7	19	17	Matt Kenseth	DEWALT Power Tools Ford	29	9	40	Sterling Marlin	Coors Light Dodge
8	24	38	Elliott Sadler	M&M's Ford	30	40	45	Kyle Petty	Georgia Pacific Dodge
9	1	12	Ryan Newman	ALLTEL Dodge	31	43	43	Christian Fittipaldi	Cheerios Dodge
10	3	42	Jamie McMurray	Havoline Dodge	32	30	4	Johnny Sauter	Kodak Easy Share Pontiac
11	10	19	Jeremy Mayfield	Dodge Dealers/UAW Dodge	33	42	74	Tony Raines	BACE Motorsports Chevrolet
12	16	1	John Andretti	Pennzoil Chevrolet	34	39	30	Steve Park	America Online Chevrolet
13	13	29	Kevin Harvick	GM Goodwrench Chevrolet	35	29	54	Todd Bodine	National Guard Ford
14	26	77	Dave Blaney	Jasper Engines & Transmissions Ford	36	38	23	Kenny Wallace	Stacker2 Dodge
15	28	97	Kurt Busch	Rubbermaid Ford	37	20	49	Ken Schrader	BAM Racing Dodge
16	37	18	Bobby Labonte	Interstate Batteries Chevrolet	38	21	32	Ricky Craven	Tide Pontiac
17	18	41	Casey Mears	Target Dodge	39	23	22	Ward Burton	Caterpillar Dodge
18	2	5	Terry Labonte	Kellogg's/got milk? Chevrolet	40	36	02	Hermie Sadler	goteamva.com Pontiac
19	7	24	Jeff Gordon	DuPont Chevrolet	41	27	88	Dale Jarrett	UPS Ford
20	32	20	Tony Stewart	Home Depot Chevrolet	42	15	99	Jeff Burton	CITGO Ford
21	17	31	Robby Gordon	Cingular Wireless Chevrolet	43	4	16	Greg Biffle	Grainger Ford
22	14	01	Mike Skinner	U.S. Army Pontiac					

MBNA AMERICA 400

September 21, 2003

Did the fates play a major role in the outcome of events leading into the 28th contest of the 2003 NASCAR Winston Cup Series season – and the race itself – or was it just a particular combination of things that culminated in a logical conclusion?

Perhaps that question is best left to philosophers or tarot-card readers, but two curious events did highlight the MBNA America 400 weekend at Delaware's capital city track: Thanks to the weather, the series points leader got an automatic No. 1 starting spot for the event; also, the year's No. 1 driver in number of races won – and a vocal critic of a new rule – ended up benefiting from it and winning yet again.

Weather watchers had a keen eye on the path of Hurricane Isabel, which had come ashore further "down south" a few days before Dover International Speedway was set to open. While things did get a tad "breezy" at the track, the storm had weakened by the time it got to Delaware and the show went on. To be on the safe side, though, NASCAR canceled all activities on Thursday and Friday, which meant the drivers would start the race based on car owner points. That put Roush Racing Ford driver Matt Kenseth on the pole.

Dale Earnhardt Jr. took the second starting berth, Kevin Harvick was third on the grid, Jimmie Johnson fourth, Ryan Newman fifth, and Jeff Gordon, Kurt Busch, Bobby Labonte, Terry Labonte and Michael Waltrip fifth through 10th, respectively.

The new regulation – the first major piece of legislation under the still-new administration of NASCAR Chairman Brian France – effectively ended the so-called "gentlemen's agreement."

"We were just trying to do the best we could with a car that was decently balanced ... and it worked in our favor."

While still a lap down to the leaders, Ryan Newman pits under caution. A flat tire before lap 50 forced Newman to pit under green, losing the lead and a lap in the process. More than 200 laps later, Newman regained his lap and began a charge toward his seventh win of the season.

That, of course, was the unwritten but widely disregarded "rule" among drivers that said they wouldn't pass each other under the caution flag. Now it was the law.

"We have monitored and continually discussed the situation regarding racing back to the yellow throughout the season and have reached the conclusion that it is time for us to take this step," NASCAR President Mike Helton said. "We will eliminate the practice completely and no longer depend on the 'gentlemen's agreement' in an effort to further ensure the safety of the competitors."

In essence, once the yellow flag was displayed drivers now had to slow immediately and line up single file behind the race leader. Anyone improving his position during the caution would be penalized, but a driver making a pass while trying to slow down would be allowed to return to his proper position. Another provision that some competitors liked but others disagreed with said that, on a caution, the first driver not on the lead lap would get one back.

One who didn't like the "free lap" idea was Ryan Newman, who came into Dover with six 2003 victories, three more then anyone else.

"There shouldn't be any awards for anyone else's (yellow flag)," the No. 12 Penske/ALLTEL Dodge driver said shortly before getting the command to start his engine. "In most situations it's bad. If they're a lap down, generally they deserve to be."

Hence, it was a bit ironic that Newman ended up benefiting from the rule to the extent he won the race.

Coming into the 400-lap event on the one-mile track, Kenseth, with 4,015 points was solidly in command of the race to the championship. He finished seventh in the Sylvania 300 at New Hampshire International Speedway for his sixth top-10 effort in the last seven events and his 21st of the year. But despite his top-10 showing, he actually lost 14 points to Earnhardt Jr. and led by 404.

Earnhardt Jr. brought his DEI/Budweiser Chevrolet home fifth in New Hampshire for his 10th top-five effort of the year, which moved him into a tie for the series lead in that category. The finish was also a personal best for him at the Loudon facility and was his first top five in the last five races.

RCR Enterprises' Harvick was third in points going into New Hampshire and he left in the same spot after finishing 13th in the Sylvania 300. With 3,552 points, he trailed Earnhardt by

59 and was 463 behind the leader. It was the fourth straight week he'd been ranked third in the standings.

Johnson's victory at New Hampshire was his third in 2003, but it wasn't good enough to move him up to fourth in series points. He, however, did close to within nine points of Harvick, and the win was his fourth top-five effort in the last five races. He'd now been ranked No. 4 in points for the fourth week in a row.

Newman finished ninth in Loudon for his eighth top-10 finish in the last 10 races. That helped move him up one spot in points, from sixth to fifth, his highest ranking of the season. Since winning at Chicago, 10 races ago, he'd improved 11 positions, and with 3,398 points, he was 145 in arrears of Johnson.

(Top) Rick Hendrick (right) consults with crew chief Robbie Loomis about the DuPont team's plan of attack on the Monster Mile. Whatever the plan was, it worked in Jeff Gordon's favor as he picked up a fifth-place finish in the race, his first top five in the last seven events.

(Above) Jamie McMurray gives us a smile while lacing up his boots before going to work at Dover. The Havoline driver had scored three top 10s in the last four races, and he continued that momentum with a sixth-place finish at Dover, further solidifying his lead over Greg Biffle in the rookie standings.

(Above) Matt Kenseth takes the green flag in front of an estimated crowd of 137,000 to begin the MBNA America 400. The starting field was set according to points after Bud Pole qualifying was cancelled due to the effects of Hurricane Isabel.

(Right) Jamie McMurray (42) tries to catch Kevin Harvick (29), but to no avail. Harvick shot into the lead on the first lap and took control, leading 133 of the first 166 circuits before settling to a fourth-place finish, his seventh top five in the last 10 events.

Gordon came in 19th at New Hampshire and the finish cost him, as he slipped from fifth to sixth in points. Still in a slump of sorts, the four-time series champion left Loudon with just his second top-25 finish in the last six races. He, however, was only 16 points behind Newman and was heading to a track that had been good to him in the past. His Dover record included four wins, including three in a row.

With a 15th-place finish at Loudon, Busch had failed to crack the top 10 for the fifth time in the previous half-dozen races, the lone exception being a win at Bristol, Tenn. The Roush driver, however, actually moved up a spot in points from eighth to seventh. With 3,323 markers his total going into Dover was the same as Bobby Labonte's. But he earned the better slot off the "tiebreaker" provision because of more season victories. Both drivers were just 59 behind Gordon.

Terry Labonte, with an 18th-place showing at Loudon, remained ninth in points, with 3,191, for the second week

in a row. He trailed his younger brother by 132 points coming into Dover and was just 22 points ahead of Waltrip, who held onto 10th in points for the second straight week. Waltrip was just one of two drivers (Johnson was the other) to be ranked in the top 10 for the entire season.

As soon as the flagman dropped the green banner to start the event, Kenseth gave up his first-place starting spot, ceding it to Harvick, who paced the first seven circuits. On lap 12, Newman went to

lap after Joe Nemechek crashed and bored a hole in the wall. When the race went green on lap 105, Todd Bodine became the first beneficiary of the new rule and got his lost lap back.

Harvick led through the 166th lap and between then and the fifth caution period, which encompassed laps 288-296, Sterling Marlin, Gordon, Earnhardt Jr., Kenseth and Tony Stewart took turns pacing the field. The fifth yellow flag was thrown on lap 287 for debris on the track, and on lap 291, Newman got his lost lap back and rejoined the action in 19th place.

Newman pitted twice more – on laps 292 and 294 – while the race was still under caution, and the strategy would carry him to the end of the race without another stop. He took the lead for the last time on the 328th lap when then-leader Tony Stewart came into the pits during the sixth yellow flag and held off several charges from Jeremy Mayfield to beat him by 1.152 seconds at the checkered flag.

the front for the first time when he got around Harvick in the third corner, but on the 45th circuit, the "Monster Mile" bit the No. 12 Dodge. A flat tire sent Newman to the pits under the green, and when he re-emerged with four fresh Goodyears, he was buried in the field a lap down.

The second yellow flag emerged on the 81st

(Left) Greg Biffle (16) tries Joe Nemechek (25) on the high side in the early going. Nemechek would suffer a flat tire that sent him into the wall and ended his day, while Biffle had a strong run to seventh, one spot behind fellow rookie Jamie McMurray.

(Below) Two-time Dover winner Tony Stewart (20) measures four-time Dover champ Jeff Gordon (24) on the inside. Both drivers put their prior success to work and broke out of recent slumps with top-five results.

Jeremy Mayfield (19) dogs Ryan Newman (12) with the laps winding down. Mayfield, who started 25th, went on a tear over the last 100 laps and worked all the way up to the race leader, but couldn't complete the pass after repeated attempts and finally settled for the runner-up spot.

Stewart, who said his last set of tires were not up to snuff, finished third, while Harvick and Gordon were fourth and fifth.

"I still believe what I said (about giving a driver back a lost lap)," Newman said. "I guess the reward part of it, from my perspective, is still opinionated. It will always be opinionated if the rule stands the way it is.

"Being able to save fuel is not really easy when you're trying to go fast. We were just trying to do the best we could with a car that was decently balanced ... and it worked in our favor."

Newman drove to his seventh win of the year, at an average speed of 108.802 mph, in 3 hours, 40 minutes and 35 seconds and won $160,460.

MBNA America 400 *final race results*

Fin. Pos.	Start Pos.	Car No.	Driver	Team
1	5	12	Ryan Newman	ALLTEL Dodge
2	25	19	Jeremy Mayfield	Dodge Dealers/UAW Dodge
3	11	20	Tony Stewart	Home Depot Chevrolet
4	3	29	Kevin Harvick	GM Goodwrench Chevrolet
5	6	24	Jeff Gordon	DuPont Chevrolet
6	18	42	Jamie McMurray	Havoline Dodge
7	19	16	Greg Biffle	Grainger Ford
8	4	48	Jimmie Johnson	Lowe's Chevrolet
9	1	17	Matt Kenseth	DEWALT Power Tools Ford
10	14	2	Rusty Wallace	Miller Lite Dodge
11	23	21	Ricky Rudd	Motorcraft/U.S. Air Force Ford
12	13	99	Jeff Burton	CITGO Ford
13	17	40	Sterling Marlin	Coors Light Dodge
14	15	9	Bill Elliott	Dodge Dealers/UAW Dodge
15	29	7	Jimmy Spencer	Sirius Satellite Radio Dodge
16	41	43	Jeff Green	Cheerios Dodge
17	33	54	Todd Bodine	National Guard Ford
18	27	88	Dale Jarrett	UPS Ford
19	20	38	Elliott Sadler	M&M's Ford
20	9	5	Terry Labonte	Kellogg's/got milk? Chevrolet
21	26	10	Johnny Benson	Valvoline Pontiac
22	16	6	Mark Martin	Viagra Ford
23	12	31	Robby Gordon	Cingular Wireless Chevrolet
24	28	77	Dave Blaney	Jasper Engines & Transmissions Ford
25	37	0	Jason Leffler	NetZero Pontiac
26	32	30	Steve Park	America Online Chevrolet
27	40	4	Kevin Lepage	Kodak Easy Care Pontiac
28	31	23	Kenny Wallace	Stacker2 Dodge
29	21	22	Ward Burton	Caterpillar Dodge
30	39	74	Tony Raines	BACE Motorsports Chevrolet
31	8	18	Bobby Labonte	Interstate Batteries/3M Chevrolet
32	36	45	Kyle Petty	Georgia Pacific Dodge
33	38	49	Ken Schrader	BAM Racing Dodge
34	30	1	John Andretti	Pennzoil Chevrolet
35	42	37	Derrike Cope	Friendly's Chevrolet
36	35	41	Casey Mears	Target Dodge
37	2	8	Dale Earnhardt Jr.	Budweiser Chevrolet
38	7	97	Kurt Busch	Brute/Rubbermaid Ford
39	43	02	Hermie Sadler	VCU Rams/Dollar Tree Pontiac
40	22	32	Ricky Craven	Tide Pontiac
41	34	01	Mike Skinner	U.S. Army Pontiac
42	10	15	Michael Waltrip	NAPA Chevrolet
43	24	25	Joe Nemechek	UAW-Delphi Chevrolet

RACE

EA SPORTS 500

September 28, 2003

One day after Dale Earnhardt Jr. had been side-lined early in the MBNA America 400 at Dover, Del. – which caused him to drop two positions in points toward the NASCAR Winston Cup Series championship – the news was a little better: He'd passed a medical checkup and had been cleared to compete at Talladega (Ala.) Superspeedway in the EA Sports 500.

Earnhardt Jr. led the 400-miler in Delaware three times for 48 laps but hit the wall late in the race because of a deflating tire and finished out of the running. He also sustained a sprained right foot and slight concussion, but after a thorough examination, Charlotte-based neurosurgeon Dr. Jerry Petty gave him the OK to compete.

"It's so cool to get into a car like this and try to figure out how to beat the best in the world."

"My foot gets a lot better every day. I've stayed off my feet," Earnhardt said. "I've been to the shop, and the guys are making sure I'm comfortable in the car.

"I love going to Talladega. It would take a heckuva lot more than this to keep me out of the race."

Little wonder. In the April event at the 2.66-mile high-banked oval, the DEI/Budweiser Chevrolet driver started from the rear of the field (because his crew changed engines) and won the Aaron's 499. It was his fourth consecutive victory at Talladega, tying him with retired drivers Buddy Baker and Darrell Waltrip. It, however, was, however, nowhere near the record number of victories at the Alabama track – 10 – set by his late father.

New rules set in place by NASCAR for the EA Sports 500 mandated a slightly larger carburetor restrictor plate combined with a "taller" rear spoiler. The idea was to allow a bit more acceleration but at the same time keeping the cars stable and less likely to go out of control. The changes didn't appear to affect Earnhardt Jr.'s thoughts

Jeff Green (43) is "hung out" on the low side while Jeff Burton (99) and Jeff Gordon (24) form a tight draft in the middle, and Michael Waltrip (15) bump-drafts Mark Martin on the outside. This kind of action was the rule rather than exception at Talladega in a race that featured 41 lead changes and had 23 cars finish on the lead lap.

about the event one way or the other. Since his father's passing in February 2001, he'd won four of the nine "plate" races run at Talladega and Daytona Beach, Fla.

"Our success shows the strength of the entire Dale Earnhardt, Inc. organization," he said. "We have always focused on the restrictor-plate races, from the engines to the guys who work on the (car) bodies hour after hour in the wind tunnel and in the shop."

Obviously, Earnhardt was also hoping to make up the loss in points suffered at Dover's "Monster Mile." After all, Talladega was his "turf."

Matt Kenseth, who finished ninth in the MBNA America 400, left the track with 4,158 points, a lead of 436 over new No. 2 runner Kevin Harvick. The Dover finish was his third top 10 in a row and seventh in the last eight races. He now had been ranked first in points for the 25th consecutive week.

RCR Enterprises' Kevin Harvick left Dover with a fourth-place finish that bumped him up a spot in points from third to second place. He'd spent the previous four weeks ranked third and was now closer to taking the lead in the standings than he'd ever been in a three-year career. His showing at Dover was his sixth top-five finish in the last eight races and 10th of the season.

The pilot of Rick Hendrick's Lowe's Chevrolet, Jimmie Johnson, also moved up a notch in the standings – from fourth to third – by finishing eighth at Dover, his fifth top-10 effort in the previous seven events. With Michael Waltrip dropping out of the elite top 10, Johnson remained the only driver to be ranked 10th or better in the standings since the first race of the year. He headed into Alabama with 3,685 points, 17 better than Earnhardt Jr. and 37 behind Harvick.

Earnhardt Jr.'s Dover experience sent him out of the race with a 37th-place finish. It was his worst showing in the previous 10 races and ended an eight-race run as the No. 2 man in points. The last time he'd ranked below third was when he fell to fifth following the Bristol, Tenn., race in March, about six months ago.

Ryan Newman continued his torrid second-half run with a victory at Dover, his record seventh of the year. It also gave him a season sweep at the "Monster Mile" and marked him as the third driver to do so in 2003. Kurt Busch won both events at Bristol, Tenn., and Johnson did the same at Loudon, N.H.

How strong had Newman been as the season wore on? In the last 17 races he'd recorded 13 top-10 finishes, including 10 in the top five, of which six were wins. The run moved him from

(Above) Dale Earnhardt Jr. (8) draws up to the rear bumper of Greg Biffle's Ford, with Tony Stewart (20) and Terry Labonte (5) keeping the pair boxed in near the apron. Earnhardt was in the midst of slicing his way through the field after having to start 38th due to a pre-race inspection penalty.

(Right) The Budweiser crew hastily patches the front end of Earnhardt's Chevrolet after he made contact with Jeff Green on pit road during the day's first caution. Despite the damage, Earnhardt powered back to the front where he eventually beat everyone but teammate Michael Waltrip.

27th in points to fifth, and with 3,578 going into Talladega, he was 90 points behind Earnhardt Jr. and just 36 in front of Jeff Gordon.

A fifth-place run in Delaware was another sign that Gordon, sixth in points with 3,542, was breaking out of his recent frustrating slump. The run was his second top-10 finish in the last three races after he managed just one in the previous seven.

Despite finishing 31st at Dover, Bobby Labonte moved past Kurt Busch in points and into seventh in the standings from eighth. The two were tied in points coming into the Delaware event, but Labonte was able to slip past Busch, who finished six places lower then he did at Dover. Engine failure in his Ford gave Busch his worst finish in his last 10 starts and left him 21 points (3,372-3,294) behind Chevrolet-driving Labonte.

Despite finishing 20th at Dover – his poorest effort in his last nine starts – Terry Labonte, with 3,294 points, was able to stay ninth in points for the third consecutive week. Tony Stewart, the defending series champion, finished third at Dover and returned to the top 10 in the standings (he was 11th) after a two-week absence. Dover was his seventh top-five finish of the season, and with 3,291 markers, he was just three behind Labonte.

In Bud Pole qualifying, Elliott Sadler got the job done quickly – his No. 38 M&M's Ford was the second car on the track – but he had to wait until 47 other drivers made their runs to accept congratulations for his run of 189.943 mph. It was Sadler's second pole win of the year and second of his career.

While the nervous Sadler secluded himself in his motorhome, rookie Jamie McMurray grabbed the No. 2 starting spot with a speed of 189.395 mph in the No. 42 Havoline Dodge. Jimmie Johnson qualified third quickest, McMurray's teammate, Sterling Marlin, was fourth fastest and Jeff Gordon, Dale Jarrett, Ken Schrader, Casey Mears, Bill Elliott and Bobby Labonte rounded out the top 10.

Earnhardt's speed of 188.382 mph would have put him 11th on the starting grid, but his Chevrolet failed to pass its "physical." The car's rear quarter panels were 5/16-inch too low to the ground, and Earnhardt had to start 38th in the race.

That didn't faze him, though. He was one of 17 drivers who swapped the lead 41 times and

(Left) Michael Waltrip slides the NAPA Chevrolet into its pit stall for a two-tire change and a full tank of gas. An infraction by his crew, however, dropped Waltrip back in the field, a deficit he erased in 29 laps before driving to his second win of the season.

(Below) Tony Stewart tries to keep his Home Depot Chevrolet in front of the Ford of Kurt Busch and Jamie McMurray's Dodge. Although Stewart was not among the 17 drivers who took a turn at the point, he was able to hang near the front and post his second consecutive third-place finish.

he ended up finishing in second place, 0.95-second behind teammate Waltrip. It was Waltrip's second win of the year – the Daytona 500 was his first – and it was the ninth restrictor-plate victory for a DEI driver in the last 12 races dating to February 2001.

"It's so cool to get into a car like this and try to figure out how to beat the best in the world," Waltrip, who led six times for 16 laps, said. "As the race unfolded, I figured out a way to make the car run better."

Waltrip wasn't kidding. He made contact with Johnson on lap 143, causing Johnson to spin and bring out the third of five yellow flags for 23 laps. Waltrip pitted for gas and ended up going to the end of the longest line. His gasman had tried to add more fuel to the car after the catch-can man had taken away his container, which was an infraction. So Waltrip had to saw his way through the field, fend off several challenges – including one from Earnhardt Jr. – before he took the lead for the final time on lap 180.

(Right, Above) Michael Waltrip (15) takes the middle position with Kevin Harvick (29) on his right and Mike Wallace on the inside. Wallace, driving a Dodge for Phoenix Racing in his 12th start of the year, grabbed his second top-10 finish of the season, the other (a ninth) coming in the Daytona 500.

(Right, Below) The NAPA Chevrolet was one of several cars outfitted with the new "escape hatch," which Waltrip uses quite effectively in his triumphant emergence in front of the frontstretch grandstands. The win was Waltrip's second of the season and the fourth of his career, all with the use of restrictor plates.

Stewart, Newman and Gordon finished third through fifth. Pole winner Sadler barrel-rolled his car five times, bringing out the final yellow on lap 182, after he was tagged by Kurt Busch while trying to avoid Earnhardt. Sadler was taken to a hospital and later released with no injuries.

Waltrip finished the event in 3 hours, 12 minutes and 17 seconds at an average speed of 156.045 mph and won $157,090.

EA Sports 500 *final race results*

Fin. Pos.	Start Pos.	Car No.	Driver	Team
1	18	15	Michael Waltrip	NAPA Chevrolet
2	38	8	Dale Earnhardt Jr.	Budweiser Chevrolet
3	11	20	Tony Stewart	Home Depot Chevrolet
4	12	12	Ryan Newman	ALLTEL Dodge
5	5	24	Jeff Gordon	DuPont Chevrolet
6	39	97	Kurt Busch	Lenox/Irwin Ford
7	30	29	Kevin Harvick	GM Goodwrench Chevrolet
8	17	32	Ricky Craven	Tide Pontiac
9	33	2	Rusty Wallace	Miller Lite Dodge
10	23	09	Mike Wallace	Miccosukee Resort Dodge
11	10	18	Bobby Labonte	Interstate Batteries Chevrolet
12	34	31	Robby Gordon	Cingular Wireless Chevrolet
13	9	9	Bill Elliott	Dodge Dealers/UAW Dodge
14	20	22	Ward Burton	Caterpillar Dodge
15	24	90	John Andretti	AOL 9.0 Chevrolet
16	2	42	Jamie McMurray	Havoline Dodge
17	42	77	Dave Blaney	Jasper Engines & Transmissions Dodge
18	13	43	Jeff Green	Cheerios/Yu-Gi-Oh! Dodge
19	6	88	Dale Jarrett	UPS Ford
20	19	23	Kenny Wallace	Stacker2 Dodge
21	7	49	Ken Schrader	BAM Racing Dodge
22	14	5	Terry Labonte	Kellogg's/got milk? Chevrolet
23	15	6	Mark Martin	Viagra Ford
24	36	16	Greg Biffle	Grainger Ford
25	27	25	Joe Nemechek	UAW-Delphi Chevrolet
26	43	1	Jason Keller	Pennzoil Chevrolet
27	28	01	Mike Skinner	USG Sheetrock Pontiac
28	26	44	Christian Fittipaldi	Bugles Dodge
29	25	98	Jason Jarrett	C.H.I. Overhead Doors Ford
30	1	38	Elliott Sadler	M&M's Ford
31	29	74	Tony Raines	BACE Motorsports Chevrolet
32	40	99	Jeff Burton	CITGO Ford
33	37	17	Matt Kenseth	Smirnoff Ice Triple Black/DEWALT Ford
34	3	48	Jimmie Johnson	Lowe's Chevrolet
35	21	60	David Green	NetZero/Haas Automation Chevrolet
36	32	21	Ricky Rudd	Motorcraft Ford
37	8	41	Casey Mears	Target Dodge
38	22	19	Jeremy Mayfield	Dodge Dealers/UAW Dodge
39	4	40	Sterling Marlin	Coors Light Dodge
40	16	00	Buckshot Jones	Crown Fiber Communications Chevrolet
41	41	10	Johnny Benson	Valvoline Pontiac
42	31	7	Jimmy Spencer	Sirius Satellite Radio Dodge
43	35	14	Larry Foyt	Harrah's Dodge

BANQUET 400

October 5, 2003

The ALLTEL Dodge the crew at Penske Racing South put under Ryan Newman swept him to his eighth NASCAR Winston Cup Series victory of the 2003 season about as efficiently as did the Kansas tornado that picked up Dorothy and Toto and deposited them in the Land of Oz.

The verbal wind created when some of Newman's staunchest rivals questioned how he'd won again stirred things up, too, but more on that later.

As the circuit left Alabama's Appalachian foothills and headed toward the flat farmlands of America's heartland, the latest version of "silly season" was also creating a breeze.

Three topics of discussion kept the competitors busy chewing the fat:

* What was Bill Elliott going to do? Would he retire at the end of the year, keep racing full time in 2004 or perhaps compete on a part-time basis?

* Who did RCR Enterprises have in mind to fill the seat in the No. 30 AOL-sponsored Chevrolet next year? Several names had come up.

* Would Hendrick Motorsports find a new crew chief for Jeff Gordon and give Robbie Loomis his "walking papers?"

While the 48-year-old Elliott was still coyly mum, his team owner, Ray Evernham, said Oct. 3 he thought he'd have a "bunch of announcements" to make in perhaps two weeks. The future of Elliott's teammate, Jeremy Mayfield, was also a bit cloudy, with the driver saying he was approaching his future "week to week, race to race ... I ain't worried about it."

When team owner Richard Childress replaced Jeff Green with Steve Park back in May, everyone knew it was a "temporary" fix. By Kansas, Childress was saying he had to "make AOL happy," while Park noted it "was time to move on."

"We go out and do the best job we can with what we've got to work with."

Team owner Jack Roush watches stoically while Matt Kenseth's Ford is prepared for action at Kansas Speedway. After suffering engine failure the week before at Talladega and falling to 33rd, his worst finish of the season, Roush had every intention of getting his DeWalt juggernaut back on track quickly. It was, however, not to be.

Rumors had his possible replacements being Ward Burton, Scott Riggs – or Mayfield!

Gordon, the four-time series champion had, going into Kansas, just one victory for the year and was dealing with an on-and-off "slump" that was keeping him from challenging points leader Matt Kenseth. He, however, laughed off the idea that Loomis might be replaced. "I believe in Robbie, and I believe in the team we have," he said.

Gordon was far from the only driver to be frustrated by "Tool Man" Kenseth. At Talladega Superspeedway, the DeWALT Ford driver endured his worst finish of the year – 33rd because of engine failure – but he still came into the Kansas event with 4,227 points, 354 more than second-place driver Kevin Harvick. Kenseth, whose previous worst finish was 22nd at Martinsville, Va., had a three-race streak of top-10 finishes snapped in Alabama.

Harvick finished seventh at Talladega for his seventh top-10 showing in the last nine events. He also led four laps in the EA Sports 500 to extend his streak to seven consecutive races of leading laps and collecting bonus points. He also gained 82 points on Kenseth.

Dale Earnhardt Jr., because of a runner-up finish in Alabama, arrived in Kansas with 3,843 points, just 30 less than Harvick. The run was his best finish since winning at Talladega in April and it was his 11th top-five finish of the season. He

also led three laps in the EA Sports 500 to mark the fourth straight race he'd paced the field and picked up bonus points. The result: He moved up a spot in points from fourth to third.

Spinouts and engine woes at Talladega dropped Jimmie Johnson down to fourth in the standings from third. It was his worst finish in the last 16 times at bat and he trailed Earnhardt Jr. by 92 points going into the Banquet 400. Johnson, however, had been in the top 10 in points for a series-

(Above) Greg Biffle (16) tries to sneak to the inside of Terry Labonte (5), who also keeps Steve Park (30) at bay on his right.

(Left) Dale Earnhardt Jr. (8), with Mike Skinner on his right in the U.S. Army Pontiac, takes the starting field under the green flag to begin the Banquet 400. Earnhardt qualified third but moved up to the front row after pole winner Jimmie Johnson fell to the rear in his backup Lowe's Chevrolet.

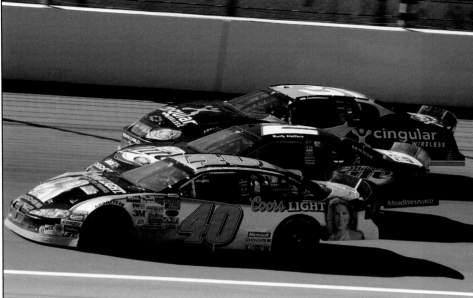

(Above) A busy pit road has Jimmie Johnson (48) in front of (in order) Greg Biffle, Jimmy Spencer and Kyle Petty. Aided by nine cautions during the race, Johnson was able to work from the back at the start to a decent seventh-place finish.

(Above Right) Sterling Marlin (40), Rusty Wallace (2) and Robby Gordon (31) use Kansas Speedway's smooth and wide surface to race three wide along the frontstretch. Wallace had recently found the consistency he had been lacking and notched his fifth straight top-10 finish, his 11th of the year.

(Right) Jeremy Mayfield awaits fresh Goodyears on a green-flag stop. His third place at Kansas continued his recent rally; it was his fifth top 10 in his last seven races after a dismal first half of the season.

leading 29 weeks, and he was the only driver to make that claim.

Newman, fifth in points with 3,738, finished fourth at Talladega for his fourth consecutive showing in the top 10, which was also his seventh top 10 in the last eight races. Although he didn't lead any laps in Alabama – it was only the second time in the last 12 races that happened – he remained fifth in points for the third straight week. He also closed to within 13 points of Johnson.

Gordon was beginning to smile again, thanks, in part, to a fifth-place finish at Talladega, where he led a race-high 47 laps. He left the track sixth in the standings for the third straight week, and

with 3,707 markers, was just 31 behind Newman and 44 in arrears of Johnson. Also, he was heading to a track where he'd won every race ever run there – two!

Despite getting caught up in a last-lap accident at Talladega, Bobby Labonte finished 11th in the race and kept his seventh-place spot in points for a second consecutive week. It marked his 20th straight week in the top 10, but with 3,528 points, he trailed Gordon by 179 and was just one ahead of Kurt Busch.

Busch's sixth-place run at Talladega was just his second top-10 showing in the previous eight contests, his 12th of the season and first since he

won at Bristol in August. However, the Roush driver had been in the top 10 all but one week the entire year.

Tony Stewart went into the 500-miler in Alabama 10th in points and he emerged ninth. In effect, he swapped spots with Terry Labonte. Stewart followed up a third-place run at Dover, Del., with another in Alabama, and he left the track with 3,456 points, 40 more than Labonte.

It turned out to be an up-and-down weekend in Kansas for Johnson. After notching the Bud Pole at a record time and speed on Oct. 3, he crashed his Chevrolet in a practice session the next day and had to start the Banquet 400 at the rear of the field in a backup car. In the race, he lost a lap early on, got it back because of the still-new "free-pass" rule and went on to finish seventh.

"When we walked in here today, Chad (Knaus, crew chief) had that look in his eye," Johnson said. "He was ready to win the pole, but I didn't think we'd go this fast."

"Fast" was a lap of 29.938 seconds at 180.373 mph around the 1.5-mile track, which easily eclipsed Earnhardt Jr.'s year-old mark of 177.924 mph. Mike Skinner was second quickest, in the U.S. Army Pontiac, with a run of 179.647 mph, and that bumped Earnhardt Jr. (179.581 mph) back to third on the grid.

Bobby Labonte and Rusty Wallace took starting spots four and five, while Jason Leffler, J. Gordon,

Bill Elliott, Jeff Green and Elliott Sadler rounded out the top 10 qualifiers.

The "Heartbreak of Qualifying" award went to point leader Kenseth, who crashed his primary car during a pre-qualifying practice session and had to dust off his backup Ford. His lap at 175.547 mph was way too slow and he had to take a provisional for a 37th-place start.

In a nutshell, the Banquet 400 turned out to be a movable feast for Newman and his "Dodge Boys." He started 11th, ran in the top 10 for about the first 80 laps and then fell off the charts until it mattered.

(Above) Bill Elliott (9) races alongside Jeff Green (43), who was making his third start for Petty Enterprises in the Cheerios Dodge. Elliott was by far the dominant driver of the day, leading 115 laps – 78 more than any other driver.

(Left) Elliott's crew sends their driver on his way while keeping an eye on their competition farther down pit road. Despite a great effort, Elliott was eventually confounded by Newman and was forced to settle for second place at the finish.

Ryan Newman (12) puts the nose of his fleet Dodge into the wind with the Intrepids of Jeff Green (43) and Jamie McMurray (42) on his flanks. Newman had the entire package at Kansas, allowing him to outrun and outlast his competition to take his eighth win of the season.

The race featured nine yellow-flag periods for 47 laps, and during the fifth, Newman and several others pitted for fuel and tires. When the race was interrupted again on lap 183, before it went green on lap 191 Newman pitted four times for tires and as much gas as could be packed into his car's fuel cell.

He was still behind the top 10 runners, but when the seventh caution went into effect on lap 202, most of the lead-lap cars pitted – but not Newman, who on lap 206 was in second place. Newman also stayed on the track through the eighth yellow-flag period. On lap 240 of 267, he passed Mayfield at the start/finish line and motored away.

Mayfield ceded second place to Bill Elliott 11 laps from the end, but Elliott could get no closer than 0.863-second to Newman at the finish. Mayfield finished third, Stewart was fourth and Gordon fifth.

Although several other drivers also rode the final 78 laps without stopping, it appeared no one could figure out how Newman could get about 5.4 miles per gallon and still be fast.

"We just beat them," Newman said. "We don't cheat. We go out and do the best job we can with what we've got to work with. When there's an opportunity to try and stretch it to the end, we try and stretch it to the end."

Newman completed the event in 3 hours, 17 minutes and 34 seconds at a record average speed of 121.630 mph. While others groused and grumbled, he accepted the winner's check of $191,000.

Banquet 400 *final race results*

Fin. Pos.	Start Pos.	Car No.	Driver	Team	Fin. Pos.	Start Pos.	Car No.	Driver	Team
1	11	12	Ryan Newman	ALLTEL Dodge	23	36	45	Kyle Petty	Georgia Pacific Dodge
2	8	9	Bill Elliott	Dodge Dealers/UAW Dodge	24	12	41	Casey Mears	Target Dodge
3	16	19	Jeremy Mayfield	Dodge Dealers/UAW Dodge	25	25	31	Robby Gordon	Cingular Wireless Chevrolet
4	14	20	Tony Stewart	Home Depot Chevrolet	26	35	74	Tony Raines	BACE Motorsports Chevrolet
5	7	24	Jeff Gordon	DuPont Chevrolet	27	9	43	Jeff Green	Berry Burst Cheerios Dodge
6	24	29	Kevin Harvick	GM Goodwrench Chevrolet	28	43	49	Ken Schrader	BAM Racing Dodge
7	1	48	Jimmie Johnson	Lowe's Chevrolet	29	2	01	Mike Skinner	U.S. Army Pontiac
8	15	42	Jamie McMurray	Havoline Dodge	30	6	0	Jason Leffler	NetZero Pontiac
9	5	2	Rusty Wallace	Miller Lite Dodge	31	26	23	Kenny Wallace	Stacker2 Dodge
10	19	21	Ricky Rudd	Motorcraft Ford	32	42	09	Mike Wallace	Miccosukee Resort Dodge
11	23	54	Todd Bodine	National Guard Ford	33	13	88	Dale Jarrett	UPS Ford
12	22	16	Greg Biffle	Grainger Ford	34	29	40	Sterling Marlin	Coors Light Dodge
13	33	99	Jeff Burton	CITGO Ford	35	20	10	Johnny Benson	Valvoline Pontiac
14	18	35	Bobby Hamilton Jr.	Wawa/Marines Ford	36	37	17	Matt Kenseth	DEWALT Power Tools Ford
15	27	7	Jimmy Spencer	Sirius Satellite Radio Dodge	37	30	25	Joe Nemechek	UAW-Delphi Chevrolet
16	34	5	Terry Labonte	Kellogg's/got milk? Chevrolet	38	41	37	Derrike Cope	GBROnline.com Chevrolet
17	4	18	Bobby Labonte	Banquet/Interstate Batteries Chevrolet	39	31	15	Michael Waltrip	NAPA Chevrolet
18	3	8	Dale Earnhardt Jr.	Budweiser Chevrolet	40	21	97	Kurt Busch	Rubbermaid Ford
19	40	1	John Andretti	Pennzoil Chevrolet	41	32	32	Ricky Craven	Tide Pontiac
20	38	6	Mark Martin	Viagra Ford	42	10	38	Elliott Sadler	Pedigree Ford
21	39	22	Ward Burton	Caterpillar Dodge	43	28	77	Dave Blaney	Jasper Engines & Transmissions Ford
22	17	30	Steve Park	America Online Chevrolet					

UAW-GM QUALITY 500

October 11, 2003

With 30 events in the books and just six left in the 2003 NASCAR Winston Cup Series season, it was fairly obvious that Matt Kenseth's dominating grasp on the series points standings was as tenacious now as it had been since he assumed it 27 races ago.

Kenseth's lock on the standings, however, was not yet all encompassing. Coming off a season-worst finish of 33rd at Talladega, Ala., the Roush Racing Ford driver had more foul luck in the Banquet 400 at Kansas Speedway when an early-race accident led to a 36th-place finish. Before that, he had just one finish outside the top 20 – 22nd at Martinsville, Va. – in his first 28 starts.

"It's about time ... the fans deserve to see the fastest car win the race for once."

Yet, coming into Lowe's Motor Speedway – the site of his first series career victory in May 2000 – with 4,282 points, he was still 259 up on Kevin Harvick. So, anything was still possible.

One thing that was settled, though, was Dale Earnhardt Jr.'s status with the team founded by his late father. On Oct. 9, it was announced Earnhardt Jr. had signed a five-year contract with the team, which was good through 2007, and that his sponsor, Budweiser, was soon expected to "re-up," too.

"I'm with the best team in the garage and that's priceless," Earnhardt Jr. said. "I feel like (it's) a pretty good deal. It's got everything both sides of the plate wanted. I can't complain."

In other news, Ricky Craven, driver of the No. 32 Tide Pontiac, inked a contract extension with PPI Motorsports that would keep him with owner Cal Wells II through 2006, and NASCAR Busch Series standout Brian Vickers would make his initial NASCAR Winston Cup Series appearance in the No. 25 Hendrick Motorsports Chevrolet at Atlanta in two weeks.

Tony Stewart (20) prepares the field for a lap-165 restart following the second of five cautions during the race. Ward Burton (22), leading the lap-down cars on the inside, had earlier announced he would be leaving the team after more than seven full seasons behind the wheel of the Caterpillar Dodge.

Also, Ward Burton would be leaving Bill Davis Racing to ink a deal with Haas CNC Racing. His replacement would be Scott Wimmer, who had won five NASCAR Busch Series races for Davis. Burton had been Davis' No. 1 driver since 1995 and had won five NWCS races, including the 2002 Daytona 500. Differences of opinion, though, had fractured the relationship, and Burton felt it was time to do something else.

Ranked second in points for the third consecutive week, Harvick, with 4,023 markers, finished sixth in Kansas for his third top-10 finish in a row and eighth in the previous 10 events. His recent surge allowed him make up 177 points on Kenseth, putting him closer than anyone had been

to the leader since early August.

With his future in the sport for the next few years now clear, Earnhardt Jr., third in points for the second consecutive week, trailed Harvick by 68 points and Kenseth by 325 heading toward his "home track" in Concord, N.C. It was the nearest in points he'd been to Kenseth since early August when he trailed by 258 following the road race at Watkins Glen, N.Y.

Ryan Newman seemed to be surviving the recent controversy over the apparently unexplainable fuel efficiency of his No. 12 Penske South Dodges and continued his tear as the most dominant driver in the season's second half. His series-leading eighth victory at Kansas was his fifth top-

(Far Left) A DeWalt crew member burns accumulated rubber off one of Matt Kenseth's used tires to take an accurate tread-depth reading.

(Left) Two-time Lowe's Motor Speedway winner Bobby Labonte (18) is chased by Bill Elliott, himself a double victor at the Concord, N.C., track. Both drivers took stints at the front of the field before settling into the top 10, with Elliott fourth and Labonte coming home sixth.

(Bottom) The field rumbles toward the initial green flag in front of 160,000 fans at Lowe's Motor Speedway to begin the UAW-GM Quality 500, the first time the event was run on Saturday under the lights.

trailed Newman by just 16 points heading to the speedway with his sponsor's name on the front gate – and a place where he dominated in May. He not only won the Coca-Cola 600, but also The Winston special non-points event the week before.

The Jeff Gordon of old emerged again in Kansas, as Hendrick Motorsports' unofficial lead driver finished fifth in Kansas City and held on to the No. 6 spot in points for a fourth straight week. He also finished fifth at Dover, Del., and Talladega, Ala., and with 3,862 points was just 40 behind his protegé but a healthy 217 in front of No. 7 man Bobby Labonte.

Labonte, despite finishing 17th at Kansas, retained his seventh-place ranking for the third consecutive week but took a dive in number of points behind Gordon and had teammate Tony Stewart breathing down his neck just 29 points behind. Stewart, with 3,616 points, displaced Kurt Busch by moving from ninth to eighth in the point race. The reigning champion registered his third consecutive top-five finish by finishing fourth at Kansas Speedway. Heading into the Lowe's Motor Speedway event, he was in his third straight week in the top 10 in points.

Kurt Busch matched his worst finish of 40th in the spring Atlanta race at Kansas because of engine failure, slipped a spot in points and trailed Stewart by 41. Terry Labonte finished 16th in Kansas but held onto the 10th spot in points by 79 over No. 11 Michael Waltrip. With 3,511 markers he left the Midwest 64 behind Busch and a distant 771 in arrears of Kenseth.

(Above) Matt Kenseth runs in front of Brian Vickers, who was making his NASCAR Winston Cup Series debut driving the Haas Automation Chevrolet. Kenseth, with an eighth-place performance, was able to "stop the bleeding" in the points that had resulted from finishes of 33rd and 36th in the previous two events.

(Right) Jeff Gordon (24) drifts up the banking a bit as Bill Elliott (9) and Jimmie Johnson try to gain ground on the inside. Both eventually did, with Johnson moving up to third at the finish ahead of Elliott in fourth, dropping Gordon back to fifth.

10 finish in a row, which included three wins. His success in Kansas City moved him up a spot in points from fifth to fourth, his career best ranking, and it was his series leading 13th top-five performance of the season. With 3,918 points, he trailed Kenseth by 364 and Earnhardt Jr. by just 39.

Jimmie Johnson finished a stout seventh at Kansas for his fifth top-10 finish in the previous seven contests but still slipped to fifth in points from fourth, a victim of Newman's surge. Johnson

If Secret deodorant's ad agency were to drop the second part of its signature slogan, "Strong enough for man. But made for a woman," the product might make an apt sponsor for Newman. After the Hoosier hotshot did it again – won a season-leading eighth Bud Pole Award to match his eight race wins – he was downright furtive in avoiding the obvious question, "What are you guys doing?"

Newman zipped around the 1.5-mile condo-enhanced speed plant in 28.930 seconds at 186.657 mph to claim his second straight Bud Pole and 15th in a 75-race career. Newman also broke the old track record speed of 186.464 mph, set by Johnson in May 2002.

Saturday night, Johnson did his best to leave Lowe's Motor Speedway with a total sweep of events for the year – he'd won the Coca-Cola 600 and The Winston in May – but the best he could do was lead the UAW-GM Quality 500 three times for 104 laps and finish third. Newman, the pole winner, tried again to use fuel mileage and tire management to his advantage in search of a ninth season victory, but after leading twice for 46 laps, he came up 0.608-second short.

The victor in an event that saw just five yellow-flag periods for 31 laps was defending NASCAR Winston Cup Series champion Stewart. The Home Depot Chevrolet driver was helped by fresher tires but said his second win of the year came simply

Gordon's speed of 186.207 mph, set in 29 seconds flat, was good enough for a second-place start in the 500-mile race, while Johnson, Bill Elliott and Kevin Lepage were third through fifth quickest.

"We're just doing what we think is right," a coy pole winner said when asked why the No. 12 ALLTELL Dodge was so fast and fuel efficient. "We were just happy to beat everybody. I didn't hold back on the first lap, but I gave it everything I had on the second. I had to really hang it out."

With that, the expression on his face resembled that of the Wal-Mart "smiley face."

"There's nothing wrong with grinning when you're winning," he said.

Stewart, Elliott Sadler, Todd Bodine, Harvick and Mike Skinner rounded out the top 10 in qualifying, while Ken Schrader, Hermie Sadler, Mark Green and Jeff Fultz failed to make the field.

because he had the quicker car.

Stewart chopped through the field like a reaper mowing down wheat and led six times for 149 of the scheduled 334 laps. Newman, who pitted a final time on lap 267, almost pulled off the win, but after Stewart made his stop on the 298th circuit, the fresh tires he received eventually paid off. Between laps 299 and 318, Stewart chopped about 7.5 seconds off Newman's lead, and when he passed him at the start-finish line on the 327th lap, the race was his.

"It's about time that the fastest car won the race with all this fuel mileage stuff all year," Stewart said. "The fans deserve to see the fastest car win the race for once."

It took 3 hours, 20 minutes and 34 seconds for Stewart complete the event at an average speed of 142.871 mph and take away the winner's share of $312,478.

Dale Earnhardt Jr. (8), with new contract in hand, challenges Todd Bodine in the National Guard Ford. With a ninth-place finish combined with Newman's second place, Earnhardt could feel the heat of the hot-running Penske Dodge driver, who left Charlotte just seven points back of Earnhardt in the standings.

(Above) After chopping nearly eight seconds off Newman's lead over just a 30-lap span, Tony Stewart is able to pull alongside the ALLTEL Dodge and challenge for the first position.

(Right) With just seven laps remaining, Stewart edged ahead coming off turn two and put his Home Depot Chevrolet solidly ahead for the final time.

(Far right) Stewart felt downright triumphant as he emerged from his car in victory lane after pulling to a 0.608-second margin of victory over Newman to take his second win of the year.

UAW-GM Quality 500 *final race results*

Fin. Pos.	Start Pos.	Car No.	Driver	Team
1	6	20	Tony Stewart	Home Depot Chevrolet
2	1	12	Ryan Newman	ALLTEL Dodge
3	3	48	Jimmie Johnson	Lowe's Chevrolet
4	4	9	Bill Elliott	Dodge Dealers/UAW Dodge
5	2	24	Jeff Gordon	DuPont Chevrolet
6	12	18	Bobby Labonte	Interstate Batteries Chevrolet
7	19	42	Jamie McMurray	Havoline Dodge
8	29	17	Matt Kenseth	Carhartt/DEWALT Ford
9	11	8	Dale Earnhardt Jr.	Budweiser Chevrolet
10	9	29	Kevin Harvick	GM Goodwrench Chevrolet
11	27	6	Mark Martin	Viagra Ford
12	32	19	Jeremy Mayfield	Dodge Dealers/UAW Dodge
13	14	2	Rusty Wallace	Miller Lite Dodge
14	30	15	Michael Waltrip	NAPA Chevrolet
15	33	40	Sterling Marlin	Coors Light Dodge
16	23	10	Johnny Benson	Zerex/Valvoline Pontiac
17	22	16	Greg Biffle	Grainger Ford
18	21	5	Terry Labonte	Kellogg's/got milk? Chevrolet
19	13	32	Ricky Craven	Tide Pontiac
20	37	99	Jeff Burton	CITGO Ford
21	5	4	Kevin Lepage	Kodak Perfect Touch Pontiac
22	16	88	Dale Jarrett	UPS Ford
23	39	21	Ricky Rudd	Rent-A-Center/Motorcraft Ford
24	34	77	Dave Blaney	Jasper Engines & Transmissions Ford
25	35	74	Tony Raines	Aaron's Dream Machine Chevrolet
26	25	7	Jimmy Spencer	75th Anniversary 3 Stooges/Sirius Dodge
27	36	43	Jeff Green	Betty Crocker/dinner made easy Dodge
28	38	22	Ward Burton	CAT Rental Stores Dodge
29	8	54	Todd Bodine	National Guard Ford
30	41	1	John Andretti	Pennzoil Chevrolet
31	40	25	Joe Nemechek	UAW-Delphi Chevrolet
32	18	23	Kenny Wallace	Stacker2 Dodge
33	20	60	Brian Vickers	Haas Automation Chevrolet
34	31	44	Christian Fittipaldi	Bugles Dodge
35	24	0	Jason Leffler	NetZero Pontiac
36	26	30	Steve Park	America Online Chevrolet
37	43	37	Derrike Cope	GBROnline.com/Friendly's Chevrolet
38	15	31	Robby Gordon	Cingular Wireless Chevrolet
39	10	01	Mike Skinner	U.S. Army Pontiac
40	42	45	Kyle Petty	Georgia Pacific/Dixie Dodge
41	17	97	Kurt Busch	Irwin/Lenox Ford
42	28	41	Casey Mears	Target/Energizer/Fujifilm Dodge
43	7	38	Elliott Sadler	M&M's Ford

SUBWAY 500

October 19, 2003

When a driver can arrive at a race track for a late-season event knowing that he has a ride locked in for at least the rest of the year, it's assumed he can breathe a little easier and run the event free of at least one distraction.

Joe Nemechek seemed to be a tentative example of that when he arrived at Martinsville (Va.) Speedway for the year's 32nd NASCAR Winston Cup Series race. Nemechek was preparing to run his last race in the No. 25 Hendrick Motorsports Chevrolet – NASCAR Busch Series driver Brian Vickers was slated to take the ride for the year's final four races – and at Atlanta he'd be behind the wheel of No. 01 MB2 Motorsports/U.S. Army Pontiac. Nemechek was replacing Mike Skinner, who had been filling in for the injured Jerry Nadeau, who was still recovering from a crash in May at Richmond, Va. The ride again would be his, in 2004, if he was ready, but until then, Nemechek was the team's driver of record.

> "I don't know what it is we hit on here this year, but right now I'm loving this place ... pretty much everything went right."

"The big thing is just getting the communications factor going, working with those guys," Nemechek said. "They've had different drivers in their cars this year. I think they're looking forward to having one guy they can get information and feedback from. I'm looking forward to being that guy."

Skinner had hoped to stay with MB2 through the rest of the season but ceded to Nemechek when he learned that the team was buying engines from Hendrick and that Vickers was originally supposed to be in the car for the final four 2003 races. Besides, he had inked a deal with the new Bang Racing team and would be returning full-time to the NASCAR Craftsman Truck Series in 2004.

Dale Earnhardt Jr. (8) chases Terry Labonte (5) through Martinsville's turn three. Labonte took the lead on the day's fourth caution when he elected not to pit and held the No. 1 position for 40 laps before the Budweiser Chevrolet driver caught him and assumed the point.

In related news, Johnny Benson had been dropped as the driver of the No. 10 Valvoline/MBV Pontiac (the team is co-owned by the principals of MB2 and the Valvoline brand) and it appeared that NASCAR Busch Series driver Scott Riggs would be the team's driver for 2004. Benson joined the team midway through 2000 and gave it one victory two years later. Riggs has four wins in NASCAR Busch Series racing and won five times in the NASCAR Craftsman Truck Series.

Did either Kevin Harvick or Dale Earnhardt Jr. stand any chance of catching series points leader Matt Kenseth and possibly challenging him for the 2003 championship? Theoretically, anything was possible going into Martinsville, but Kenseth's lead in the standings — he had 4,424 points vs. 4,157 for Harvick and 4,100 for Earnhardt Jr. — meant his rivals would have to go "flat out" for the rest of the season and hope Kenseth would encounter problems.

Kenseth, however, had ended a two-race downward skid with an eighth-place finish in the UAW-GM Quality 500 at Lowe's Motor Speedway, allowing him to pick up eight points on Harvick. After finishing 33rd at Talladega, Ala., and 36th at Kansas, the run at Charlotte was just what the No. 17 DeWalt-sponsored Ford driver needed.

At LMS, Harvick came home 10th for his fourth straight finish in the top 10. He also extended his grip on the No. 2 spot in points for the fourth consecutive week. Earnhardt Jr. finished one spot better than Harvick — and one lower than Kenseth — at LMS for his third top-10 showing in the previous five races, and for week No. 3, was third in points, 57 behind Harvick and a distant 324 in arrears of Kenseth.

Earnhardt also had to worry about Penske

Racing South's Ryan Newman, who, in the ALLTEL Dodge, came "calling" at LMS with a runner-up finish to Tony Stewart. The run was his sixth consecutive top-10 finish and ninth in the last 10 events – a tear that moved him from ninth to fourth in points. With 4,093 points, he was just seven behind Earnhardt Jr. and 64 in back of Harvick.

Jimmie Johnson, ranked fifth in points for the second straight week, finished third at LMS for his sixth top-10 effort in the last eight races. Included was a victory in New Hampshire. As he was just 21 points behind Newman and 28 in back of Earnhardt, he was helping to make things interesting in the final stretch.

Jeff Gordon, sixth in points with 4,017, had been a model of consistency in his last four races,

finishing fifth in each. The run in the UAW-GM 500 was his 12th top-five finish of the year, putting him just two behind Newman in that category. Also, he was looking to sweep both Martinsville races in the same season, something last accomplished by Rusty Wallace in 1994.

Defending series champion Stewart was in a good mood after winning at LMS. It was his second victory of the year, his fourth consecutive top-five effort and it advanced him from eighth to seventh in points. He, however, was just one point up on Bobby Labonte (3,801-3,800), who fell to eighth in the standings from seventh with a sixth-place run at Charlotte. Labonte had been seventh in the NASCAR Top 10 for three straight weeks but was heading to a track where he'd had a modicum of success in recent years.

Jeff Burton (99) holds his inside position ahead of Jeff Gordon in the DuPont Chevrolet, while Ward Burton (22) looks for a way to challenge on the outside. W. Burton, making his last start behind the wheel of the Caterpillar Dodge, did all he could to go out on a positive note by qualifying on the front row at Martinsville, but a tangle with Kenny Wallace before the midpoint of the race took him from winning contention.

Terry Labonte came into the nighttime run at LMS 10th in the standings and left in ninth. Although he ended up 18th in the UAW-GM 500, his fifth consecutive finish outside the front 15, he left in better shape than Kurt Busch, who was ninth in points but fell to 10th. Busch crashed out of the 500-miler, finishing 41st, but with 3,615 points was just five behind T. Labonte.

Three marks down, one to go: When Gordon notched the Bud Pole position for the Subway 500 with a lap of 20.220 seconds at 93.650, it was nowhere near the record mark (95.371 mph), set three years ago by Stewart, but it didn't really matter. He had won the spring event at Martinsville – from the pole – and now he was poised to notch a total sweep of events at the 0.542-mile track for the year.

"The laps were good and smooth, and I just tried to get as clean a (run) as possible on that last lap," Gordon said. "Temperatures cooled down a bit for qualifying. The last time we were here we picked up two-tenths (of a second) from where we practiced, and I was hoping we could do that again.

"That's exactly what we picked up."

Ward Burton raised quite a few eyebrows by lapping the track at 93.180 mph and taking the second starting position. It was also his best qualifying run of the year, which was ironic in that this would be his last race in the Bill Davis-owned Caterpillar Dodge. He was leaving the team before the year was out under less than ideal circumstance.

"It's been a hard week, but we'll go out there and give it the best we can for the last race," noted the laconic Virginian.

Earnhardt Jr. knocked off a lap of 93.015 mph for third place, and he was the only other driver to exceed the 93 mph mark. Kenny Wallace and Harvick were fourth and fifth quickest, respectively, while Jimmy Spencer, Rusty Wallace, Newman, Sterling Marlin and Jeff Green completed the fastest 10 in time trials.

After all the framin,' bammin,' loopin' and spinnin' was over the guy who was the center of

(Above) Dale Jarrett (88) fends off a challenge from Kevin Harvick in the GM Goodwrench Chevrolet. Jarrett, who started at the back of the field in a backup UPS Ford, battled all the way up to 11th after 500 laps, while Harvick started fifth and dropped to seventh at the finish.

(Below) Dale Earnhardt Jr. (8) and Bill Elliott (9) look for somewhere to go on the grooved concrete that makes Martinsville's 12-degree-banked corners. Earnhardt, in fourth at the finish, grabbed his fourth top 10 in the last six events, while Elliott's ninth place gave him three straight top-10 results.

Jeff Gordon (24) leads the way for Jimmie Johnson and Tony Stewart after a late-race restart. Gordon led the race two times for a dominating 313 laps, including the final 206, and gained his second win of the year, both coming at the Virginia short tack.

attention in victory circle had this to say: "What a great day for us, a great weekend. I wish we could race at Martinsville every weekend."

Yep, it was Gordon, who made a clean sweep of things for the year at the rural Henry County oval. Gordon led the first 107 laps and the final 206 to take a 1.036-second win over teammate Johnson. Gordon joined Busch (Bristol), Johnson (New Hampshire) and Newman (Dover) in winning both races at the same track in 2003, and he gave Chevrolet its first Martinsville sweep since Darrell Waltrip did way back in 1989.

Gordon, for the most part, avoided all the spin-outs that slowed the race 15 times for 119 laps. He took the lead away from Nemechek two laps after the 10th caution ended, made his last stop for service under the 11th, came back onto the track in first place and was never headed.

"I don't know what it is we hit on here this year, but right now I'm loving this place," he said. "I had a handling race car, great pit stops, and pretty much everything went right."

Gordon drove to his second win of the year in 3 hours, 53 minutes and 14 seconds at an average speed of 67.658 mph and won $183,018.

Subway 500 *final race results*

Fin. Pos.	Start Pos.	Car No.	Driver	Team
1	1	24	Jeff Gordon	DuPont Chevrolet
2	26	48	Jimmie Johnson	Lowe's Chevrolet
3	16	20	Tony Stewart	Home Depot Chevrolet
4	3	8	Dale Earnhardt Jr.	Budweiser Chevrolet
5	8	12	Ryan Newman	ALLTEL Dodge
6	31	5	Terry Labonte	Kellogg's/got milk? Chevrolet
7	5	29	Kevin Harvick	GM Goodwrench Chevrolet
8	17	42	Jamie McMurray	Havoline Dodge
9	28	9	Bill Elliott	Dodge Dealers/UAW Dodge
10	21	99	Jeff Burton	CITGO Ford
11	39	88	Dale Jarrett	UPS Ford
12	41	30	Steve Park	America Online Chevrolet
13	14	17	Matt Kenseth	DEWALT Power Tools Ford
14	23	6	Mark Martin	Viagra Ford
15	12	21	Ricky Rudd	Motorcraft Ford
16	4	23	Kenny Wallace	Stacker2 Dodge
17	35	41	Casey Mears	Target Dodge
18	2	22	Ward Burton	Caterpillar Dodge
19	19	16	Greg Biffle	Grainger Ford
20	22	25	Joe Nemechek	UAW-Delphi Chevrolet
21	11	01	Mike Skinner	U.S. Army Pontiac
22	18	49	Ken Schrader	SEM Products Dodge
23	33	74	Tony Raines	BACE Motorsports Chevrolet
24	10	43	Jeff Green	Cheerios/Betty Crocker Dodge
25	32	45	Kyle Petty	Georgia Pacific Dodge
26	15	15	Michael Waltrip	NAPA Chevrolet
27	34	0	Jason Leffler	NetZero Pontiac
28	38	38	Elliott Sadler	M&M's Ford
29	7	2	Rusty Wallace	Miller Lite Dodge
30	43	02	Hermie Sadler	James Madison University Pontiac
31	40	1	John Andretti	Pennzoil Chevrolet
32	27	32	Ricky Craven	Tide Pontiac
33	30	19	Jeremy Mayfield	Dodge Dealers/UAW Dodge
34	29	10	Johnny Benson	Valvoline Pontiac
35	24	4	Kevin Lepage	Kodak Pontiac
36	37	31	Robby Gordon	Cingular Wireless Chevrolet
37	25	77	Dave Blaney	Jasper Engines & Transmissions Ford
38	6	7	Jimmy Spencer	Sirius Satellite Radio Dodge
39	13	97	Kurt Busch	Rubbermaid Ford
40	36	54	Todd Bodine	National Guard/Subway Ford
41	20	18	Bobby Labonte	Interstate Batteries Chevrolet
42	42	37	Derrike Cope	PHM/Friendly's Chevrolet
43	9	40	Sterling Marlin	Coors Light Dodge

BASS PRO SHOPS
MBNA 500

October 27, 2003

Bill Elliott surprised some people ... er, sort of ... four days before the running of 33rd race of the 2003 NASCAR Winston Cup Series season at Atlanta Motor Speedway when he said he had an announcement to make.

The consensus was that the 48-year-old Georgian, who had been a part of the series since 1976, was at last going to tell the public about his plans for 2004 and beyond. Namely, was he going to make 2003 his final year in racing? Or would he run some sort of part-time schedule in 2004 with Evernham Motorsports and Dodge, perhaps combining it with a "farewell" tour?

Instead, the lanky redhead introduced a line of snack food bearing his name. On the bigger question, he was as coy as a Southern belle with her face obscured by a sunbonnet and church fan.

"If I had something to say, I'd tell you," Elliott said. "I don't have all the answers. When we do, then we'll be able to say something."

"This reminds me a little bit of 2000 where we ended the season on a real positive note ... "We're very excited about the way things are right now."

Team owner Ray Evernham said he had been feeling out several potential candidates for the seat in the No. 9 Dodge should Elliott retire, but he had no firm commitments from anyone. As for Elliott, he was not pressuring him or pushing him to make up his mind.

"I really don't think that he's jacking everyone around," Evernham said. "I'm not bugging him about it because he knows I have options. When he makes that decision, he'll let me know. I really don't believe he's made it yet."

The same day Elliott was telling people about his foray into the world of comestibles, Evernham and his other driver, Jeremy Mayfield, were publicly renewing their vows. Mayfield had "pursued

Jeff Gordon rolls to his third win of the season, his second in as many weeks. The victory extended his recent surge to six straight finishes of fifth or better and put him in position to gain valuable spots in the late-season point standings.

other options to see what was out there" (as did his boss), but the two got together Oct. 22, and Mayfield signed a contract renewal good through at least 2005.

"He (Evernham) and I are pretty strong-minded at times," Mayfield said. The more we talk, the better things are. When we don't talk, they're not good. What we had to do was sit down and talk things out."

Matt Kenseth, who came into the Atlanta 500-miler with a series-leading 23 top-10 finishes, had a mediocre day in Martinsville, Va., and finished 13th in the Subway 500. It was his third showing outside the top 10 in his last four starts, but the damage was minimal. He lost just 27 points to Kevin Harvick, and with just four races left had a lead of 240 points over the No. 2 man in the race

for the crown. With 4,548 markers in his wallet, Kenseth had now been the leader for 29 straight weeks.

Harvick survived the rigors of the Subway 500 with a seventh-place finish and headed to Georgia with 4,308 points. The run at Martinsville was his fifth consecutive top-10 finish, and he trimmed 223 points off his deficit during the run. To his credit, the RCR Enterprises pilot had been ranked second in points for the fifth week in a row.

Dale Earnhardt Jr., third in points for the fourth consecutive week, had a productive day at the Martinsville half-miler, finishing fourth. The showing there marked his 12th top-five finish of the season and his fourth top 10 in the last six races. At Martinsville, he led twice for 61 laps, marking the seventh straight race in which he'd earned bonus points. With 4,265 points, he was 45 behind Harvick and 283 in back of the leader.

Ryan "Winning Man" Newman had another victory elude him in Virginia, but he did register a series-leading 15th top-five finish with a fifth-place performance that gave him a points total of

4,248. It was also his fifth straight top-five and sixth in his last seven starts, which includes three wins. He, however, did not lead a lap in the Subway 500, marking only the third time in the last 15 events he hadn't earned any bonus points.

Jimmie Johnson was the "first loser" at Martinsville, finishing second to teammate Jeff Gordon, for his fifth top-10 performance in the last six races. With 4,242 points, he held onto fifth place in the championship standings for the third week in a row and edged to within six points of Newman and 23 of Earnhardt. Heading to Atlanta, Johnson was the only driver to stay in the top 10 in points for the entire season.

If anyone had to be in a great mood going into the MBNA 500, it was four-time champion Jeff Gordon, who captured both the pole and the race at Martinsville, Va., giving him a clean sweep of both NASCAR Winston Cup events and pole starts there for the year. The win, his second of the season, was his 13th top-five effort of the year and fifth in a row. With 4,202 points, Gordon held on to the sixth spot in the standings for as many

(Top Left) With his NASCAR Winston Cup Series debut at Charlotte behind him, Brian Vickers came to Atlanta ready to take the wheel of his full-time ride for 2004, the No. 25 Chevrolet from Hendrick Motorsports.

(Top Right) Everything was a "go" for Ward Burton at Atlanta as he climbed into the cockpit of the NetZero Pontiac after finishing his tenure with Bill Davis Racing last week at Martinsville.

(Above Left) Dale Earnhardt Jr. was wondering if he could continue his recent hot spell and close the gap in the standings on second-place Kevin Harvick over the final four races of the season.

(Above) Bill Elliott confers with crew chief Mike Ford regarding his setup at Atlanta. Although the media was more interested in Elliott's plans for the future, Bill was determined to build on strong runs of late and try to capture a win before the season drew to a close.

(Below) Ryan Newman (12) takes charge in the early laps ahead of Bobby Labonte and Dale Earnhardt Jr. Newman posted his ninth Bud Pole of the season in grand fashion by turning the fastest lap of the year, 194.295 mph, and had a good run going before his day came to an abrupt end when he was tagged by Earnhardt Jr. in the closing laps.

(Below Right) Crew members retreat down pit road to attend to their drivers and cars as the rain begins falling on Sunday afternoon. The precipitation forced officials to complete the 500-mile distance on Monday.

(Bottom) Joe Nemechek stops for service in the U.S. Army Pontiac from MB2 Motorsports. Nemechek made his first run in the car at Atlanta and had a solid performance, qualifying eighth and finishing 10th.

straight weeks and put him within striking distance of the three drivers in front of him.

Joe Gibbs Racing teammates Tony Stewart and Bobby Labonte held onto the seventh and eighth spots, respectively, in the chase for the championship following the 500-lap event at Martinsville. Stewart finished third in the Subway 500 for his fifth consecutive top-five finish and left the track with 3,971 points, 231 behind Gordon. The five-race tear also pushed him from No. 11 to No. 7 in points for the second consecutive week.

Labonte, thanks to a blown engine in his Chevrolet, ended up with a disastrous 41st-place finish in Virginia but managed to hold onto the No. 8 spot for another week. It matched his second-worst showing of the year – the Daytona 500 – and he trailed Stewart by 131 points. He however, was heading to a track where he'd won four of the last seven fall races.

En route to a sixth-place finish in the Subway 500, Terry Labonte might have left a little milk in his pits for the silent Elliott. Labonte ended a five-race run without a top-10 finish in his best showing since winning the Southern 500 at Darlington in August. It also marked his seventh straight week in the NASCAR top 10, and heading to "Hotlanta" he trailed his brother by just 65 points.

Elliott, with a finish of ninth in Virginia, collected his third showing of 10th or better in a row and shot from 12th to 10th in points. With 3,685 markers in his wallet, the "ol' redhead" had also cracked the top 10 for the first time in over a year.

The one thing Elliott couldn't do, though, was "crack" the Bud Pole position for the Bass Pro Shops 500. The best he could coax out of his Dodge was a lap at 192.969 mph, which put him

fifth on the starting grid. That was nowhere near Newman's pole-winning run of 194.295 mph, which also happened to be the fastest lap anyone in the series had run all year, as well as his ninth Bud Pole of the season.

"That dadgum Ryan, I can't beat him," Elliott groused. "I'm just glad (qualifying) is over."

Bobby Labonte was the only other driver to come anywhere near the Dodge-driving wunderkind. He took the No. 2 starting spot at 194.016, while Dale Earnhardt came in third at 193.319. Brian Vickers got his feet wet in NWCS

competition with a fourth-place effort of 193.272, while Elliott Sadler, Todd Bodine, Joe Nemechek, Johnson and Harvick rounded out the fastest 10 qualifiers.

In the race, 12 drivers swapped the lead 28 times and Newman, Harvick, Earnhardt Jr. and Elliott Sadler paced the first 36 laps. Rain then brought out the second of 10 yellow flags for 63 of 325 laps, and that yellow turned to red when it became obvious the wet stuff wasn't going away.

The event was resumed Monday morning and the drivers got down to business. Stewart led the

(Above) Jeremy Mayfield (19) and Jimmy Spencer (7) match their Dodge Intrepids in their tussle for position. Mayfield celebrated his contract extension with Ray Evernham with his 10th top-10 finish of the season, a seventh, while Spencer posted his fourth top 10, this time in ninth.

(Left) Kevin Harvick (29) moves to the outside to challenge Bobby Labonte (18), while Tony Stewart and Bill Elliott try to close in from behind. Atlanta master Labonte led on six occasions, but could do no better than fifth over the final laps.

Jeff Gordon (24) stays squarely in front of Jimmy Spencer (7) while he chases Dale Earnhardt Jr. (8) from behind. Gordon and Earnhardt each took five turns at leading, but it was Gordon who climbed from his car to the cheers of his teammates in victory lane (below right).

most laps – 109 vs. 66 for B. Labonte and 55 for Gordon – but at the finish it was Gordon at the stripe for his second straight win and third of the year. Stewart was closing in during the waning laps, but when Newman was tagged by Earnhardt Jr. on lap 322, and crashed, the race was slowed for the last time and ended under the yellow.

Officially, Gordon took 3 hours, 55 minutes and 2 seconds to win at an average speed of 127.769 mph. In racing, overnight delays don't count.

"This reminds me a little bit of 2000 where we ended the season on a real positive note," said Gordon who collected $249,978. "We're very excited about the way things are right now."

Bass Pro Shops MBNA 500 *final race results*

Fin. Pos.	Start Pos.	Car No.	Driver	Team		Fin. Pos.	Start Pos.	Car No.	Driver	Team
1	19	24	Jeff Gordon	DuPont Chevrolet		23	38	99	Jeff Burton	CITGO Ford
2	24	20	Tony Stewart	Home Depot Chevrolet		24	30	10	Johnny Benson	Valvoline Pontiac
3	9	48	Jimmie Johnson	Lowe's Chevrolet		25	25	45	Kyle Petty	Georgia Pacific Dodge
4	5	9	Bill Elliott	Dodge Dealers/UAW Dodge		26	43	49	Ken Schrader	1-800-CallATT Dodge
5	2	18	Bobby Labonte	Interstate Batteries Chevrolet		27	36	35	Bobby Hamilton Jr.	U.S. Marine Corps/Wawa Ford
6	3	8	Dale Earnhardt Jr.	Budweiser Chevrolet		28	14	41	Casey Mears	Target Dodge
7	15	19	Jeremy Mayfield	Dodge Dealers/UAW Dodge		29	1	12	Ryan Newman	Mobil 1/ALLTEL Dodge
8	17	97	Kurt Busch	Rubbermaid/Sharpie Ford		30	28	23	Kenny Wallace	Stacker2 Dodge
9	22	7	Jimmy Spencer	Sirius Satellite Radio Dodge		31	42	21	Ricky Rudd	U.S. Air Force/Motorcraft Ford
10	8	01	Joe Nemechek	U.S. Army Pontiac		32	41	22	Scott Wimmer	Caterpillar Dodge
11	37	17	Matt Kenseth	Smirnoff Ice Triple/DEWALT Ford		33	32	5	Terry Labonte	Kellogg's/got milk? Chevrolet
12	31	88	Dale Jarrett	The UPS Store Ford		34	27	16	Greg Biffle	Grainger Ford
13	29	0	Ward Burton	NetZero Pontiac		35	26	32	Ricky Craven	Tide Pontiac
14	12	4	Kevin Lepage	Kodak Perfect Touch Pontiac		36	20	30	Steve Park	America Online Chevrolet
15	18	42	Jamie McMurray	Havoline Dodge		37	35	77	Dave Blaney	Jasper Engines & Transmissions Ford
16	40	40	Sterling Marlin	Coors Light Dodge		38	13	15	Michael Waltrip	NAPA Chevrolet
17	6	38	Elliott Sadler	M&M's Ford		39	39	6	Mark Martin	Viagra Ford
18	33	74	Tony Raines	BACE Motorsports Chevrolet		40	23	37	Derrike Cope	PHM/Friendly's Chevrolet
19	21	2	Rusty Wallace	Miller Lite Dodge		41	34	02	Hermie Sadler	Zapf Creations Chevrolet
20	10	29	Kevin Harvick	GM Goodwrench Chevrolet		42	7	54	Todd Bodine	National Guard Ford
21	16	31	Robby Gordon	Cingular Wireless Chevrolet		43	4	25	Brian Vickers	UAW-Delphi Chevrolet
22	11	1	John Andretti	Pennzoil Chevrolet						

CHECKER AUTO PARTS 500
presented by Havoline

November 2, 2003

Perhaps you can it up to the normal tension that tends to build up as a long and competitive NASCAR Winston Cup Series season winds to a conclusion, but it seems that along the way somebody always runs afoul of a rule or two and the result in some sort of sanction.

A lapse in judgment on the part of driver Kurt Busch during the Subway 500 in Martinsville, Va., caught up with the Roush Racing driver a few days later when NASCAR officials revoked his annual credential or "hard card" for actions detrimental to racing. During the race, Busch's Ford developed an oil leak. When he entered pit road he purposely, according to NASCAR, "spun the car around in a reckless manner," causing people to jump out of his way. Busch was summoned to the NASCAR mobile office after the race but, for whatever reason, failed to appear.

> "What a great day! It's been so long since we've won an 'open' race ... We've run so well this year and have come so close a bunch of times."

Hence, at the Atlanta event, his credential was cancelled for the rest of the season. That meant Busch had to pick up a paper credential at the NASCAR Registration trailer and a separate "Hot" garage pass at the NASCAR trailer for all remaining races.

Ward Burton's debut in the No.0 Haas CNC Racing Pontiac at Atlanta was less than auspicious. Inspectors found an unapproved modification to car's carburetor during an opening-day inspection, and team crew chief Tony Furr was socked with a $25,000 fine. Burton was docked 25 driver points, while team while Gene Haas lost as many owner points.

The crowd of over 100,000 on hand for the Checker Auto Parts 500 spills onto the nearby hillside next to beautiful Phoenix International Raceway in Avondale, Ariz.

NASCAR
Winston Cup
Series

Pontiac's first NASCAR Winston Cup Series victory came on Feb. 17, 1957 when Cotton Owens drove one to victory in a 160-mile event on the long-defunct Beach & Road Course in Daytona Beach, Fla. Unless a Pontiac driver could win one of the three remaining races in 2003, Ricky Craven, who won at Darlington, S.C., in March, would go down in history as the final driver to bring the make into an NWCS victory lane. That's because, on Oct. 24, a General Motors spokesman announced Pontiac would be pulled from competition for good at the end of the year.

No concrete reason was given, but in so many words, it appeared Pontiac might cease producing passenger cars that could qualify as being "NASCAR legal." The series teams affected by GM's decision - all whom tentatively were expected to switch to Chevrolet in '04 - were Haas CNC'; Morgan-McClure; PPI; MBV and MB2.

Chevrolet drivers Dale Earnhardt Jr. and Kevin Harvick were getting a bit edgy. No matter how hard they tried, neither could get near enough pointswise to pose a threat to the No. 17 DEWALT Power Tools Ford pilot Matt Kenseth.

Kenseth, with a series-leading 23 top-10 finishes in 33 starts, just missed another by finishing 11th in the rain-delayed MBNA 500 at Atlanta. Going into the one-mile track in Phoenix,

(Above) Ryan Newman (12), starting in the No. 1 position for the 10th time in 2003, leads the field through turns three and four before taking the green flag to begin 312 laps on the one-mile Phoenix oval. Starting next to Newman is Brian Vickers, who bested 41 other drivers in just his third career NASCAR Winston Cup Series qualifying run.

(Left) Veterans Ricky Rudd (21) and Jeff Burton race side by side through the low-banked turns at PIR. Burton, who won back-to-back races here in 2000-01, put together a much-needed top-10 finish, just his second in the last eight races.

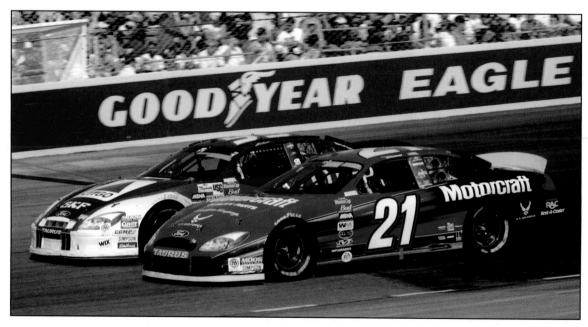

(Above) Matt Kenseth (17) chases his teammate and car co-owner, Mark Martin, into the first turn. Both Roush drivers posted top-10 results in the race, with Martin taking 10th and Kenseth climbing all the way to seventh after starting the event from the first provisional spot, in 37th.

(Below) Michael Waltrip (15) takes a single-file pack into the first turn at speed. Waltrip did not lead a lap, but did drive to fifth at the finish in his bid to regain a top-10 spot in the points before the end of the season.

Harvick's run of five consecutive top-10 finishes came to an end at Atlanta, where he ended up 20th. It marked just the third time in the last 13 events he was not 10th or better, and it was his worst finish since he ran 25th at Pocono, Pa., in July. On the up side, going into the "Valley of the Sun" he was just four points behind Earnhardt.

Jimmie Johnson's third-place run at Atlanta was his third consecutive top-five performance and sixth in the front 10 in the last seven races. After spending the last three weeks ranked fifth in points, he moved up to fourth with 4,412 markers. He also remained the only driver to stay in the top 10 from the first race to the present.

The Georgia rain most certainly was no pain for Jeff Gordon, who won the 500-miler there for his third victory of the year and second in a row. Atlanta was his 14th top-five effort of the year. After six consecutive weeks at No. 6, he moved up to fifth in points with 4,382 and positioned himself to gain even more in the final three events of the season. Heading to Phoenix, he was only 30 points behind Johnson, 34 in back of Harvick and 38 in arrears of Earnhardt Jr.

Ryan Newman's luck ran a bit short at Atlanta because of a late-race accident and he dove from fourth to sixth in points. The finish marked only the third time in the last 16 events he had not posted a top-10 effort, and he now found himself with 4,329 points, 53 behind Gordon and 83 in back of Johnson.

his point lead over Earnhardt Jr. was 258 (4,678-4,416) and 262 more than third-ranked Harvick. For Kenseth to clinch the championship prior to the season finale at Homestead, Fla., he'd have to exit Phoenix with a lead of 371 points or make sure the spread was 186 following the penultimate event in Rockingham, N.C.

Earnhardt Jr. finished sixth at Atlanta for his fourth top-10 effort in the previous five races. After spending the last four weeks ranked third in points, he dislodged Harvick and jumped up one spot. Earlier in the season, he held onto the No. 2 spot for 17 weeks.

Teammates Tony Stewart and Bobby Labonte, with 4,151 and 4,000 points, respectively remained seventh and eighth in the standings. Stewart continued his late-season roll with a runner-up finish to Gordon at Atlanta, his sixth consecutive top-five run. During the stretch that began at Dover, Del., he won at Lowe's Motor Speedway, finished second once, third three times and fourth once. Going into Phoenix, he trailed Newman by 178 points.

Labonte ran fifth at Atlanta for his second top-10 finish in the previous three races. The performance was his 11th top five of the season and first since he ran fifth at Daytona in July.

After finishing fourth at Atlanta, Bill Elliott upped his points total to 3,845 and moved up a spot in points from 10th to ninth. The Atlanta result was fourth consecutive top-10 finish and his eighth in the top five for the year. He left Georgia trailing B. Labonte by 155 points and had to keep an eye on Bobby's older sibling, Terry. The older Labonte's 33rd-place showing at Atlanta was his worst showing since finishing 39th at Bristol, Tenn., in March and he slipped from ninth to 10th in points. He, however, was just six points behind Elliott and felt good about the upcoming event in Phoenix.

Newman somewhat made up for whatever heartbreak he felt at Atlanta by taking center stage in the desert. In Bud Pole qualifying, he toured the one-mile oval in 26.931 seconds at 133.675 mph and secured the No. 1 starting spot for the race. The pole was his season-record 10th and 17th in a 78-race career. It was also the third time in the previous four events, the No. 12 ALLTEL Dodge landed on the inside front row.

"Three of the last four? I didn't think about it," Newman said. "But it doesn't get old. It will always be a great confidence builder for the team.

"It doesn't get old."

His rivals - especially those in the Hendrick Motorsports stable - might wish it would "get old" for the Penske South flash. The Hendrick trio of rookie Brian Vickers, Johnson and Gordon were the second through fourth fastest qualifiers, respectively, and Vickers' lap speed of 133.640 mph was impressive.

Rusty Wallace secured the fifth spot on the starting grid, while the top 10 were rounded out by Stewart, Busch, Dave Blaney, Casey Mears and Joe Nemechek. Derrike Cope and Brandon Ash failed to qualify, and none of the starters were bumped to the rear of the field.

At the end of the 312-lap event, it was a smiling Earnhardt Jr. - heck he was grinning like Alice's Cheshire cat! - in victory lane. That it was his ninth career victory and second of the year was notable. What was news, though, was it was his first victory in a non-restrictor-plate event since Dover, Del., in September 2001.

"What a great day! It's been so long since we've won an 'open' race," Earnhardt said. "We've run so well this year and have come so close a bunch of times."

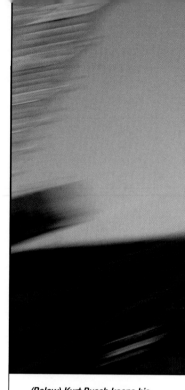

(Below) Kurt Busch keeps his Rubbermaid Ford in front of Jimmie Johnson's Lowe's Chevrolet and the ALLTEL Dodge of Ryan Newman. Busch led 98 of the first 173 laps and took the lap-leader bonus but yielded positions to Johnson and Newman in the second half of the race.

Dale Earnhardt Jr.'s No. 8 Chevrolet was a blur over the second half of the race as he set out in pursuit of the leaders. Over the last 100 laps, Earnhardt showed great skill and patience while tracking down then-leader Jimmie Johnson. With 51 laps to go, the Budweiser Chevrolet moved inside the Lowe's Monte Carlo at the end of the backstretch and took the point for good, giving Earnhardt his second win of the year, the ninth of his career.

Earnhardt took on four tires on lap 211 during the race's six of 10 cautions for 66 laps and was set from thereon out. He had led lap 39 and laps 86-120, and when he passed Johnson on the backstretch during the 262nd circuit, the event was his. Johnson was 0.735-second behind at the finish, and he was trailed by Newman, Busch and teammate Michael Waltrip.

Earnhardt completed the event in 3 hours, 19 minutes and 11 seconds at an average speed of 93.984 mph and left the desert track $203,017 richer.

Checker Auto Parts 500 presented by Havoline *final race results*

Fin. Pos.	Start Pos.	Car No.	Driver	Team	Fin. Pos.	Start Pos.	Car No.	Driver	Team
1	11	8	Dale Earnhardt Jr.	Budweiser Chevrolet	23	43	4	Kevin Lepage	Kodak Perfect Touch Pontiac
2	3	48	Jimmie Johnson	Lowe's Chevrolet	24	8	77	Dave Blaney	Jasper Engines & Transmissions Ford
3	1	12	Ryan Newman	ALLTEL Dodge	25	26	23	Kenny Wallace	Stacker2 Dodge
4	7	97	Kurt Busch	Rubbermaid/Sharpie Ford	26	23	09	Mike Wallace	Miccosukee Resort Dodge
5	17	15	Michael Waltrip	NAPA Chevrolet	27	34	49	Ken Schrader	BAM Racing Dodge
6	37	17	Matt Kenseth	DEWALT Power Tools Ford	28	32	14	Larry Foyt	Harrah's Dodge
7	4	24	Jeff Gordon	DuPont Chevrolet	29	39	88	Dale Jarrett	UPS Ford
8	27	99	Jeff Burton	CITGO Ford	30	19	5	Terry Labonte	Kellogg's/got milk? Chevrolet
9	28	22	Scott Wimmer	Caterpillar Dodge	31	10	01	Joe Nemechek	U.S. Army Pontiac
10	12	6	Mark Martin	Viagra Ford	32	31	31	Robby Gordon	Cingular Wireless Chevrolet
11	15	40	Sterling Marlin	Coors Light Dodge	33	5	2	Rusty Wallace	Miller Lite Dodge
12	22	42	Jamie McMurray	Havoline Dodge	34	13	29	Kevin Harvick	GM Goodwrench Chevrolet
13	2	25	Brian Vickers	UAW-Delphi Chevrolet	35	36	45	Kyle Petty	Georgia Pacific/Brawny Dodge
14	18	9	Bill Elliott	Dodge Dealers/UAW Dodge	36	24	18	Bobby Labonte	Interstate Batteries Chevrolet
15	25	16	Greg Biffle	Grainger Ford	37	42	43	Jeff Green	Cheerios Dodge
16	33	1	John Andretti	Pennzoil Chevrolet	38	38	32	Ricky Craven	Tide Pontiac
17	30	21	Ricky Rudd	Motorcraft Ford	39	40	30	Steve Park	America Online Chevrolet
18	6	20	Tony Stewart	Home Depot Chevrolet	40	29	7	Jimmy Spencer	Sirius Satellite Radio Dodge
19	41	74	Tony Raines	BACE Motorsports Chevrolet	41	20	0	Ward Burton	NetZero Pontiac
20	14	38	Elliott Sadler	Pedigree Ford	42	9	41	Casey Mears	Target Dodge
21	35	10	Johnny Benson	Valvoline Pontiac	43	16	19	Jeremy Mayfield	Dodge Dealers/UAW Dodge
22	21	54	Todd Bodine	National Guard Ford					

POP SECRET MICROWAVE POPCORN 400

November 9, 2003

As is not that unusual in a sport filled with highs and lows, for some NASCAR Winston Cup Series race teams, the 2003 season had, with only two events left, been one rife with success and pleasant surprises. For others, however, the year had been long and arduous with more missed opportunities, lack of luck and disappointment than seemed to be fair.

One team in the latter category was Robert Yates Racing, founded in Charlotte in the late 1980s and now headquartered in suburban Mooresville, N.C. Its "lead" driver, Dale Jarrett, who had given team owner Robert Yates a series championship in 1999, found himself with just one victory in 2003 and mired 26th in points. Elliott Sadler, brought in to replace Ricky Rudd at the first of the year, was just three spots higher than Jarrett in points and surprisingly had won nothing.

> "I'm going to retire eventually ... but as good as we're running right now ... it makes it harder in one respect. I still feel good ... ."

Jobs were changed and people left but nothing seemed to work. Engine specialist Doug Yates (the owner's son) started the season as the team's general manager but, shortly before the 34th event of the season at Rockingham, he went back to the engine room while veteran racer Eddie D'Hondt was brought in as the new GM. Yates also promised more changes and swore he'd have his operation up to snuff, at least by the start of the 2004 season.

"Silly Season" rumors also swirled around supposed driver and other changes at Richard Childress Racing. The fate of drivers Ken Schrader and Tony Raines, among others, was a continued topic of discussion and, of course, there was the "what will Bill Elliott do" story, which refused to go away.

Even Elliott's team owner, Ray Evernham, was beginning to wonder what his organization would look like in 2004. Hence a ray of sunshine cast aside some of the "shadows of doubt," when Elliott and his Dodge team performed flawlessly on Nov. 8 and won the 36th

Bill Elliott gives a victory wave to the Rockingham faithful after he and his team completed a nearly perfect weekend. Elliott not only won his first race of the season, the 44th of his storied career, but his crew captured pit-road bragging rights by winning the Union 76/Rockingham World Pit Crew Championship held on Saturday.

NASCAR
Winston Cup
Series

USG

BNA

ACK
SE

M

NASCAR
RACE CAR
NASCAR
Winston Cup

Bud
POLE AWARD

MECHANIX WEAR

WM
WASTE MANAGEMENT

Holley
HP CARBS

GOODYEAR
BELTS & HOSE

ESEL
GRAMES

DGE

SIEMENS

SIEMENS

Valvoline

EVERNHAM
MOTORSPORT

PPG

UAW

9

annual Union 76/Rockingham World Pit Crew Competition. Led by crew chief Mike Ford, Elliott's crew, completed a four-tire, 14-gallon stop in a record 16.725 seconds.

The win was special in that it was the last such contest. Always held at Rockingham the day before the track's fall event and sponsored since the first by the producers of Union 76 racing

gasoline, the race itself had been eliminated from the schedule and the fuel supplier was leaving the sport at year's end.

"What's really neat is this is something I knew (the team) wanted to do," Evernham said. "It's a goal they set several months ago, and here they sit today. I'm really proud of them."

It was also a portent of things to come. In yet another "Cinderella story," Elliott would go on to win the race itself the next day. It would be his first series victory since August 2002, 50 races ago, and would come at the track where he made his NWCS debut in 1976.

With 4,828 points going into the Pop Secret 400, Matt Kenseth, discounting incredibly horrible luck, all but had a lock on the 2003 NASCAR Winston Cup Series championship. There were several combinations that would hand

(Above Left) Larry Foyt (14) chases Matt Kenseth's DeWalt Ford into the turns. Kenseth, who qualified 23rd for the race, did not lead a lap during the day but stayed close to the front and picked up a solid fourth-place finish, easily good enough clinch the title.

(Below Left) Jeremy Mayfield (19) gets a solid jump on the rest of the lead-lap cars on the restart following the fourth of 10 cautions during the day. Ward Burton (0), in second on the restart, dives to the inside while the rest of the lead-lap cars are caught on the outside.

(Below) Sterling Marlin (4) holds his own with Michael Waltrip (15) and a double-wide pack bearing down from behind. Marlin took 10th on the day, his first top 10 the last 15 events.

(Far Right) The CITGO crew hustles through a tire change for their driver, Jeff Burton. The team appeared to be gaining momentum in the late season, posting a seventh place at Rockingham, their third top 10 in the last four events.

him the title, but basically all he had to do in the next two races was average 72 points per race; finish 30th or better; lead a lap and finish 31st or better or lead the most laps and finish 33rd or better. If he could extend his point lead to at least 186 after Rockingham, none of that would matter. The crown would be his.

Kenseth's nearest challengers heading to "The Rock" were Dale Earnhardt Jr. (4,600 points), Jimmie Johnson (4,587) and Jeff Gordon (4,528), meaning the battle for the runner-up spot in the standings was still shaking out. Earnhardt Jr. remained second in points after winning at Phoenix, Ariz., and had scored four straight top-10 finishes beginning recently at Lowe's Motor Speedway.

Johnson finished second to Earnhardt Jr. at Phoenix and had climbed from fourth to third in

points. He'd scored five straight top-10 finishes, extending a streak that began at Kansas, and had been ranked in the NASCAR Top 10 in all 34 races run to date.

With a seventh-place showing in the Checker Auto Parts 500 in Arizona, Gordon jumped from fifth to fourth in points. He'd also posted his seventh consecutive top-10 finish and had 19 top 10s for the year.

The season's top race winner, Ryan Newman, finished third at Phoenix and moved up a notch in points from sixth to fifth. In the last nine events, he scored in the top 10 eight times, and with 4,499 markers was threatening Gordon.

The news for Kevin Harvick after Phoenix could have been better. He ended up 34th at the finish and fell from third to sixth in points. It was his second consecutive finish of 20th or worse and he

headed to Rockingham with 4,477 markers, just 22 in back of Newman and 51 behind Gordon.

Tony Stewart finished 18th in Arizona but kept his seventh-place spot in the standings. Although he'd scored 16 finishes in the top 10, in 2003, he was a distant 217 points behind Harvick with two races left.

The situation was about the same for Stewart's teammate, Bobby Labonte. He was 18 spots behind Stewart at the end of the Checker 500 but held onto eighth in the NASCAR Top 10 with 4,055 points. Kurt Busch claimed fourth in the Phoenix race and moved up two notches in points from 11th to ninth. That put him, with 3,983 points, just 17 in front of the No. 10 man, Bill Elliott, who had finished 14th in the Phoenix race, dropping him from ninth to 10th in the standings.

The 46th – and final – driver though, was a different story. Newman secured his 11th Bud Pole of the season with a lap of 155.577 mph, and the best anyone else could muster was Jeremy Mayfield, who secured the third position at 153.307. Tony Raines matched Mayfield, who got the third spot because he had more points. Elliott came in fifth fastest at 154.840 mph but after his crew swapped engines in his Dodge, he had to start at the end of the field.

"We've been fast here before, but we haven't been fast for a long run," said Newman, whose car was painted to match one in which the late Mark Donohue gave team owner Roger Penske his first

(Upper Left) Jimmie Johnson continued his torrid late-season surge with a strong runner-up finish to Elliott. It was his second-straight second-place result, the fifth consecutive finish of second or third, and his 11th top 10 in the last 14 events.

(Left, Below) Tony Stewart picked up 20 positions during the race to finish ninth, adding to his personal string of seven top 10s in the last eight races, six of those being among the top four.

When it came to adding up top-10 finishes, no one did it any better than Matt Kenseth. His fourth-place finish in the race brought his season total to 25, good enough to hoist the champion's trophy with a race still remaining on the schedule.

Rick Hendrick's latest "discovery," Brian Vickers, almost scored a Rockingham "double," at least as far as qualifying was concerned. After winning the pole for Saturday's NASCAR Busch Series race, the Target House 200, Vickers was the first driver to attack the track in Bud Pole qualifying for the Pop Secret 400. He ripped off a lap at 155.505 mph and then watched 44 others fail to beat his speed.

(Top) Bill Elliott brings his Dodge into the pits where his crew awaits his arrival. The recently-crowned pit-road champs proved their muster, helping Elliott come from the very back of the pack at the start to the very front before the halfway point.

(Above) Once he reached the front, he led 140 of the remaining 206 circuits and finished with a 1.2-second margin of victory. Ryan Newman, driving a specially-painted ALLTEL Dodge, fell to fourth at the end behind Jeremy Mayfield (19) in third.

NWCS victory in 1973. Newman provided win No. 50 for Penske earlier this year at Michigan.

Back of the pack or not, Elliott didn't take long to remember the nuances of the 1.017-mile Rockingham track. After the first of 10 yellow-flag periods for 65 laps, the No. 9 Dodge was ninth in the running, and when the second yellow ended on lap 90 he was seventh.

Elliott kept improving his position as the event wound on. He was running fifth on lap 118 (after caution No. 5), third following the sixth, and he took the lead for the first of five times for 140 laps on lap 186, leading through 243. He also led laps 245-254, 320-329, 331-368, and when he won the race off pit road after the ninth caution, he was on his way. At the finish, Elliott was 1.230 seconds in front of Jimmie Johnson, while Mayfield battled for third.

Kenseth didn't lead any laps, but it wasn't necessary. A fourth-place run handed him the championship, and now he could relax a little bit as he thought about the season finale at Homestead-Miami Speedway in South Florida.

"I'm going to retire eventually," Elliott said, "but as good as we're running right now ... it makes it harder in one respect. I still feel good, and I still feel like we can do the things we need to do."

Elliott completed the race in 3 hours, 34 minutes and 44 seconds at an average speed of 111.677 mph and won $207,648.

Pop Secret Microwave Popcorn 500 *final race results*

Fin. Pos.	Start Pos.	Car No.	Driver	Team	Fin. Pos.	Start Pos.	Car No.	Driver	Team
1	5	9	Bill Elliott	Dodge Dealers/UAW Dodge	23	7	2	Rusty Wallace	Miller Lite Dodge
2	18	48	Jimmie Johnson	Lowe's Chevrolet	24	2	25	Brian Vickers	UAW-Delphi Chevrolet
3	3	19	Jeremy Mayfield	Dodge Dealers/UAW Dodge	25	6	01	Joe Nemechek	U.S. Army Pontiac
4	23	17	Matt Kenseth	DeWalt Power Tools Ford	26	37	22	Scott Wimmer	Caterpillar Dodge
5	1	12	Ryan Newman	ALLTEL Dodge	27	22	77	Dave Blaney	Jasper Engines & Transmissions Ford
6	4	74	Tony Raines	BACE Motorsports Chevrolet	28	42	14	Larry Foyt	Harrah's Dodge
7	9	99	Jeff Burton	CITGO Ford	29	25	10	Johnny Benson	Valvoline Pontiac
8	14	18	Bobby Labonte	Interstate Batteries Chevrolet	30	36	1	John Andretti	Pennzoil Chevrolet
9	29	20	Tony Stewart	Home Depot Chevrolet	31	35	23	Kenny Wallace	Stacker2 Dodge
10	31	40	Sterling Marlin	Coors Light Dodge	32	33	45	Kyle Petty	Georgia Pacific/Brawny Dodge
11	10	16	Greg Biffle	Grainger Ford	33	39	41	Casey Mears	Target House Dodge
12	20	5	Terry Labonte	Kellogg's/got milk? Chevrolet	34	38	30	Steve Park	America Online Chevrolet
13	26	8	Dale Earnhardt Jr.	Budweiser Chevrolet	35	21	42	Jamie McMurray	Havoline Dodge
14	8	7	Jimmy Spencer	Sirius Satellite Radio Dodge	36	28	49	Ken Schrader	BAM Racing Dodge
15	34	29	Kevin Harvick	GM Goodwrench Chevrolet	37	11	15	Michael Waltrip	NAPA Chevrolet
16	27	54	Todd Bodine	National Guard Ford	38	32	88	Dale Jarrett	UPS Ford
17	19	97	Kurt Busch	Rubbermaid Ford	39	30	32	Ricky Craven	Tide Pontiac
18	13	0	Ward Burton	NetZero Pontiac	40	24	21	Ricky Rudd	Motorcraft Ford
19	41	43	Jeff Green	Pop Secret Dodge	41	12	6	Mark Martin	Viagra Ford
20	17	31	Robby Gordon	Cingular Wireless Chevrolet	42	40	4	Kevin Lepage	Kodak Easy Share Pontiac
21	15	38	Elliott Sadler	M&M's Ford	43	43	37	Derrike Cope	Friendly's Chevrolet
22	16	24	Jeff Gordon	DuPont Chevrolet					

RACE

FORD 400

November 16, 2003

R.J. Reynolds Tobacco Co. and its Winston brand – the prime sponsor of NASCAR's top series for 33 years – got a champions' sendoff before the final race with its backing, the Ford 400 at Homestead-Miami Speedway in South Florida.

Richard Petty, who won the circuit's first official NASCAR Winston Cup championship in 1971 and retired as a driver at the end of 1992, took a ceremonial final victory lap around the newly revamped track in honor of RJR's many years of contributions. Then as an added treat, professional tennis champion Serena Williams waved the green flag over the 43-car field to start the final event of the Winston era.

"With two to go, I said, 'I want this win more than he does, maybe' ... (But) there was no way, unless something happened, that I was going to pass him."

Homestead-Miami Speedway opened in 1995 and staged its first NWCS event four years later. The track had been redesigned once to "round off" its rectangular configuration, and earlier this year it was radically reworked to create corners with 18-20 degrees of banking, up from the original six. Drivers who tested on the new layout generally gave the track their seal of approval.

Homestead-Miami effectively was a brand-new venue from the "git-go." Practice speeds were up, and Raybestos Rookie of the Year candidate Jamie McMurray blazed around the 1.5-mile layout in time trials to win his first career Bud Pole position with a record lap time of 29.816 seconds at 181.111 mph, breaking the old record of 156.440 mph, set by Steve Park in 2000.

Bobby Labonte was second fastest in Bud Pole qualifying with a posting of 29.879 seconds at 180.729 mph. Brian Vickers equaled Labonte's run but was placed third in the lineup, as Labonte's car owner had more points. Ryan Newman took the fourth starting spot at 180.717 mph, Jeff Gordon, at 180.210 mph was fifth quickest, and Kevin Harvick, Kurt Busch, Joe Nemechek, Jeremy Mayfield and Jimmie Johnson rounded out the top 10.

Newly crowned NASCAR Winston Cup Series Champion Matt Kenseth faces the cameras and microphones before completing his season at Homestead-Miami Speedway, a scene that would play itself over many times in the coming weeks.

Not to take anything from Chip Ganassi Racing Dodge driver McMurray, but everyone broke Park's mark. Jeff Burton's lap of 176.188 mph put him 36th on the starting grid. Matt Kenseth, Dale Earnhardt Jr., Robby Gordon, Mark Martin, Sterling Marlin, Ricky Craven and Kenny Wallace got into the race with provisional starts, while Ken Schrader, Kyle Petty, Mike Wallace, Derrike Cope and Rich Bickle all failed to find a berth in the event.

When told his first pole was historic because it was for the last race under the Winston/RJR banner, McMurray flashed a boyish grin and quipped, "My dad is big into stuff like that. I think that's neat, but I didn't care if (his first pole) came in the first race or the last one. I'm just happy to have one!"

Kenseth, of course, had wrapped up the championship with a fourth-place finish at Rockingham, N.C., but a ton of money and prestige was on the line to see who would take second- through 10th-place honors and join

Kenseth on the stage at the final NASCAR Winston Cup Series Awards Ceremony in New York in early December. Going into the Ford 400, 667 points separated the top nine drivers (excluding Kenseth), and the final event's outcome could shake some things up a bit.

Johnson came out of Rockingham with a second straight runner-up finish and 4,762 points. The result was also his fifth consecutive showing in the top three and it moved him from third to second in points, 38 ahead of Earnhardt Jr., who had slipped to third because of a 13th-place result in North Carolina.

After notching a season record 11th Bud Pole of the season at "The Rock," Newman finished

fifth in the Pop Secret 400, for his 17th top-five finish of the year, also a series high. He also rose to fourth in points from fifth and with 4,659 heading into Homestead, he was 34 up on Jeff Gordon.

Gordon's day at "The Rock" was ... in a word ... rocky. He finished 22nd in the 400-mile event and dropped to fifth in the standings from fourth. With 4,625 points, he was 99 behind Earnhardt Jr. and 137 in back of his teammate, Johnson.

Harvick, who was Kenseth's toughest late-season pursuer until scoring poorly at Atlanta and Phoenix, found himself battling to get back into the top five. A 25th-place finish at Rockingham moved him to within 30 points of Gordon and 64

(Above) Richard Petty, the original NASCAR Winston Cup Series champion was honored at Homestead and took a lap in a replica of his 1971 Plymouth (top) provided by the folks at Winston. The cars may have changed over the years, but not King Richard's patented smile.

(Left) All in all, it wasn't a bad weekend for Jamie McMurray. He set the track record in his Havoline Dodge to win his first career Bud Pole Award, and, with his top-10 finish, put the wraps on his Raybestos Rookie of the Year title.

(Right) Jeremy Mayfield (19) trails the stout Lowe's Chevrolet driven by Jimmie Johnson, who needed a strong finish to retain his second-place standing in the points. Johnson did just that, taking third place at the end to claim "best of the rest" behind champion Kenseth.

(Below Right) Bill Elliott (9) keeps his Dodge glued to the inside as he comes upon Johnny Bensons' Valvoline Pontiac. Benson was making his last start for the MBV team and gave them a welcome fourth-place finish, their best of the year.

of Newman. Going to Florida with 4,595 points, he had a comfortable lead of 197 over seventh-place Tony Stewart.

Stewart, however, kept his seventh-place ranking for the fifth consecutive week by finishing ninth at Rockingham and also shaved 20 points off his deficit to Harvick. Bobby Labonte, the champion in 2000, came home eighth in the Pop Secret 400 and remained at a "static" eighth in series points, with 4,197. Bill Elliott's first victory of the 2003 season in that event kept him in the NASCAR Top 10 for the fourth consecutive week. It also gained him a spot in the rankings at the expense of Busch.

Busch faltered at Rockingham, finishing 17th, making his fight to stay in the top 10 all that harder. Ranked 10th in points or better for 32 of 35 race weeks, Busch headed into the season finale with 4,095 markers. The defending champion at Homestead-Miami found himself 56 points behind Elliott and 102 in back of Labonte.

R.J. Reynolds officials on hand at Homestead for the final race under their purview got an event to remember. The new track layout allowed the

racers to run three wide, dice for position and keep the filled-to-capacity house (almost 72,000) too busy watching the action to do much else.

One byproduct was a record 10 caution-flag periods for 60 of the event's 267 laps, and the new asphalt contributed at least partially to shredded tires that sent Michael Waltrip, Brian Vickers, Jeremy Mayfield and Greg Biffle into the wall, causing, in order, yellow flags on laps 73, 120, 140 and 198.

Kenseth, championship in hand, went into the event hoping to at least challenge for a second win in 2003, but he did not get much of a chance to move through the field from his 37th-place start. On the 29th lap, the engine in his No. 17 Ford let go and he finished in last place. Had it not been the year's final event, he could have packed up and left, but he, of course, had to stick around to participate in the post-race champion's celebration.

The adage about auto racing being a humbling sport rang true at Homestead. From a 20th-place start, Elliott wasted little time in showing every-one that any thoughts of retirement might be premature. He took the lead for the first time on lap 47 and went on to dominate the event. His red No. 9 Dodge paced the field on laps 75-87, 92-121, 133-142 and 144-201. He relinquished the lead to Tony Stewart on the 202nd circuit but regained it again on lap 216 and left everyone else in his wake.

Then on the final lap, for Elliott, the racer's nightmare came true. He cut a right-rear tire and in less than a mile went from pursuing his second-straight victory to an eighth-place finish. Bobby Labonte was in a position to pounce on

(Above) Bobby Labonte, in his Interstate Batteries Monte Carlo, tries to keep up with Bill Elliott's Dodge Dealers Intrepid. "Awesome Bill" was earning his nick-name at the front of the field, dominating the event until a cut tire on the final lap abruptly ended his bid for a second straight win.

(Left) Kevin Harvick (29) and Jeff Gordon (24) duel through Homestead-Miami's newly banked turns in a battle for position. They were also in a fight for position in the points, entering the race with Gordon in fifth, one spot ahead of Harvick. At the finish, both advanced one position due to a 37th-place DNF by Ryan Newman.

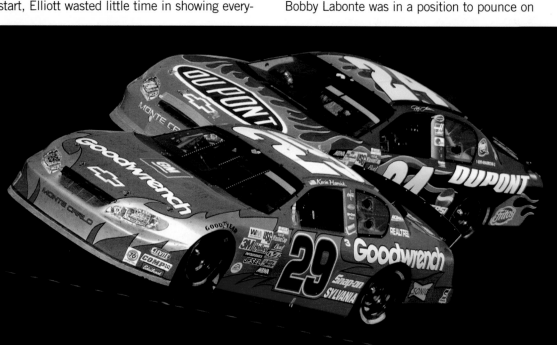

(Above) Bobby Labonte gets a real "lift" from crew chief Michael McSwain in victory lane after somewhat of a surprising win, their second of the year.

(Above Right) In a celebration of their own, champion Matt Kenseth lets the bubbly fly while team owner Jack Roush clutches the rather large $4.25 million check presented by R.J. Reynolds for winning his first NASCAR Winston Cup Series title.

Elliott's misfortune - and he did. His second win of the year came at the end of a 3-hour, 25-minute and 37-second race that netted him $331,058.

Harvick was 1.749 seconds behind in second place, Johnson finished third, Johnny Benson, in a final run for his team, was fourth and Jeff Gordon was fifth.

"It was an unfortunate ending," Elliott said. "You win them sometimes like that, although I don't think I've ever won one like that. We've done an awesome job this year."

"With two to go, I said, 'I want this win more than he does, maybe,'" Labonte noted. "(But) there

was no way, unless something happened, that I was going to pass him.

"That's got to be tough. Bill is such a great guy, and obviously he had the car to win."

In the final battle for points, Johnson ended up second, just 90 markers behind Kenseth. Earnhardt Jr., J. Gordon and Harvick were third through fifth in the standings, while Newman, Stewart, B. Labonte and Elliott sixth through ninth. Terry Labonte finished the race 15th and grabbed the No. 10 spot away from Busch, who had a troublesome day and ended up finishing 36th in the final NASCAR Winston Cup Series race.

Ford 400 *final race results*

Fin. Pos.	Start Pos.	Car No.	Driver	Team	Fin. Pos.	Start Pos.	Car No.	Driver	Team
1	2	18	Bobby Labonte	Interstate Batteries Chevrolet	23	11	2	Rusty Wallace	Miller Lite Dodge
2	6	29	Kevin Harvick	GM Goodwrench Chevrolet	24	38	8	Dale Earnhardt Jr.	Budweiser Chevrolet
3	10	48	Jimmie Johnson	Lowe's Chevrolet	25	16	7	Jimmy Spencer	Sirius Satellite Radio Dodge
4	21	10	Johnny Benson	Valvoline Pontiac	26	32	88	Dale Jarrett	UPS Ford
5	5	24	Jeff Gordon	DuPont Chevrolet	27	15	41	Casey Mears	Target Dodge
6	9	19	Jeremy Mayfield	Dodge Dealers/UAW Dodge	28	18	77	Dave Blaney	Jasper Engines & Transmissions Ford
7	13	20	Tony Stewart	Home Depot Chevrolet	29	42	32	Ricky Craven	Tide Pontiac
8	20	9	Bill Elliott	Dodge Dealers/UAW Dodge	30	39	31	Robby Gordon	Cingular Wireless Chevrolet
9	1	42	Jamie McMurray	Havoline Dodge	31	30	21	Ricky Rudd	Motorcraft Ford
10	41	40	Sterling Marlin	Coors Light Dodge	32	24	0	Ward Burton	NetZero Pontiac
11	34	54	Todd Bodine	National Guard Ford	33	40	6	Mark Martin	Viagra Ford
12	27	22	Scott Wimmer	Caterpillar Dodge	34	3	25	Brian Vickers	UAW-Delphi Chevrolet
13	19	74	Tony Raines	Speed Racer on SPEED Channel Chev.	35	25	16	Greg Biffle	Grainger Ford
14	36	99	Jeff Burton	CITGO Ford	36	7	97	Kurt Busch	Rubbermaid Ford
15	14	5	Terry Labonte	Kellogg's/got milk? Chevrolet	37	4	12	Ryan Newman	ALLTEL Dodge
16	12	14	Larry Foyt	Harrah's Dodge	38	33	02	Hermie Sadler	Sadler GM Chevrolet
17	8	01	Joe Nemechek	U.S. Army Pontiac	39	17	00	Mike Skinner	Bacardi Silver/Raz Chevrolet
18	31	4	Kevin Lepage	Kodak Perfect Touch Pontiac	40	26	43	Jeff Green	Chex by Petty Dodge
19	35	30	Steve Park	America Online Chevrolet	41	23	15	Michael Waltrip	NAPA Chevrolet
20	28	90	Ron Hornaday	Childress Vineyards Chevrolet	42	22	1	John Andretti	Pennzoil Chevrolet
21	29	38	Elliott Sadler	M&M's Ford	43	37	17	Matt Kenseth	DeWalt Power Tools Ford
22	43	23	Kenny Wallace	Stacker2 Dodge					

REFLECTIONS

THE NASCAR WINSTON CUP SERIES 2003

(Above) The fans at Bristol Motor Speedway in August, on hand for the Sharpie 500, were treated to a "flying" display of patriotism, as this skydiver came to earth prior to the start of the race.

(Left) Support for the nation's servicemen and women was evident in Bobby Labonte's pit!

(Below) Casey Mears was caught here in a reflective moment with the Stars and Stripes as a backdrop.

(Left) Pocono Raceway CEO Dr. Joseph "Doc" Mattioli joined the Rudd family, Ricky, Linda and Landon, before the driver's 700th consecutive NASCAR Winston Cup Series start in late July at the Pennsylvania superspeedway.

(Below Left) There's only one Jimmy Spencer! The outgoing and loquacious driver acknowledges his fans prior to the start of a race.

(Below) Kurt Busch had a successful 2003 season, in the No. 97 Roush Racing/Sharpie Ford, with 14 top-10 finishes in 36 races, including four victories.

(Top) The No. 8 didn't escape unscathed during a long and arduous season!

(Above) Jimmie Johnson acquitted himself well for his team owners, Rick Hendrick and Jeff Gordon. He won three races, finished 17 more times in the top 10 and ended up second in series points.

(Left) The driver of "Car No. 8" attracted autograph seekers wherever he went during the 2003 season. Driving again for the team founded by his late father, Dale Earnhardt Jr. finished a career-best third in 2003 NASCAR Winston Cup Series points.

(Above) Mike and Angela Skinner were a popular couple with fans and competitors alike. Skinner decided to return to the NASCAR Craftsman Truck Series in 2004. His wife authored a best-selling book dealing with the lives of racing people.

(Above Right) Bobby Labonte enjoys a lighter (Hulk) moment with his 9-year-old son, Tyler, before a race.

(Right) Ryan Newman (center) approached racing as a serious business all year and his no-nonsense attitude paid off with a series leading eight race victories and 11 Bud Pole Awards.

(Top left) Jack Roush and Mark Martin enjoy a "lighter" moment before a race. Their protégé, Matt Kenseth, gave Roush Racing its first NASCAR Winston Cup Series championship.

(Above left) Bill Elliott enjoys a quiet moment of privacy and contemplation before the year's last race at Homestead, Fla.

(Above) Kevin Harvick celebrates his only victory of the year – the Brickyard 400 at Indianapolis. Harvick finished the year fifth in points.

(Left) Jeff Gordon flashes that "winning" smile that's made him so popular with the fans. The four-time NASCAR Winston Cup Series champion won three races in 2003 and finished fourth in points.

(Above) Ready for the fans: The army of souvenir and racing collectibles trailers that follow the circuit from race to race create their own community while at the track.

(Right) Veteran racer Terry Labonte enjoyed one of his best seasons in recent years. He won the fabled Southern 500 for the second time in his long career and finished 10th in points.

(Far right) Robby Gordon en route to victory at Watkins Glen, N.Y., in August. The RCR Enterprises driver also won the road race at Sonoma, Calif., in June.

(Above) Tony Stewart surprised Kyle and Pattie Petty late in the season with a $1 million donation for their Victory Junction Gang Camp for critically ill children. The camp will open in 2004.

(Far left) A member of Stewart's team performs a "plug check." Spark plugs can give the trained eye a glimpse of engine performance.

(Left) Jaime McMurray ended the year 13th in overall points with as many finishes in the top 10. Most important, though, was he was named the series' Raybestos Rookie of the Year.

(Above) Rookie driver Tony Raines ran hard for BACE Motorsports in its first season of NASCAR Winston Cup Series competition. Raines missed just one race all year and finished third in Rookie of the Year competition.

(Below) The champ and his hardware: Matt Kenseth enjoys the trophy he received that symbolizes his greatest racing accomplishment – winning the 2003 NASCAR Winston Cup championship.

AUTOGRAPHS